Acoustic Communication

COMMUNICATION AND INFORMATION SCIENCE

A series of monographs, treatises, and texts
Edited by
MELVIN J. VOIGT
University of California, San Diego

William C. Adams • Television Coverage of the Middle East
William C. Adams • Television Coverage of International Affairs
William C. Adams • Television Coverage of the 1980 Presidential Campaign
Alan Baughcum and Gerald Faulhaber • Telecommunications Access and Public Policy
Mary B. Cassata and Thomas Skill • Life on Daytime Television
Hewitt D. Crane • The New Social Marketplace
Rhonda J. Crane • The Politics of International Standards
Herbert S. Dordick, Helen G. Bradley, and Burt Nanus • The Emerging Network Marketplace
Glen Fisher • American Communication in a Global Society
Oscar H. Gandy, Jr. • Beyond Agenda Setting
Oscar H. Gandy, Jr., Paul Espinosa, and Janusz A. Ordover • Proceedings from the Tenth Annual Telecommunications Policy Research Conference
Edmund Glenn • Man and Mankind: Conflict and Communication Between Cultures
Gerald Goldhaber, Harry S. Dennis III, Gary M. Richetto, and Osmo A. Wiio • Information Strategies
Bradley S. Greenberg • Life on Television: Content Analyses of U.S. TV Drama
Bradley S. Greenberg, Michael Burgoon, Judee K. Burgoon, and Felipe Korzenny • Mexican Americans and the Mass Media
Cees J. Hamelink • Finance and Information: A Study of Converging Interests
Robert Landau, James H. Bair, and Jean H. Siegman • Emerging Office Systems
John S. Lawrence and Bernard M. Timberg • Fair Use and Free Inquiry
Robert G. Meadow • Politics as Communication
William H. Melody, Liora R. Salter, and Paul Heyer • Culture, Communication, and Dependency
Vincent Mosco • Broadcasting in the United States
Vincent Mosco • Pushbutton Fantasies
Kaarle Nordenstreng • The Mass Media Declaration of UNESCO
Kaarle Nordenstreng and Herbert Schiller • National Sovereignty and International Communication
Harry J. Otway and Malcolm Peltu • New Office Technology
Ithiel de Sola Pool • Forecasting the Telephone
Dan Schiller • Telematics and Government
Herbert I. Schiller • Who Knows: Information in the Age of the Fortune 500
Jorge A. Schnitman • Film Industries in Latin America
Indu B. Singh • Telecommunications in the Year 2000
Jennifer Daryl Slack • Communication Technologies and Society
Dallas W. Smythe • Dependency Road
Sari Thomas • Studies in Communication Volumes 1–3
Janet Wasko • Movies and Money

In Preparation:

Bruce Austin • Current Research in Film
Heather Hudson • Telecommunications and Development
James Larson • Television's Window on the World
Kenneth Kraemer and William Dutton • Modeling as Negotiating
John Lawrence • The Electronic Scholar
Armand Mattelart and Hector Schmucler • Communication and Information Technologies
Vincent Mosco • Proceedings from the Eleventh Annual Telecommunications Policy Research Conference
Everett Rogers and Francis Balle • The Media Revolution in America and in Western Europe
Herbert I. Schiller • Information and the Crisis Economy
Keith R. Stamm • Newspaper Use and Community Ties
Robert S. Taylor • Value–Added Processes in Information Systems
Tran Van Dinh • Diplomacy and Communication in a Changing World
Tran Van Dinh • Independence, Liberation, Revolution
Georgette Wang and Wimal Dissanayake • Continuity and Change in Communication Systems

Acoustic Communication

Barry Truax
Simon Fraser University
Burnaby, British Columbia, Canada

Ablex Publishing Corporation
Norwood, New Jersey 07648

Second Printing 1994

Printed in the United States of America.

Library of Congress Cataloging in Publication Data

Truax, Barry
Acoustic communication.

(Communication and information science)
Bibliography: p.
Includes index.
1. Sound. 2. Communication. 3. Electro-acoustics.
I. Title. II. Series.
QC225.15.T78 1984 534 84-20372
ISBN 0-89391-263-8
ISBN 0-89391-307-3 (pbk.)

Ablex Publishing Corporation
355 Chestnut Street
Norwood, New Jersey 07648

To
R. Murray Schafer
and
the memory of Glenn Gould

Contents

Introduction

For many people in contemporary society, sound and hearing are simply taken-for-granted phenomena of little special significance to daily life, except as they occur in the forms of oppressively loud noise or technological innovation, as in the latest in audio and computer technology. Change for the better or worse seems as inevitable as it is uncontrollable by the individual. Whether our response is to resist or indulge in such change, we are caught up in a profoundly altered environment whose dynamics we do not understand. If we look to traditional intellectual disciplines for insight, we stumble not only on their esoteric language, but also on a tradition that deals with sound in isolation from real-world environments. Such disciplines may tell us how sound behaves in a particular, usually idealized context, but they are incapable of showing how sound connects us to the environment and to others, how it affects human behavior, or what the impact of urbanization or technology will be on such relationships. In short, what affects us most is what we seem to know the least about.

This book is an introduction to a new approach to the very old topic of sound. I use the term "acoustic communication" because it is the most general way to describe all of the phenomena involving sound from a *human* perspective. After all, a scientist may study "vibratory motion," but the individual experiences its effects as a form of communication. The relatively youthful field of communication studies provides a useful framework and set of concepts for understanding a complex system such as the one which sound creates between people and the environment. It is surprising (to me at least) that no one has applied communicational concepts to the field of sound before, at least not systematically. Just as the public tends to take sound for granted, communication specialists tend to assume that listening and sound-making work the same way they always have, and therefore they study social behavior at a more abstract level. Both groups may hear the contemporary soundscape in which they live, but neither seems inclined to *listen* to it with much sensitivity.

Listening is the key issue in communication via sound because it is the primary interface between the individual and the environment. It is a path of information exchange, not just the auditory reaction to stimuli. I used the term "soundscape" above, not just as a synonym for "acoustic environment," but as a basic term of acoustic communication. It refers to how the individual and society as a whole *understand* the acoustic environment through listening. Listening habits may be acutely sensitive or distractedly indifferent, but both interpret the acoustic environment to the mind, one with active involvement, the other with passive detachment. Moreover, listening habits create a *relationship* between the individual and the environment, whether interactive and open-ended, or oppressive and alienating. It is possible that two individuals in the same sound environment might have contrasting relationships to it. What is different is the *pattern* of communication in each case.

The communicational approach also contributes the very useful notion of *context* and stresses its importance to the understanding of messages. A sound means something partly because of what produces it, but mainly because of the circumstances under which it is heard. Even an emergency signal such as a fire whistle does not have its usual meaning if it occurs in a small town with a volunteer brigade at the regular time of their evening practice. The impact of electronic technology on sound (what we will call "electroacoustic" technology) has a profound effect on communication because, among other things, it can take a sound out of its original context and put it into any other. Even music becomes an environmental sound when it is produced by a loudspeaker, and we may react to it with annoyance when it seems inappropriate in its new context. We have lost the sense of magic that our grandparents felt when they first heard a radio bringing sound from far away into their homes. Today, radio often functions as a stimulant to get us through a boring or frustrating situation; its out-of-context sound becomes the new "environment" on which we may come to depend.

Acoustic communication attempts to understand the interlocking behavior of sound, the listener and the environment as a *system* of relationships, not as isolated entities. The listener is also a soundmaker, and even the sound of one's own voice comes back to the ear colored by the environment. With sound, everything interacts with everything else. Sound also results in other forms of behavior on the part of the listener, including reactions that may seem unrelated to aural experience. The worker stressed by noise may have trouble communicating with friends and family. Noise may also disrupt sleep or other activity and cause extra mental and physical stress that, in combination with other sources of tension, can lead to complex physiological and psychological problems. Fortunately, the systemic nature of acoustic communication can also lead, through similar chain reactions, to positive change. In fact, one of our goals in analyzing systems of acoustic communication will be to arrive at principles for "acoustic design."

We will find that acoustic systems of communication are vulnerable to changes of a particular kind, namely those that attack the forces which keep it balanced. Conscious intervention in the form of design strategies is needed to alter a downward course of deterioration. However, we will ask if such intervention need always take the form of "experts" imposing solutions, or whether there are means whereby the individual can bring about change and regain control.

In the second half of the book we will deal with the impact of electroacoustic technology on communication, and to a certain extent we will draw a parallel between the problems of noise and the manipulative effects of the media and audio technology. Both seem to be forces outside of the individual's control, and both seem inextricably tied to our notions of "progress." The comparison is not accidental because at their very basis, the models on which they are based are similar. The acoustician understands sound as a series of energy transfers from source to listener; similarly, the audio engineer treats audio systems as a series of signal transfers and manipulations.

Our communicational approach will analyze the implications of electroacoustic communication on the listening process, the community and the possibilities for design. What does it mean for sound to become a physical object on tape or disk? How does listening change when sounds are more likely to be repetitions than originals? What happens when audio products and services become part of the consumer process and are controlled by a multi-billion dollar industry? And perhaps most significant of all, how can we distinguish what is original and of lasting value from what is merely a technical novelty?

In contrast with the utopian optimism of audio technophiles who never question the inexorable march of technology, or the traditionalists who would prefer to ignore its existence entirely, we will assess the benefits and disadvantages of the new audio environments more objectively. Most of the time, technology seems to work as a "zero-sum" operation—for every advance there is a corresponding price. Much of part II will be devoted to auditing the balance sheet of technology. But once we have seen the exact nature of its impact, we will be able to discover what can change the *pattern* of communication, not just its content. The audio industry thrives on what is new as a driving consumer force, but what constitutes significant change? So-called alternatives exist on the sidelines, but are these "poor cousin" imitations of conventional media products? Does the inherently artificial nature of electroacoustic communication invalidate its options, or does it offer distinctly new possibilities for human awareness?

Another similarity between a discussion of noise and audio technology is the difficulty one encounters with subjective likes and dislikes. If the tone of an argument seems critical, whether of urban noise, AM radio or amplified music, there are always those who will say "But I like it!" just as there are those who will readily agree and say "There, I told you so!" People clearly have strong prejudices about what they hear. Just as some people are more sensitive to sound and noise, others regard the styles of music they listen to or the audio products they consume as an important part of their "lifestyle." Those who do not share their preferences are regarded unsympathetically. What I must ask of the reader, therefore, is to try to see beyond this type of reaction, to look to the larger pattern and not get "hung up" on specific content. The whole theme of the book is not to judge particular sound as good or bad, but to see the pattern of how it functions. It matters little to the argument here what you choose to listen to, or what not to listen to. If this book changes your understanding of how sound and listening work, and how they are affected by changes in the soundscape and technological innovation, it will have achieved its purpose.

Because of the newness of the communicational approach to the field of sound studies, I have thought it necessary to use the first chapter to go into a more detailed and theoretical discussion of how it differs from the traditional approach. The general reader may wish to proceed directly to chapter 2 where we examine various aspects of the listening process. Since this book is accompanied by no sound examples, they will have to come from the reader/listener's own experience, both remembered and current. For any argument based on perceptual experience, the only true verification and understanding will come from actual practice. It has been my experience in teaching this subject that by simply drawing attention to the listening process, most people quickly realize how little they know about it and how often it is ignored. Once begun, listening takes its own course with the individual. But experience often leads to questions of "why" and "how," and this is where the ideas and models presented in this book may prove valuable.

In chapter 3 we will turn to the always fascinating topic of voice and human soundmaking. Nothing is more revealing of a person than the voice. However, its development and effective use seems to be discouraged early on by society, and school systems in particular, no doubt because of the visual and literary bias of the printed word. The voice as the key to self-image and self-confidence gets traded for prowess in more intellectual fields. But here again, a little conscious redirection of attention and a bit of factual knowledge can help to reorient oneself toward this incredibly important tool of individual and interpersonal communication.

Our discussion becomes more theoretical in chapter 4 with a discussion of the three major systems of acoustic communication: speech, music, and soundscape. Although each system has its own traditional patterns of organization and specific characteristics, we shall try to step back from these details to gain a perspective of them as forming a continuum. Many current developments have tended to blur the boundaries between the conventional categories. Perhaps the greatest change has occurred in the field of contemporary music which has moved both towards language and the environment in its remarkable expansion during this century. In addition, recent research into brain processes and the specialization of its two hemispheres has shed new light onto how it handles various kinds of auditory input.

In chapter 5 we shift the perspective from the individual listener to the larger social unit, and introduce the idea of the "acoustic community" to describe environments in which sound plays a formative role. We will analyze what contributes to a positively functioning acoustic environment, one that binds the community together in contrast to forces that weaken community ties. Case studies will be used both to illustrate the problems of field work, and to suggest some innovative approaches to it. The analysis will also include an alternative way of thinking about the problem of noise. Most literature deals with its "effects," instead of looking to its causes or examining how it functions within the community. In fact, the whole topic of noise has become so complex that we will devote an entire chapter to devising a fresh approach to this troublesome problem.

Included in the discussion of noise in chapter 6 is an account of its "deaf spots"—the myths and fallacies that surround it and make it difficult to understand. In fact, one can even speak of the "ideology" of noise because it has become such an ingrained part of our social structure and habitual ways of thinking. There is an interesting parallel to be drawn between medical models and our concept of noise as a "disease" for which we seek a "cure." The industry that surrounds its study and control is similar to that surrounding, and therefore dependent on, diseases such as cancer. Both our ways of thinking about the problem and our methods of institutionalizing it have become so entrenched that they quite possibly *prevent* a solution from being found! From a communicational perspective, however, the factors that promote change in an acoustic system become apparent, and we will use them to map out a path towards positive change.

The last chapter in part I is devoted to the definition and principles of acoustic design. By taking the entire continuum of acoustic systems as our vantage point, we will try to generalize the principles by which they ensure effective communication. Design does not necessarily imply intentional manipulation, so even the natural soundscape can inspire us with the beauty of its construction. The wisdom of an "acoustic ecology" is to integrate the listener within the soundscape. Just as we are not separate from nature, we are not isolated from the soundscape "out there." Its design is of our own doing, and therefore it is our responsibility.

Understanding the traditional forms of acoustic communication makes it easier to assess the complete impact of technology on its processes. Therefore the second half of the book is devoted to rethinking the topics of the first half on the basis of that impact. In chapter 8, we see that the essence of electroacoustic technology is to change the entire basis on which sound functions. The "audio signal" into which the sound wave is transformed obeys few of the "rules" of traditional acoustic behavior. Therefore, it is not surprising if it completely changes the nature of communication, both for the individual and the society. Constraints are broken and new possibilities are created. But what is their price, and if sound is no longer constrained by traditional forces, what takes their place? Is the split between a sound and its source, or what we will call "schizophonia," a sign of disintegration for the listening process and human communication?

In chapter 9 we will look at the "double-edged sword" of technology more closely to see what problems accompany its extensions. Its products produce a new soundscape by changing both the sounds that populate it and social patterns of communication. To understand the changes fully, we will have to introduce a certain amount of technical terminology related to electroacoustics, but we shall attempt to do so in the clearest manner possible with the emphasis on implications, not engineering. Chapter 10 will do much the same for the listening process by examining how its nature is fundamentally changed by audio technology. What are the implications when the listener becomes a consumer of audio products and services? Do not the processes that extend listening possibilities also simplify them in certain ways? In some cases, technology makes active listening more analytical, but in others, it encourages completely distracted listening habits. More seriously, audio media are used as a surrogate to fill the gaps left by environments and jobs that are unfulfilling and meaningless. Psychological dependency, commoditization and a vulnerability to the inculcation of values are some of the problems faced by the new listener.

In chapter 11 we turn to a more detailed analysis of a particular case of the audio media, namely radio. Consistent with the rest of the book, we will avoid judgments based on content alone. In fact, we will argue that an understanding of how radio functions in people's lives requires a broader basis of analysis. The relation between form and content holds the clue. We will present a new approach to the analysis of the *structure* of radio that clarifies how it attracts and maintains the attention of its audience, even when they are engaged in other activities. Such distracted forms of listening seem to be increasingly common, and so it is enlightening to understand how communication can be designed to be effective with such listeners. It also makes us aware of how vulnerable we are to media manipulation, and of the need for alternatives.

In chapter 12 we turn to the larger perspective of the impact of electroacoustic sound on the community and the soundscape. We deal both with the introduction of loudspeakers into the environment and the redefinition of the "acoustic community" as a market. The changes go beyond those brought about by radio and television to include the recent introduction of computer and video technology in telecommunications and two-way videotext systems. On what basis will these new kinds of electroacoustic "communities" be defined? We will also provide some background information on the size and extent of two sectors of the international audio industry, namely those devoted to disk recording and background music.

Having sketched out the new roles (and predicaments) of the listener and the soundscape as a result of electroacoustic technology, we will turn our attention in the last two chapters to the question of alternatives. What can the individual do to regain control, what are the true alternatives that counterbalance the problems introduced by technology, and what are the principles of electroacoustic design? In chapter 13 we will summarize a fairly wide range of experimental activity that various individuals have carried out over the past 35 years in investigating the new possibilities of electroacoustic technology. First there are those based on the "document in sound" which explore the tape medium through the radio documentary, aural history, and the conventional disk recording. Then there is the broader and less well-known field of electroacoustic music where we will use our concept of the continuum of sound between speech, music, and soundscape to show how all three are creatively used and explored. We will look at representative work in the areas of the "text-sound" composition, electronic and computer composition with "abstract" sound material and finally, the unique form of the "soundscape composition" which not only uses environmental material, but also plays on the listener's environmental experience in order to enhance it.

In the final chapter, we will attempt to generalize from such examples the differences in the process and practice of electroacoustic design that make it an extension of traditional acoustic forms. It is not just a matter of different sounds and different structures (though these are considerable). The composer/designer can now control the communicational environment in which the work is to function in ways that were not possible before. Even more exciting is the possibility of designing the compositional process itself. Whereas traditional methods constrain the composer to work in certain ways, and therefore to some extent to think accordingly, the electroacoustic composer has greater freedom of choice in selecting a working method.

Analog and digital techniques, interactive and automated systems, real-time and non–real-time synthesis, deterministic and stochastic control, as well as the use of memory storage and complex algorithms are all part of the repertoire from which the composer can now choose to be part of the working method. In fact, we will argue that the new electroacoustic design environment is progressively bringing about some very fundamental changes in the traditional roles of the instrument designer, composer, performer, and listener. In particular, the split between composer and performer that has been fairly rigorous since the 19th century can be reintegrated in the future as a direct result of technology. The potential of electroacoustic technology to extend human communication through sound is its main justification, and the book intends to leave the reader with a greater appreciation of how that potential may be realized.

The range of topics covered by the book is quite large in order to suggest the general applicability of the communicational model. However, the constraints of space have dictated that examples and citations of specific work are kept within modest limits. Those familiar with specific fields will realize that I have only touched their surface, and even that many important contributors to them have not been mentioned. The reader may also be frustrated when further information on an interesting point is not forthcoming. Such sacrifices have been made to keep the book readable and its theme coherent. Once its basic ideas have been grasped, applications and extensions should be readily apparent.

Related literature in the field that uses a communicational model is, unfortunately, not abundant. I have included as many references as possible, and the bibliography contains a selection of representative work. However, the tradition of writing about sound and hearing has been almost exclusively from the scientific point of view, that is, based on the factual information about how sound behaves. At the popular level are such overviews as J. R. Pierce's *Man's World of Sound* (Pierce, 1958), with the unfortunately sexist connotation of its title, Stevens and Warshofsky's *Sound and Hearing* in the Time-Life series (Stevens & Warshofsky, 1965), and Denes and Pinson's *The Speech Chain* which is a good introduction to vocal sound (Denes & Pinson, 1963).

More recently we have a technically detailed book by Frederick A. White with the somewhat misleading and unfortunate title *Our Acoustic Environment* (White, 1975) which contains an excellent summary of scientific information on acoustics, psychoacoustics, noise control, and the physiological and psychological effects of noise, but only a page and a half on communication. Beyond that there is no lack of books on acoustics—general, musical, and architectural—as well as those which attempt to bridge specific gaps, such as that between psychoacoustics and music (Roederer, 1975). Similarly, many excellent books on noise exist (e.g., Kryter, 1970; Bragdon, 1970; Burns, 1968; Baron, 1970), but in general, they tend to deal with the negative effects of noise without a corresponding model of how sound functions positively in the environment.

A unique attempt to break out of this one-sided approach came with R. Murray Schafer's *The Tuning of the World* (Schafer, 1977), and the present volume includes many of his ideas and terms. However, as inspiring as that book is, it is largely descriptive of historical trends and other soundscape phenomena, and does not provide a coherent model for their analysis. Still, it is a useful place to start and the present volume can be seen as an extension of the same material from a communicational perspective, particularly with regard to the impact of technology. Schafer's work is closely related to that of the World Soundscape Project, a research and educational endeavor devoted to soundscape study which he founded at Simon Fraser University, and with which I worked for a number of years (Truax, 1974; Giansante, 1979; Zapf, 1981a; Torigoe, 1982). Although some of its publications are still available, I have quoted from them frequently as the reader may not be familiar with their ideas and terminology. By way of acknowledging other debts, I should also mention the profound influence that Otto Laske's work has had on my thinking. Although his seminal work, *Music, Memory and Thought* (Laske, 1977) is too theoretical for the general reader, his cognitive approach to musical behavior has had a lasting impact on my thinking about soundscape studies.

Lastly, a few words about language. Technical terms cannot be avoided in a book such as this, but I have tried to give brief definitions of the less familiar ones I have used. The reader may wish to refer to my *Handbook for Acoustic Ecology* (Truax, 1978), which is a compendium of terminology, for more extensive explanations. Throughout the book I have attempted to follow the American Psychological Association's guidelines for nonsexist language. I have also chosen not to use "he/she" and "his/her" constructions, both because I think they are awkward and in practice they have proved unnecessary. In the Introduction to the *Handbook*, I remarked on the equally prevalent visual bias of language. Unfortunately, I don't think one can avoid its influence entirely, but we can refrain such inappropriate excesses as those in a recent book on *Listening* which states that "listening scholars currently view the the creative aspect of listening in a different light" (Wolvin & Coakley, 1982, p. 50). Language is a powerful form of communication, and we should try to be as sensitive to the nuances of words as we are to the sounds of acoustic communication.

Barry Truax

Acknowledgements

A book of this sort does not spring from a void; it is the result of a 10-year process of teaching and research during which countless students and colleagues have contributed to my thinking on this subject. With their help, numerous areas that impinge upon acoustic communication have been opened up to me, and although the synthesis is my own, I am indebted to them all. However, a few individuals deserve special mention for their specific contribution to this volume.

First I would like to thank Dr. William Leiss, chairman of the Department of Communication, S.F.U., for his enthusiastic support and encouragement of this project; his confidence bolstered mine in no small way. I am also most indebted to many individuals whose work I have incorporated into the text, and who have brought many useful examples to my attention. These include my colleagues in the World Soundscape Project who provided much of the groundwork for the ideas developed here; Prof. Bengt Hambraeus who provided the Swedish mountain recordings referred to in chapter 3; James Fields who worked on the English village study quoted in chapter 5; Michelle Rohatyn who did the daycare study in the same chapter; Alan Shapiro who brought the Navaho and Hopi soundmaking to my attention; and David Brown who introduced me to the writings of Jacques Lusseyran.

Several people have kindly read portions of the manuscript and offered valuable suggestions. Among these are Pete Anderson, Ian Angus, Ken Barron, Lou Giansante, Guenther Krueger, Jean McNulty, Imbert Orchard, Melvin Voigt, and Hildegard Westerkamp. Finally, I would like to thank Simon Fraser University for its sabbatical year support without which this book would never have been written, and my colleagues in the Centre for the Arts who have tried to understand why a composer would insist on a social science perspective to sound, and those in the Department of Communication who graciously tolerated their own perspective being infiltrated by a musician's point of view. My interactions with these people and with all of my students continue to be a source of great inspiration and support.

I.

Sound, Listening, and Soundscape

1

Acoustic Tradition and the Communicational Approach: Energy Transfer and Information Processing

If we wish to understand sound and its behavior generally, as implied by the term "acoustic communication," and we turn to the traditional disciplines that study it, we find that they are scattered institutionally throughout the arts and sciences, engineering, and medicine. Moreover, each discipline or specialization concerns itself with only a particular aspect of the entire subject, and often no attempt is made to bridge the arbitrary gaps between them. Each discipline has also developed its own terminology and concepts through which it expresses its knowledge, and like all specialized subjects, acoustics uses a great number of abstract ideas that often seem removed from the perceptual immediacy of the acoustic world that surrounds us.

Books on acoustics, following the general development of the discipline, have come to rely more and more heavily on visual representations of their subject matter. One almost comes to think that the two-dimensional wave diagrams that populate these books, showing undulating lines moving around a horizontal one, must actually correspond to what's happening in the air (or the "medium" as it is always generalized), instead of being simply a convenient representation of a three-dimensional phenomenon in only two. One only has to go back to the writings of the 19th-century acousticians with their ingenious demonstrations of acoustic principles through sounding experiments, or their examples drawn from such real-world experience as Tyndall's observation that "the day was acoustically clear; at a distance of 10 miles the horn yielded a plain sound,"[1] to understand how far the modern scientific approach has led us away from everyday perception.

A great deal can be learned, of course, from both the theoretical and experimental achievements of acoustics, but it can also leave us wondering whether such knowledge has been placed beyond the public's reach and comprehension. At the same time, environmental noise is an ever present

[1]John Tyndall, *Contemporary Review*, 1874, p. 826; note that the distance referred to is in nautical miles.

problem over which one feels one has little control. The essentials of scientific knowledge seem not to have filtered down to the level of general public awareness, and, too often, decisions are left to "experts" who speak only a technical language.

The scientific method has achieved its results through an experimental methodology that allows observable phenomena to be studied in isolation from the variables that normally complicate most situations. For results to be verifiable they must be able to be replicated at any time and place, and this constraint necessitates a type of study where each variable can be controlled. The environmental context in such a study is essentially idealized. Problems in the contemporary world seem increasingly to involve complex interactions at many levels simultaneously, and techniques designed for ideal situations often fail when applied in actuality. Although I am not claiming that scientific procedures cannot be devised or adapted to contemporary problems, I am suggesting that at least in the realm of sound, such methods have been slow to emerge, and the answers offered thus far are fragmentary at best and all too often, ineffectual. This book is an attempt to sketch out a new framework for understanding acoustic contexts in all of their subtlety and complexity. It presents a communicational model to show how sound, in all its forms and functions, defines the relationship of the individual, the community, and ultimately a culture, to the environment and those within it. However, in order to understand the potential of the communicational approach, it is necessary to examine it in the context of the traditional models, and therefore we will present first a brief survey of the basis of physical acoustics and the related model of signal processing.

The Energy Transfer Model

To go more deeply into the sources of the gap between traditional knowledge and contemporary problems, we can begin by examining the model on which most disciplines dealing with sound have been based, namely the energy transfer model. With the advent of electronic technology, the model has become that of signal transfer, but we can see that the same principles are embodied in it as well. The energy transfer model deals with acoustic behavior as a series of energy transfers from source to receiver. It examines how these transfers occur, how efficient they are, and what variables affect them. The energy originates with a vibrating object that radiates its energy to the air or through any object with which it is in contact. The most common example quoted is probably that of the tuning fork which sounds faint when struck, but becomes clearly audible when placed on a table or other object with a large surface area. Acoustics tells us that the energy transfer in the first case is inefficient (it's called an impedance mismatch). In the second case where a greater surface area is involved by "coupling" the fork to the table, the energy transfer is more efficient, and since less energy is lost in the transfer to the air, the sound is more clearly heard. Similarly, we discover that the outer parts of the ear (the auricle and pinna) are especially well suited for the transfer of energy from the air to the narrow auditory canal, because they act as a kind of funnel to direct the sound waves in the appropriate direction.

Once the energy has radiated from the source, it propagates through the "medium," normally air or water, with varying speeds and other characteristics. A denser medium where the molecules are closer together, such as water or metal, allows the energy to travel more quickly. In air, the speed of sound through a warmer air mass is greater than through a cooler one, and so on. Environmental acoustics also studies how different frequencies behave during propagation, a subject that will be dealt with as "response" characteristics later on. When the sound wave comes into contact with objects, its energy is transmitted through the object, absorbed within it, or reflected from it with varying degrees of efficiency depending on frequency.

On arrival at the ear, the sound becomes the subject of study for *psychoacoustics* which examines the chain of energy transfers as the sound wave is transmitted from the outer ear via the eardrum to the bones of the middle ear called the ossicles. This transmission involves the transfer of energy from the air to a solid, a process which the eardrum through the course of its long evolution from the equivalents found in fish and reptiles is remarkably adept at performing. The actual distance moved by the eardrum in response to the slightest vibration which can be heard is less than a wavelength of light, i.e., it can not be seen, even with a microscope! The bones of the middle ear are attached to the oval window of the spiral-shaped cochlea which is filled with a fluid that can transmit the energy from the mechanical vibration of the stirrup, the last of the bones of the middle ear. The sound energy in the cochlea creates a bulging of the basilar membrane located within the cochlea, and the shearing motion of this membrane against the thousands of tiny hair cells in the organ of Corti activates them to produce electrical impulses which travel via the auditory nerve to the brain. It is through the firing of the hair cells that the first level of analysis of the sound wave occurs in terms of frequency and intensity, or more generally, in terms of the energy distribution (or "spectrum") of the sound. Once analysis is involved, it seems appropriate for psychoacoustics to use a signal processing model to describe the operation of the auditory system.

Psychoacoustics documents the processing of incoming sound waves by the auditory system to extract usable information for the brain, in other words, the process called hearing. To do so, it has relied in the past quite heavily on a model drawn from 19th-century psychophysics, namely the stimulus-response model. The founder of modern psychophysics, Gustav

Fechner, attempted to understand how the brain formed subjective impressions based on the magnitude of external stimuli. For instance, how does our concept of "heftiness" relate to objective measures of weight? Fechner discovered that there was a systematic relationship between the magnitude of the stimulus and that of the subjective response. In fact, he suspected that there was a universal logarithmic relationship between the two for many, if not all, stimuli, i.e., that larger and larger stimuli were required to produce equal increments in the corresponding subjective sensation. Although modern work has refined the nature of this principle, we can see that Fechner's concept generated several new ideas. First, it allowed subjective reactions to be scaled and therefore made amenable to scientific study. And secondly, it allowed the concept of energy transfer to be extended into the realm of individual experience by treating it as a "stimulus" with dimensions called parameters which transfer to the corresponding dimensions of subjective "response."

Thus came about the modern scientific distinction between the "objective" acoustic parameters, such as intensity, frequency and waveform, and their psychoacoustic, "subjective" counterparts, namely loudness, pitch and timbre, respectively, which describe the brain's response to those parameters (Plomp, 1976; Roederer, 1975; Tobias, 1972; Moore, 1982). This distinction allows us, for instance, to ask what is the smallest change in the objective stimulus that produces a perceptual change, a measure called the "just noticeable difference" (jnd). Or, we can ask, as did Fechner, whether the relation between stimulus and response is linear (i.e., equal changes in stimulus produce equal changes in response), or whether it is logarithmic as described above.

More subtly, psychoacoustics determines what are the physical (i.e., acoustic) characteristics of a stimulus that result in a single sensation or a double one (e.g., one tone or two, based on frequency difference). Masking experiments, for instance, determine the conditions under which one sound, by virtue of its intensity or frequency content, makes it difficult or impossible to hear another sound. The time variable is also considered: how long must a sound last or be separated from another for a certain type of percept to occur? Such data, collected over many subjects, tends to show a statistical unity of response; that is, within certain, fairly narrow statistical limits, individuals perceive sound in generally the same way, according to the psychoacoustic parameters as defined. Just as with the concept of energy transfer, response to stimuli can be rationalized as essentially known, quantifiable behavior.

Although contemporary psychoacoustics is developing the concept of the "percept" as the end result of auditory processing (McAdams & Bregman, 1979), the enduring influence of the psychophysical stimulus-response model can be seen even in such a peripheral area as the noise study. The objective of such studies seems simple enough—to document subjective reac-

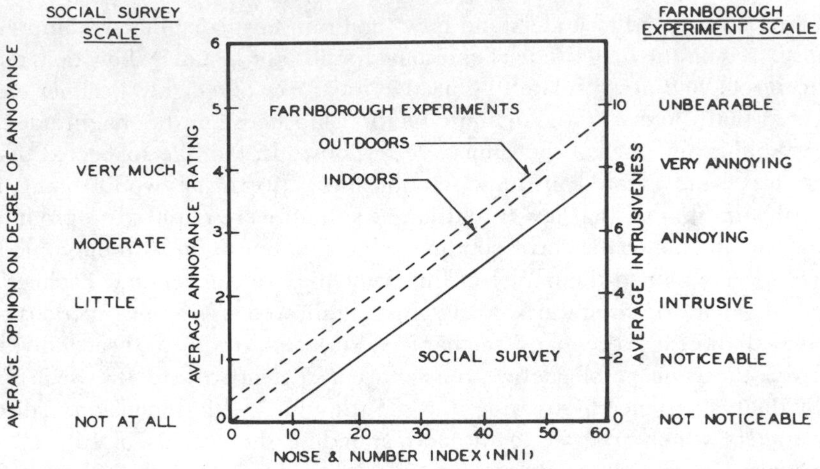

Fig. 1. Relations between annoyance rating and Noise and Number Index obtained from social survey and Farnborough experiments (from Wilson Committee on the Problem of Noise, *Noise: Final Report,* Cmnd 2056, London, HMSO, 1963, p. 208, used by permission).

tion to noise, in particular its magnitude. Not surprisingly, the result of such studies is often a plot of subjective reaction, usually related to a concept like "annoyance," against the magnitude of the "stimulus." This plot of the subjective on the vertical axis and the objective on the horizontal frequently yields, again not too surprisingly, a straight line, linear relationship! Equal increments of noise seem to produce equal increments of public response, such as in the 1960 Wilson study of Heathrow airport that proposed the Noise and Number Index.[2] The results, as in Fig. 1, show the degree of annoyance in a linear relationship to the scale for noise measurement which they have proposed. Instead of the usual approach of quantifying subjective response, the noise study devises a method for measuring noise levels that produce subjective reactions on a linear scale. In terms of the energy transfer model, the concept of annoyance is the final dissipation of "heat" in what has been a long series of energy transfers from source to listener!

By comparison, one of the many American systems, the Community Noise Equivalent Level, originating in California,[3] creates a vertical scale (Fig. 2) on a somewhat more pragmatic basis: the number and vociferousness of complaints, progressing to threats of legal or community action. Here

[2]Wilson Committee on the Problem of Noise, *Noise: Final Report*, Cmnd 2056, London: HMSO, 1963, p. 208.

[3]U.S. Environmental Protection Agency, *Community Noise*, document NTID300.3, 1971.

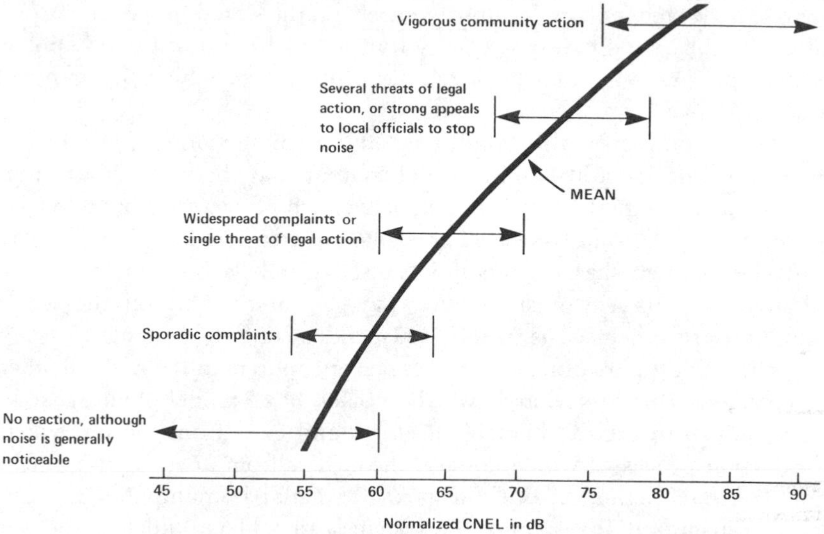

Fig. 2. Community reaction as a function of normalized CNEL values as calculated from case histories (after U.S. Environmental Protection Agency document NTID 300.3, "Community Noise," 1971).

the choice of vertical scale takes on political overtones, and the clear imperative of the system seems to be for those in authority to keep the noise level, or at least its rate of change, within limits that preserve community equilibrium and quiescent adaptation.

Signal Processing

Similarly, the entire field of electroacoustics, the result of the application of 20th-century technology to sound, constitutes a sub-discipline of electrical engineering, i.e., audio engineering. It is concerned with the energy transfer from acoustic to electrical forms, a process called transduction, as well as the subsequent processing and/or storage of the resultant audio signal. The related process of radio transmission codes an audio signal into an electromagnetic carrier wave which is transmitted to a distant receiver instantaneously—another energy and signal transfer process. It is generally assumed that the electroacoustic process ends with the conversion of the signal back into acoustic, audible form via a loudspeaker.

The term "electroacoustic," as used here, is the one which in my opinion best embodies the essential nature of audio engineering, that is, the application of electrical and electronic technology to the processing or synthesizing of sound, the latter being the electronic generation of sound without an original acoustic source. It is significant, however, that the current emphasis of audio technology is almost entirely on the signal processing aspects and not on the actual points of energy transfer, i.e., the transduction process via microphones and loudspeakers, the problems of which are generally thought to have been solved.

The emphasis on the "audio signal," from the present perspective, suggests an intentionality and sense of content that the more neutral term "energy" lacks. Signals travel in channels which of necessity include a certain level of background noise. The signal is intentional and desired, and should be distinguishable from the "noise" which is both inevitable and undesired. Signals are presumed to "have" content, and yet the way in which they are processed is usually independent of that content.

These and many other paradoxes one encounters in the audio field can be understood through what I call the "black box" model of electroacoustics, as shown in Fig. 3. The signal enters and exits from the box via the transduction processes which convert the energy from acoustic to electrical forms and back again. Inside the box, the signal is manipulated, stored, and/or transmitted. The aim of the system is to achieve "fidelity" between the input and output signals, that is, to make them indistinguishable, at least ideally. Interestingly enough, early advertisements for the gramophone, just as with certain brands of magnetic tape today ("is it live or is it. . . ?"), emphasized the "you won't be able to tell the difference" quality of their products. One advertisement showed the friends of a famous opera singer of the day seemingly baffled as to whether they were listening to their acquaintance live or on record. Judging by what we now hear in these original recordings, the imagined psychological sense of "realism" must be attributed to factors other than technical fidelity!

Perfect fidelity, of course, is technically impossible to achieve because every stage of the signal transfer process inevitably adds noise or distortion to

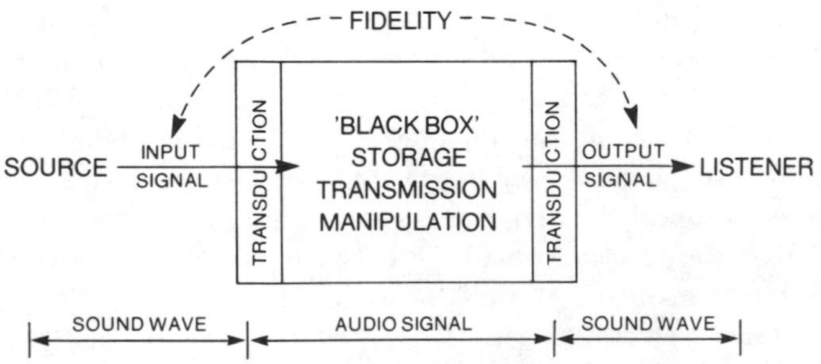

Fig. 3. The "black box" model of electroacoustics, showing the transduction of the sound wave into an audio signal, and back again into a sound wave with intermediate stages of storage, transmission, or manipulation.

the signal, however slight (or gross, judging by what is commonly heard over cheap loudspeakers daily). Thus, like the "true satisfaction" of the advertisements or the promises of other types of slogans, fidelity is unattainable, hence safe and unquestionable. What is significant, however, is that if true fidelity were attainable, the technology would become *transparent*. That is, if there were no difference between the original and reproduced signals, the result would be the same as if there had been no technological intervention at all. The technology would therefore be neutral, in the sense of being independent of, and therefore not responsible for, the content of the material it processes or the implications of its uses. Such "neutrality," as we shall see in part II, is far from the reality that has come about through the audio industry. We will examine the implications of technology on patterns of acoustic communication, and the new role into which the individual and the community are cast, in the second half of the book.

From this cursory overview of the traditional scientific approach to sound and hearing, it should be clear that it operates to a significant extent within a model of a linear chain of energy or signal transfers, much as the early models of communication processes posited a source-channel-receiver chain. Out critique of the tradition is not to deny the value of its knowledge or techniques (in fact we will constantly invoke them). Rather, it is intended to establish the limits of traditional thinking, and to clarify the concerns and goals of an interdisciplinary model of acoustic communication. Moreover, we are interested in creating a model which will provide new insight into problems which the traditional approach is incapable of solving, and design criteria which that approach cannot furnish.

A Communicational Approach

First of all, a communicational approach to acoustics deals with the exchange of *information*, rather than the transfer of energy. In other words, it does not deal with sound in isolation from the cognitive processes that understand it. In any of the cases of energy or signal transfer described earlier, the components of the system can be regarded individually—the tree falling in the forest creates a momentary series of energy transfers whether it is heard or not. Within a communicational framework we will be much more concerned about the information communicated by the sound of that tree.

Whereas hearing, in the end role of receiver in the linear model, is the processing of acoustic energy in the form of sound waves and vibration, *listening* is at the core of a communicational model. It can be defined simply as the processing of sonic information that is usable and potentially meaningful to the brain. Similarly, whereas the "sonic environment" can be regarded as the aggregate of all sound energy in any given context, we will use the term "soundscape" to put the emphasis on how that environment is understood by those living within it—the people who are in fact creating it. The individual listener within a soundscape is not engaged in a passive type of energy reception, but rather is part of a dynamic system of information exchange. Because of its importance, we will return to the concept of listening in the next chapter.

Secondly, a communicational approach includes the notion of *context*. The exchange of information is highly dependent on context, whereas the transfer of energy is not. For example, the acoustic study of sound propagation in an environment is normally carried out independent of social and cultural context. In such studies, noise behaves the same whether those it affects are poor or rich, used to it or not, capable of controlling it or dependent on it. The most attention such circumstances receive are as "correction factors" by which noise scales have to be adjusted so that the reported annoyance corresponds to the measured noise level and can be predicted from it. In a communicational approach, context is essential for understanding the meaning of any message, including sound.

Similarly, the "black box" model of electroacoustic communication, as in Fig. 3, completely ignores the fact that the context of the original source and the reproduced signal are entirely different. The concept of fidelity puts the emphasis on the quality of the signal, and therefore completely ignores the fact that there can be no "fidelity" in context between the original and the reproduced sound. Hence, a voice or music may be reproduced in any other space or time, whether appropriate or not, and often such reproduction seems paradoxical since it is "out of context." Take the example of hearing a hundred-piece orchestra in an elevator, or a hockey game on the beach! Our familiarity with such paradoxes may lessen their irony, but the arbitrariness of context remains fixed within the electroacoustic experience. On the other hand, when such devices as radio were first introduced, wonderment at the "magic" of hearing a disembodied voice over impossibly large distances was instilled in the first listeners. Before audio technology, no sound had ever been heard twice, exactly the same, nor had any sound ever been heard outside its original context.

The communicational significance of any sound can only be judged within its complete context in the broadest environmental, social and cultural sense. In fact it is through context that we understand how a sound functions. In the following sections we will examine how, within the traditional acoustic environment, the inseparability of every sound from its context makes it a valuable source of usable information about the current state of the environment. Moreover, in terms of a community, sounds not only reflect its complete social and geographical context, but also reinforce community identity and cohesion. Sometimes they are a frequent, almost subconscious reminder of context, and at other times they provide the uniqueness of occasion that reflects a community's individuality.

Thirdly, a communicational model will not deal with linear chains of energy or signal transfers, but with systems of related elements operating at different hierarchic levels. Instead of thinking of sound as coming from the environment to the listener and perhaps being generated back again, we will think of it as mediating, or creating relationships, between listener and environment. We can show this mediating function of sound as in Fig. 4, where it is placed at the top of the triangle to indicate this role.

Acoustic experience creates, influences and shapes the habitual relationships we have to any environment. The relationship may be highly interactive, even therapeutic, but it may also become alienating and both physically and mentally oppressive as in the case of noise. The relationship may be one that brings people together and binds the community, or one that isolates the individual and threatens the sense of shared experience that characterizes every community, no matter how it may be defined.

Through electroacoustic means, entirely new patterns of communication occur, bridging space and time, creating sources of power and control, and thus creating new relationships between people and their environments. In fact, one could say that technology creates new communicational environments that have few of the limitations of normal geographical ones. The listener is no longer a humble "receiver" at the end of a long and complex communicational channel, but becomes instead a member of a mass audience, a consumer market, or a target subgroup. Technology can create relationships that are repetitive, addictive, and a surrogate masquerading as a "real" relationship. When we come to an analysis of radio in part II, we will find that be being designed for the distracted listener engaged in other activity, radio attempts to fill the gaps left by jobs and environments that are not complete in themselves. It offers an alternative, seemingly more meaningful relationship, the consumption of which it in turn can use for its own commercial or other ends. However, technology also creates the possibility of innovative and artistic experiences through the artificial constructions of sound now possible, and it is these alternatives that we will return to in the last few chapters of the book.

Finally, through a communicational approach, we hope to establish useful criteria for *acoustic design*. The so-called "applied" fields of traditional disciplines, e.g., architectural acoustics, acoustical engineering, and audio engineering, have contributed extensive knowledge concerning the optimum

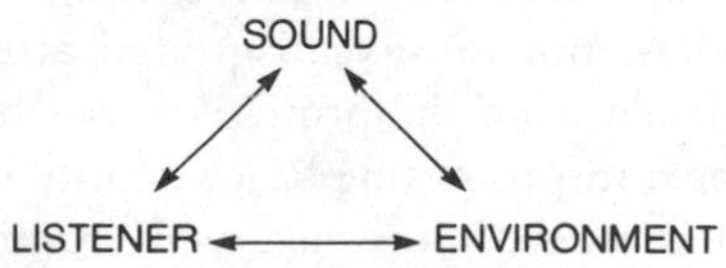

Fig. 4. The mediating relationship of listener to environment through sound.

methods for controlling sound waves and audio signals. Their design goal is that the desired stimulus will arrive at the receiver and the undesired noise will not, or at least not in such quantities as to obscure the desired signal or create undue annoyance. The techniques used by traditional disciplines are obviously useful, but they do not lead to design criteria that go beyond the question of the appropriate control of signals to ask what kind of environment is desirable, meaningful, or beneficial—not just one that can be adapted to. Hence their failure to provide solutions to obviously malfunctioning situations where anything other than "objective" factors are involved, such as employee psychology, listening habits, government policy, zoning practice, economic and political forces, and so on.

We should keep in mind that the applied disciplines were never intended to offer solutions to these more complex problems. In fact, their most conscientious practitioners are quite aware of the limitations of traditional methods and constantly use personal knowledge to extend the benefits of their "objective" techniques. Our critique of the limitations of the traditional disciplines is intended to help us create a new model and theoretical framework for thinking about contemporary problems. We hope to build upon past knowledge by extending the conceptual basis on which it rests. For instance, a communicational model establishes acoustic design as what H. A. Simon calls a "science of the artificial," the knowledge about how artifacts function to fulfill certain goals, as distinct from the natural sciences which describe how things are (Simon, 1969). If we shift our focus from the sound wave and the audio signal as the artifact to the soundscape, where sound mediates relationships between the individual and the environment, we will be able to understand the intricacies of how sound *functions,* not simply how it behaves. Functionality, rather than simply aesthetic quality or the absence of annoyance, becomes the criterion for design.

Acoustic design, in the most general sense, seeks to modify the functional relationships within the listener-environment system. It may involve changing the sound environment itself, but because the listener is always included within the system, it may also mean modifying the listening or thinking habits of the listener as part of the design strategy. In this sense, design is less of a manipulative process than that in which the "expert" imposes predetermined criteria onto an environment. It may be as simple as the listener(s) choosing to modify the way in which sound is creating functional relationships within an environment. It may use new technology or invoke traditional models, not in any misguided attempt to turn back the clock, but in order to learn from the principles that have been successful in balancing a soundscape and promoting functionality in the past. Our analysis will reveal the vulnerability that acoustic environments have to degradation which no natural forces appear to be able to counteract. Therefore, conscious, thoughtful, and informed design becomes a necessity if we are to regain control of the soundscape and make it function to our benefit.

2

The Listener

Both in theory and practice, listening is the crucial interface between the individual and an environment. It is also a set of sophisticated skills which appear to be deteriorating within the technologized urban environment, both because of noise exposure which causes hearing loss and physiological stress, and because of the proliferation of low information, highly redundant, and basically uninteresting sounds which do not encourage sensitive listening. To understand the basis of acoustic communication, we need to examine the nature of listening more carefully.

Hearing and Listening

Hearing is well documented as a sensitivity to physical vibration within certain ranges of frequencies and intensities. In the human case, the ranges are quite large. For instance, with intensity, the dynamic range is larger than that of any audio system that processes sound. This range extends from the threshold of hearing, the slightest intensity level that excites the auditory system, to the threshold of pain, the intensity level that causes acute discomfort. The difference in intensity between the two levels is on the order of magnitude of a trillion to one, a range that is so large that a logarithmic scale has been devised to reduce it to a difference of 120 on the decibel (dB) scale. On such a scale, each doubling of intensity is measured as 3 dB.

Our sensitivity to this range of possible sound intensities is constantly changing, somewhat similarly to how the eye adjusts itself by changing the size of the iris to accommodate variable light levels. In the auditory system, the changes are called threshold shifts, which refer to an increase or decrease in the lowest sound level (or threshold) which can be heard at any moment. In contrast, the absolute threshold of hearing is a statistical measure of the best hearing level of younger people with undamaged hearing. The auditory system responds to the average noise level of any environment by shifting its sensitivity—even for normal environments of modest level. One only has to remove all extraneous noise from an environment, dim the lights, and concentrate on one's hearing to experience the gradual dropping of the hearing threshold that progressively brings minute sounds into prominence. At least 15 minutes is required to bring hearing to its most sensitive state, a duration similar to the adjustment period for a low light environment.

Threshold shift allows a certain degree of protection of the auditory system against high sound levels. This protection, however, is only temporary and cannot prevent the irreparable damage that occurs if the noise level is too high and experienced for too long a time. A large threshold shift, which is brought about by a saturation of the hair cells mentioned in the previous chapter, must be followed by a period of aural "rest," in order for the hair cells to be rejuvenated. Otherwise, deprived of nutrients, they die and cannot be replaced. We will return to the specific problems created by noise in chapter 6. For now, it will suffice to understand that the range of hearing sensitivity is potentially very large, but that it is constantly being adapted to the ambient environment, which can damage the auditory system with high noise levels.

The corresponding range of frequency sensitivity of the auditory system is also large, though it is well known that many animals have an extended high frequency range. The usual description of the audio range, or range of audible frequencies, is that it extends from 20 to 20,000 Hz, where the unit of the Hertz is one cycle per second. In practice, the upper range is seldom above 18 kHz (i.e., 18,000 Hz) for the young adult, and with noise exposure and age, it drops dramatically. At the low frequency end, there is a range where the sensation of pitch starts to disappear, and below it, the sense of physical vibration takes over. This range is between 20 and 25 Hz, and corresponds to the region where the brain cannot distinguish separate events because they are closer than about 50 milliseconds (i.e., they occur with a frequency of 20 Hz). Individual pulses or cycles of the sound wave can be *felt* below 20 Hz because of their ability to cause vibration and stimulate bodily resonances. Frequencies in this range are termed "infrasonic," since they are too low to be heard as having a pitch (Tempest, 1976). Therefore, the low end of the range of hearing sensitivity creates a link between hearing in the conventional sense, and the experience of rhythm (i.e., separate, pulsed events) and bodily sensation.

It is interesting to speculate as to why the human auditory system evolved this kind of sensitivity to physical vibration within a certain range of frequencies and a large range of intensities. In the case of the visual system, it seems more than coincidental that the range of visible frequencies, out of all those present in the electromagnetic spectrum, is centred on one of the fairly narrow bands which the earth's atmosphere transmits. Its opaqueness to other, very harmful types of radiation permitted life to develop on earth in the first place. The narrow visible frequency band coincides with that which is strongly emitted by the sun, namely around the frequency of yellow. The extremely small wavelength of light allows it to reflect off objects and convey information about the most minute characteristics of the object, such as color and texture. Therefore, we can generalize (and simplify) the nature of visual perception as a faculty that allows detail to be observed at a distance. Because of the extreme speed of light, all such detail seems to come to us instantly, giving an immediate "report" of the details of an environment.

Sound vibration, by contrast, requires physical objects and a physical medium of transfer. Moreover, it is quite slow (e.g., in a millisecond, sound travels about a foot, whereas light travels 186 miles). Sound is created by the physical motion of objects in the environment, and as acoustics tells us, it is the result of energy transfers. Although the sound wave reflects every detail of the motion of its source, its travel through an environment—reflecting from and being absorbed by all objects—is influenced by the general configuration of the environment. In a sense, the sound wave arriving at the ear is the analogue of the current state of the physical environment, because as the wave travels, it is changed by each interaction with the environment. Whereas vision allows us to scan an environment for specific detail, hearing gives us a less detailed, but more comprehensive image of entire environment in all directions at once.

Moreover, because of the relative slowness of sound propagation, not all acoustic information comes to us instantly. The various differences in time of arrival at the ear provide information about the spatial relationships within the environment. These effects are generally termed "echo" and "reverberation," but to appreciate their extreme subtlety we have only to think of the way in which a blind person maneuvers through an environment by hearing how sound is reflected off objects. Imagine "hearing" an open door because of the absence of reflection, or discerning the size and type of a tree simply on the basis of the kind of reflections it gives!

> After I went blind, I could never make a motion without starting an avalanche of noise. . . . Whenever I took a step, the floor cried or sang—I could hear it making both these sounds—and its song was passed along from one board to the next, all the way to the window, to give me the measure of the room. If I spoke out suddenly, the windowpanes, which seemed so solid in their putty frames, began to shake, very lightly of course but distinctly. . . . I could hear the smallest recession in the wall from a distance, for it changed the whole room. Because this nook, that alcove were there, the wardrobe sang a hollower song. . . . As I walked along a country road bordered by trees, I could point to each one of the trees by the road, even if they were not spaced at regular intervals. I knew whether the trees were straight and tall, carrying their branches as a body carries its head, or gathered into thickets and partly covering the ground around them. (Lusseyran, 1963, pp. 22, 32)

In general, we may say that hearing is a sensitivity to both the detail of physical vibration within an environment and its physical orientation as revealed through its modification of those vibrations. The evolutionary development of the auditory system presumably occurred because such information contributed to the survival potential of the species.

Listening

On the other hand, our model of listening begins with the survival value implicit in the ability to *interpret* information about the environment and one's interaction with it, based on the detail contained within those physical vibrations. Compared to the vast amount of knowledge available concerning the physical behavior of sound that determines what the brain receives, our knowledge of how we extract and *use* acoustic information seems quite limited. And yet, the extraction of this information is so habitual and immediate to us—compared with how difficult it is for us to explain why something sounds the way it does—that we can easily take it for granted. Perhaps our lack of explicit awareness of how much we rely on routine acoustic information makes it difficult for us to grasp the implications of environmental changes that subvert and threaten the process. We may have the feeling that something is missing and that perhaps the new situation is not satisfactory, but we don't know why.

We will begin to seek answers to these questions by examining the listening process more carefully. First, we should recall that whereas hearing can be regarded as a somewhat passive ability that seems to work with or without conscious effort, listening implies an active role involving differing levels of attention—"listening for," not just "listening to." The level of attention may be casual and distracted, or in a state of readiness, and its scope may be global (a general "scan" of the entire environment) or focussed on a particular source to the exclusion of other sounds. However, in each case, listening can be consciously controlled. It can also produce categories of perceptual immediacy such as "background" and "foreground" which do not necessarily correspond to physical distance; that is, a distant sound may seem more prominent in an environment than a closer one.

A general characteristic of cognitive processing that seems to lie at the basis of listening is the detection of difference. Sound is predicated on change at every level. At the micro level, sound pressure must oscillate in order to be detected as sound. The sound wave comprises small variations in pressure around the constant atmospheric pressure. At the macro level, a constant pattern or loudness in a sound quickly produces a psychological reaction called "habituation." In terms of information theory, the degree of repetitiveness in a message is termed "redundancy." It also corresponds to the degree to which information is predictable, i.e., in conformity to past experience. Even at the neurological level, a constant stimulus results in a decreased firing rate of the neurons. Therefore, we may characterize the first stage of cognitive processing as the detection of change. Detail is important, but only when it presents new information.

However, the amount of detail involved in even simple acoustic situations is very large, and the differences which the brain can detect are often very small. Therefore, a certain amount of screening of the incoming information is required to reduce the amount of data to that which may be significant, for instance, by reference to the memory of past experience. From a communicational point of view, this type of screening is best characterized by what Bateson calls "the difference that makes a difference" (Bateson, 1972, p. 453). It is at this point that the distinction between signal processing and information processing becomes apparent. Signal processing may involve analysis that yields data about certain parameters of the sound, but information is created and communication takes place only through the cognitive ability to distinguish what is *significant* about the results of that analysis.

Listening to the Past

A theoretical understanding of listening is greatly complemented by examining what listeners have to say, particularly about experiences in the past. The World Soundscape Project (WSP) calls these "earwitness accounts," and frequently the memories of older people about the sounds of the past are amazingly vivid even after decades. The way in which sounds are stored in memory, not separately, but in association with their original context, betrays a fundamental aspect of the listening process. Consider this reminiscence from *The Vancouver Soundscape* describing Vancouver in the 1920s:

> You could even tell the difference between the various delivery carts just by listening to the horses. The iceman had a couple of very heavy cobs drawing his cart, and the coalman had a pair of substantial Percherons which always walked. But Drysdales, a drygoods store . . . had a light cart and a couple of beautiful lightweight horses. They would prance along at a much gayer rate. The Chinese vegetable men had funny old carts with very lazy horses, which would just clob, clob, clob along. (WSP, 1978a, p. 18)

Each sound is clearly associated with a different delivery vehicle passing by and making stops. Differences in their sounds provided useful information, and patterns of association were quickly built up that stayed in the memory nearly a half century later. It is not difficult to imagine why. Each sound was associated, first of all, with one of the essentials of life in those days: ice, coal, clothing, food. A person waiting for a delivery would be listening for one of these sounds, comparing it to past experience and differentiating it from those with which it might be confused. Secondly, we can surmise that the person had a personal acquaintance with each of the delivery people; the sound connoted not only an immediate necessity, but also a personal relationship associated with it. Today, not only have the sounds changed, but so has the social and economic context that included home delivery. Moreover, many neighborhood sounds, although they may be distinctive, seldom involve familiarity with the person producing the sound, given the transience of urban dwellers, and the impersonality of many newer neighborhoods. Therefore, such sounds are more likely to be treated as annoyances and not as relevant information.

Another quote from the same source concerns the sound of foghorns that is common along the coast:

> The foghorns made dismal, gloomy sounds. They all had different tones and sounded at different intervals. We heard them as we went to sleep and again first thing in the morning. But despite the fact that they were mournful, we seem to remember them as somehow comforting. (WSP, 1978a, p. 19)

Here the relation of the listener to the sound is less immediate and dependent than that of a boat captain, for instance, but the experience seems no less important. The person was obviously familiar with the signalling codes of each horn, though the explicit information conveyed seems less important than the symbolic function which the sound acquired. The sound was heard at specific times of day, times when the listening process was probably less cluttered with other matters. The symbolic significance of the sound seems to have outweighed its possible disruption of sleep; in fact, the repetitive pattern of the horn acted as a kind of lullaby and seemed to be a comforting reminder of safety from the potential dangers of the night and the natural elements. We may be tempted to think that such associations could surround any sound, but this quotation suggests that the particular quality of the sound ("mournful") with its human associations, no doubt related to the deep resonances and drooping pitch that characterized many such horns along the coast, matched its function ("comforting") in a way that made it not only pleasing, but memorable.

Finally, we observe the most explicit type of listening situation, that in which information of immediate relevance is sought through active listening and a "testing out" of the environment through acoustic participation:

> [The boat captains] used to get their position by echo whistling. They'd give a short whistle and estimate the distance from the shoreline by the returning echo. If the echo came back from both sides at the same time they'd know that they were in the middle of the channel. They could recognize different shorelines by the different echoes—a rocky cliff, for example, would give a clear distinctive echo, whereas a sandy beach would give a more prolonged echo. They could even pick up an echo from logs. Nowadays, if the radar breaks down, they have to put out an anchor. Their ears aren't trained to listen their way through the fog. (WSP, 1978a, p. 17)

Aside from the implications that modern technology has changed our relationship to the environment, and that our dependence on it may be fragile, we find in this quote an example of the most basic function of listening—the survival value implicit in detecting information about the environment through acoustic cues. The specific technique involved here, called "echolocation," is exactly analogous to that used by bats in bouncing high frequency clicks off their prey or other objects. In experiments this ability is revealed to be effective even when the object has the thickness of a human hair (Griffin, 1959, p. 93)! The blind person's use of a tapping cane or sharp footfall achieves the same effect. Although the "hostile environments" through which we maneuver today are more likely to be heavily trafficked streets, this type of listening (which is still needed for survival) frequently includes having to block out a great deal of irrelevant information in order to hear what is important. A greater mental effort is required for it to work, and the net result, accumulated over thousands of routine daily situations, is both the fatiguing, physical stress of noise, and the disinclination to listen attentively.

Listening-In-Search and Listening-In-Readiness

The above three quotations reveal what we may call three "levels" of listening attention. In the echolocation example, listening is at its most active, involving a conscious search of the environment for cues. We can term this level of listening as "listening-in-search." Detail is of the greatest importance, and the ability to focus on one sound to the exclusion of others (an ability termed "cocktail party effect" when it occurs in fairly noisy situations), is central to the listening process (Moray, 1969). The analytic nature of this kind of listening suggests a comparison to dominant hemisphere (or "left brain") types of processes, which are also used in language processing.

The delivery cart example shows an intermediate kind of listening, that in which the attention is in readiness to receive significant information, but where the focus of one's attention is probably directed elsewhere. This type of listening, which we will call "listening-in-readiness," depends on associations being built up over time, so that the sounds are familiar and can be readily identified even by "background" processing in the brain. Perhaps the most extreme case in which such listening operates is when one is sleeping. The classic example is that of the mother being wakened by her baby's cry, but not by trucks or other noises. Subtle differences in familiar sounds convey information that is more important in judging the sound than simple identification. Even when a sound is unfamiliar or unexpected, this type of listening is ready to treat it as new information and evaluate its potential significance.

Listening-in-readiness also requires a favorable environmental situation for it to be effective. The brain is adept at pattern detection, but a minimum signal-to-noise ratio is required so that the desired signal may be separated from any competing noise. Situations where signal detection is difficult or impossible may be termed "lo-fi" environments, by analogy to electroacoustic signals of poor quality, high noise, and distortion. The complementary situation, the "hi-fi" environment, is one in which all sounds may be heard clearly, with whatever detail and spatial orientation they may have. Such an environment is, by definition, balanced and well "designed," whether the design is intentional or the result of natural causes. Within the "hi-fi" environment, the listening process is characterized by interaction. One does not have to "fight" the environment to make sense of it. Rather, it invites participation and reinforces a positive relationship between the individual and the environment. The "lo-fi" environment, in contrast, seems to encourage feelings of being cut off or separated from the environment. The person's attention is directed inwards, and interaction with others is discouraged by the effort to "break through" that is required. Feelings of alienation and isolation can be the result.

The exchange of acoustic information in a soundscape can also be thought of in terms of "feedback" concepts to describe the types of communicational relationships produced by "hi-fi" and "lo-fi" environments. The sound made by a person takes on the characteristics of the environment through the processes of reflection and absorption described earlier. Therefore, what the listener/soundmaker hears is a simultaneous image of self *and* environment. Unlike the passive quality of "being seen," the listener must make an active gesture to "be heard." The feedback of acoustic information is necessary for orientation, and in the most general sense, the awareness of self in relation to others.

There are few situations where such feedback does not operate. One is the anechoic chamber which is constructed to eliminate all reflected sound by making every surface as absorbant as possible. The lack of feedback may seem disorienting at first, since it is normally taken for granted. Sounds seem hyper-localized. They come with needle-like directness and disappear as soon as they travel a different course. However, it is only the sense of environmental space that is distorted. One can experience one's own sounds, and those of others, directly and without environmental coloration. This sense of "removal" from the environment may even seem a positive experience, similar to meditation.

The lo-fi environment, however, is similar only in that one receives little feedback from one's own sounds as well as others', either directly or indirectly. A simple measure of the situation is whether one can hear one's own footsteps in such an environment. If not, one is acoustically "cut off" from the most basic connection one has to an environment, and the extent of one's personal "aural space" is reduced to less than that of human proportions. In communicational terms, "negative feedback" is what allows a course of action to be modified based on the information received about its results. It is, in fact, a positive process that allows behavior to be guided and kept in control. Many occupations and common tasks involve hearing the results of our actions. We need to hear how well the nail is hit, how a motor is responding, and what sounds denote malfunction. The lo-fi environment destroys the fundamental basis which permits effective acoustic communication.

Listening-in-search and listening-in-readiness are basic processes which must be practised daily, like any skills. We may be able to adapt to environments in which such skills are thwarted by substituting other modes of communication, or by adapting our behavior, even if in a negative fashion. But if we experience fewer and fewer environments where acoustic communication skills can be practised, and children grow up learning fewer of those skills in the first place, what will be the long-term implications? It is these questions which have more importance than the particulars of our response to any given situation. For instance, one may say one likes the noise and hubbub of the city; to a city-raised person it is a reminder of home, and the action and excitement on which one thrives. The "quiet" of the countryside (today, an increasingly romantic illusion) may seem intolerable by comparison. These personal associations miss the point. If we as a society are moving farther and farther away from an acoustic orientation to our lives, what are the long-range implications of the loss of the relationships and patterns of communication which that orientation supported?

Background Listening and the Keynote Sound

The above quotation about hearing foghorns last thing at night and again in the morning describes a different level of listening that we commonly experience. It can be called "background listening" because the sound usually remains in the background of our attention. It occurs when we are not listening for a particular sound, and when its occurrence has no special or immediate significance to us. However, we are still aware of the sound, in the sense that if asked whether we had heard it, we could probably respond affirmatively, as long as the event were not too distant in the past. Therefore, this type of listening differs from "subliminal" perception which is defined as the total lack of conscious awareness of a perception, but with later behavioral evidence that something has been experienced at a subconscious level (Dixon, 1971). Whether subliminal perception exists for sound is still controversial, whereas the experience of background listening occurs all the time.

Perhaps the most common reason for sounds to be heard in background listening is that they are a usual occurrence, and therefore expected and predictable. They may be singled out for attention if the need should arise, but normally they aren't specifically noticed. The World Soundscape Project has classified some of these sounds as *keynote* sounds by analogy to the musical use of the term where the key of a piece is its fundamental tonality, or tonal center, to which all other pitches are related. In certain types of music, the keynote or "tonic" is constantly sounded as a drone in order to make the relationship of the other pitches more apparent, and to reinforce the image of a tonal center in the listener.

The reason for any sound being termed "keynote" is not because of any characteristic it has itself, but rather because of the way in which it is habitually perceived. Thus, a keynote sound may be part of the ambience, i.e., at a low, constant level, such as electrical hum or distant traffic; but it may also be a sound signal, i.e., a sound that stands out in an environment and is clearly distinguishable from the ambient noise. Examples of the latter type of keynote would be the sound of an ambulance siren near a busy hospital, the sound of train whistles to nearby residents, or the regular ringing of bells at fixed time intervals, as often occurs in European communities. To the visitor, such a sound may be noticed as a signal, but to the permanent resident, it is habitually experienced as a background sound. The foghorn in the above quotation seems to have functioned as a keynote sound, and yet we note the permanence of the experience in memory and its positive associations, long after it may have disappeared.

Keynote sounds paradoxically seem to be unimportant in perceptual terms, but precisely because of their prevalence, they reflect a fundamental characteristic of the environment. Just as the natural elements form the keynote sounds of traditional societies, the ubiquitous presence of traffic, electrical hums, and air conditioning reveals the dependence which modern society has on its technological base. We can hear this dependence in the sound of environments practically anywhere in the industrialized world. In terms of figure-ground relationships, the keynote sound is the "ground" against which all other sounds are heard. And like any ground, the keynotes of our environments set off and influence our perception of its "figures" or signals.

It is significant that all of the three instances of modern keynotes mentioned above (traffic, hums, and air conditioning) are examples of flat-line or steady sounds. Their constancy of intensity level makes them easy for the brain to adapt to because they show little change, and certainly none that seems to make a difference. Even when the sound contains a regular pulsation, the same kind of habituation is possible. Traffic and air conditioning are also examples of "broad-band" sounds, that is, sounds whose spectrum or energy content is continuously distributed over a fairly large range of frequencies. When that range is the entire audible spectrum and the distribution is uniform, the sound is called "white noise," by analogy to white light which contains all visible frequencies. The sound pressure variation of a broad-band sound is random, unlike a pitched sound where it is cyclic. The redundancy and predictability of the broad-band spectrum makes it easy for the brain to adapt to such sounds. The electrical hum, though periodic in waveform, achieves the same type of redundancy simply because of its artificial origin, i.e., unlike natural sounds, its waveform is perfectly regular and unchanging. This phenomenon will be explained further in chapter 9. Therefore, the most common sounds of the modern environment are low information, high redundancy sounds to which the brain can easily adapt.

However, the easy adaptability to a keynote sound is not necessarily a reason for its acceptability. For instance, it has recently been claimed that the masking qualities of such sounds as white noise make them desirable for open office areas in order to cover up the more distracting sounds of typewriters, ringing phones, conversations, and so on.[1] It is true that the "startle reaction" produced by unpredictably occurring transient sounds can be annoying, and that a steady or predictable sound is less distracting, if one has to accept one or the other. However, there are other implications to the nature of keynote sounds that only become apparent when they are considered within a communicational framework.

The presence of a steady level of sound reduces what we may call the "acoustic horizon" of an environment, that is, the farthest distance from which sound may be heard. The steady sound masks low level sounds, thereby producing a reduced sense of space. In the most extreme case, each individual is surrounded in a cocoon of sound with no aural contact with others. There is also an accompanying reduction in the variety of sounds that will be heard, because only a few of the stronger ones will rise above the ambient level. Subtle differences in existing sounds become blurred; the environment becomes bland. Although it might appear that concentration could be improved through the introduction of masking sounds, we must keep in mind that the inevitable increase in noise level also causes more physiological stress and greater fatigue at the end of the day. Beyond a certain point, the higher noise level also results in increased performance errors, because of the extra load of information processing when the brain has to shut out noise (Finkelman, 1975). We will return to the details of these problems in chapter 6.

For now, it will suffice to note that background listening is an important part of the listening process, but one that has associated with it particular problems. When background noise levels increase too much, there is extra stress on the body and a greater information load on the brain. The introduction of low information background sounds suggests a trend towards homo-

[1] "Acoustical Environment in the Open-Plan Office," Report prepared by the American Society for Testing and Materials, 1978. Distributed by the Engineering Dept., Soundolier Inc., 9380 Watson Industrial Park, St. Louis, MO. 63126. See also *Environment and Behavior*, 1982, *14* (3, 5).

geneous environments with poor acoustic definition. Such environments do not encourage more active types of listening, and their prevalence may prevent listeners from experiencing any alternative. Moreover, once background listening becomes a habit, it is ready for exploitation by the media. The power of long-term subconscious association can be tapped for commercial ends through frequent keynote-like repetition, as we shall see in part II.

Listener Preferences and Attitudes

The listening phenomena described thus far depend on specific types of relationships of the listener to the environment, and cannot be derived entirely from the sounds themselves. For instance, it would be very difficult for an objective, acoustic analysis to determine whether a given sound is a keynote, and certainly it would be impossible for such an analysis to account for the importance a sound has to a community. At best, one could conduct listener surveys, but the difficulty listeners have in articulating attitudes and types of listening experience would prove to be a limitation. Analysis of the physical characteristics of a sound can only support an understanding of the communicational patterns within an environment by informing us of the "ground rules" for acoustic behavior—when masking will occur, what factors affect propagation, how the makeup of this sound differs from that one, and so on. The way in which a sound *functions* for the listener depends on its social and environmental context.

There is a strong tendency, however, to want to label sounds as being good or bad on the basis of listener preference, and efforts to combat noise pollution often lead us to believe that if only we could get rid of certain offending sounds, all would be well. A certain small community, in its zeal to combat noise pollution, wanted to suppress a local factory whistle because it was loud. The equating of loudness to pollution in this case ignores the way in which the sound functions in the community, probably as a useful community signal that reflects an important institution and contributes to community identity. Another way to consider the problem would be to ask what the result would be if all "loud" sounds were removed from the community and the result happened to be a dull, homogeneous environment of low level hums and drones! The lack of acoustic information and interesting sonic relationships would hardly produce a balanced soundscape.

How then are we to evaluate the endless variations of reported listener preferences and dislikes? Do they constitute a reliable basis for the design of an environment? Listener preferences are certainly of interest, particularly when compared cross-culturally, as in R. M. Schafer's *The Tuning of the World* where they are documented for several countries (Schafer, 1977). Most sound preferences seem to depend on learned associations. Scolding parents and the sound of the school bell are often disliked by children, though the latter may provoke nostalgia in later years. People in tropical countries often dislike the more violent sounds of nature, especially wild animals, because of the danger they represent, whereas natural sounds are generally the favorites in northern countries. Beyond the preferences that are common within a country, there are purely individual patterns of association based on personal experience—sounds that remind one of pleasant or unpleasant memories and therefore evoke a conditioned response.

Although such associations are obviously important for the listener, it is the concern of a communicational model to account for general patterns of listening that result in observable behavior, not simply subjective reactions. For instance, how does a sound become a "taboo" or produce a phobic reaction? Under what conditions do people tolerate or accept an obviously intrusive sound? When does a sound become a "sound romance"? And, moreover, how do these types of reactions, which are based on habitual ways of understanding sound, affect individual and community behavior?

Most patterns of like and dislike for sound stem from personal and prevailing social attitudes. Consider the neighborhood where residents dislike the screeching of tires or motorcycles passing, but tolerate the obviously louder sound of jets flying overhead. There are some objective characteristics of a sound that account for the response it evokes (such as the startle reaction produced by a sharp, percussive sound, or the grating effect of sounds with a lot of high frequency components). However, the response to screeching tires and the like seems to be conditioned mainly by the person's attitudes towards the kind of people making the sound. If aircraft have become a common occurrence for the neighborhood and the residents have come to accept them, the lack of protest can be attributed both to a psychological habituation (the perennial phrase "you get used to it"), and to some form of rationalization that the airline industry is good for the community, necessary for the economy, and is being responsible by making a reasonable effort to minimize annoyance. Good advertising and public relations work on the part of the soundmaker can usually achieve this type of community perception.

Similarly, certain sounds acquire a "taboo" status based on prevailing social, moral, aesthetic, or religious grounds. The use of swear words, religious terms, certain body sounds, breaking the silence on solemn occasions (or traditionally on Sunday in Western society), are all viewed with social disapproval. Noise legislation of the traditional nuisance type has attempted to control such activities as street music (particularly in previous centuries), vendors, barking dogs, noisy trades and industry, radios and loudspeakers, and even carpet beating. The history of such taboos, as summarized in (Schafer, 1977), provides an interesting insight into changing aural perceptions and community attitudes. The proscription of any sound clearly gives it power, whether it is the sound reserved for a special occasion (the bell in a religious festival or the emergency warning signal), or that disapproved of under any circumstances. The latter provides those rebelling against social norms with a powerful weapon to use in protest. In every case, phobic reactions toward sound betray social attitudes.

The romance that builds up around the "disappearing" sound from the past is the counterpart to the phobia that usually surrounds a new sound, particularly when it replaces an older, more familiar one. (We will deal with the importance of preserving historical and unique "soundmarks" in our discussion of the acoustic community in chapter 5.) The romance associated with a past sound arises from a nostalgia for a time and circumstance that no longer exists. The sound seems romantic because it has the power both to evoke the past context and to idealize it. As suggested earlier, sounds and their original context are stored in memory as patterns. Recalling the context may revive a memory of the sound, and the sound, if heard again, usually brings the entire context back to life. (Smell seems to operate similarly for some people). However, the memory of both the sound and its context has been idealized. One seldom remembers the flaws in the sound or the noises that came with it, just as one seldom remembers the negative features of an experience as acutely as they seemed at the time. The mind discards irrelevant detail; hence, the sound "resonates" in the memory, much as the past becomes idealized as the "good old days" for many people.

The idealization of sound in the listener's memory is a practical fact for which the sound effects person is grateful (Beeby, 1966). One doesn't have to recreate the *exact* sound or environment for it to be evocative. Generally, a tape recording of an actual sound is less effective than a skillful simulation that simplifies and idealizes it. Those engaged in producing artificial environments on record and tape ("The Perfect Seascape" type of muzak) also realize that the artificial is "better" when appealing to memory and fantasy. Likewise, commercials, film soundtracks, and radio plays exploit the listener's ability to generate an "ideal" memory image based on many actual experiences. Like Tony Schwartz's "responsive chord," such an auditory image may resonate when struck appropriately (Schwartz, 1973).

One can perceive a common thread running through all of the varied aspects of the listening experience described in this chapter. The auditory system is constantly ready for new information about the environment and compares it to stored experience. Patterns in the incoming signal may be found that match those in storage (since in our model, it is only the "pattern" that is stored and not the sound itself). The sound pattern has connected with it layers of association built up over the years, and frequently these associations have a predictable, fixed quality, namely that a particular pattern of sound always produces the same response: phobia, annoyance, pleasure, intrusion, rejection, evocation of the past, and so on. These habitual responses lead to certain types of behavior, and hence to a particular relationship of the person to the environment. Thus, the pattern of sound *mediates* that relationship.

Of course, patterns of behavior, including listening, can be changed. Something can intervene in the process that disrupts or modifies it. Entirely new experiences may necessitate the formation of new concepts. The breakdown in functionality of a given pattern of behavior may cause it to be replaced by another. Or, the intervention of a third party who may do nothing more than say "Listen!" may start a process of change that can have untold benefit. Whatever the reason, all developments that shape the acoustic relation of the person to an environment will occur at the crucial interface called listening, and all design criteria that are to be effective must proceed from an intimate understanding of the listening process.

3

Voice and Soundmaking

The first sounds to which the ear is exposed as it develops in the fetus are human sounds, and from that point onward, the voice and human soundmaking are the sounds to which we are most sensitive as listeners. We seem to have an unflagging interest in the endless variations of verbal production, including not only speech and singing, but also the wider range of nonverbal elements that complement them. The brain is as adept at recognizing voices and interpreting countless subtle levels of expression, as it is oriented towards recognition of human faces. From the moment of birth, the acquisition of communicative auditory and vocal skills proceeds quickly and efficiently, based largely on the human sounds that are produced and received. The development and extension of such skills continues for a lifetime, even after basic language skills are mastered. In many ways, human soundmaking sets the norms for human acoustic communication.

If "the proper study of mankind is mankind itself," then surely the study of systems of acoustic communication must take human soundmaking as its starting point. Indeed, the literature on linguistics in its broadest sense is truly enormous, but it is rather unfortunate that the emphasis on every aspect of language, from the physiology of the voice through phonetics to theoretical and comparative linguistics, has overshadowed the sounding basis on which all of it depends, namely how human soundmaking functions in communication. It was remarked in chapter 1 that physical acoustics has developed farther and farther away from its basis in aural experience by creating intellectual concepts, theories, equations, and visual representations of its subject matter with which to think and talk about it. The same is true to a slightly lesser extent in linguistics. Most books or articles on the subject refer in print to spoken artifacts which the reader is assumed to be able to reproduce in "the mind's ear," and recently, the emphasis on automated speech synthesis has required linguistic theory to be put to the aural test (Cole, 1980; Laske, 1974a). Typically, the results of the latter show that aurally convincing speech production is difficult to produce and that the ear is tremendously sensitive to distortion and levels of semantic implication.

However, many remarkable attempts have been made over the last few decades to restore the importance of the aural basis of communication. Peter Ostwald's pioneering work in describing human soundmaking and its pathologies from a psychiatric perspective must be mentioned (Ostwald, 1963a, 1973). Don Ihde, in his *Listening and Voice,* has proceeded from a phenomenological point of view to understand human sound by careful observation of subjective experience (Ihde, 1976). Walter Ong (1982) has described the dynamics of an orally-based culture and shown how its basis in sound and hearing affects patterns of thought and communication in comparison to literate cultures based on writing and print. In addition, the growing literature on interpersonal and nonverbal communication is slowly starting to include some analysis of human soundmaking, usually through the concept of "paralanguage" which refers both to nonverbal acts (e.g., vocal noises, whistling, humming, cries, etc.) and to the acoustic structure of utterances that give them specific expression (Leathers, 1976; Mehrabian, 1972; Trager, 1958). Paralanguage is generally grouped with other aspects of nonverbal communication such as kinesics (i.e., body and facial movement), proxemics (i.e., interpersonal distance) and other forms of sensory communication (Birdwhistell, 1970; Key, 1975). In this chapter we will not attempt a summary of this work, or of linguistics, but instead will attempt to place human soundmaking within the framework of basic processes of acoustic communication. In the next chapter, we will compare it to other systems whereby sound is organized.

Voice and the Whole Person

Most of the more accessible accounts of voice production deal with it as the "speech chain" (Denes & Pinson, 1963), tracing the physiological mechanisms by which the body produces vocal sound, starting with the air stream from the lungs which is set in vibration by the vocal cords and shaped into articulated sound by the vocal tract. There is obvious value in isolating each of the component mechanisms in order to understand their functional roles separately, and the resultant models of the entire system are often the starting point for simulation and synthesis. For acoustic communication, the significance of the voice is that, first of all, its production is a reflection of the whole person, and that secondly, soundmaking is a primary means of communication by which the person's concept of self and relationships to others, including the environment, are established.

The concept of the voice reflecting the whole person is a simple one that we use every day when we detect the state and mood of a person by noting large or small differences in the voice, even if a commonplace statement or verbal gesture is being made. Psychoanalysts and psychiatrists, particularly those following Ostwald's lead, may use such information, both subjectively and through analytical documentation, to detect disturbed patterns of communication (Reik, 1949). The blind person, through knowing others primarily by voice, is usually extremely sensitive to small changes that betray mood and or anxiety. The reasons for the voice revealing this information are fairly straightforward.

Because vocal production depends, first, on breath support, any physiological or psychological stress that affects breathing will immediately be revealed in voice quality. The cause may be temporary, in the sense of being a transient condition. For instance, it may be the result of particular stress that causes shallow breathing with poor diaphragm support, hence a thin sounding voice. Or, the vocal affect may be a long-term manifestation of personality, changeable only through therapeutic intervention. For instance, Ostwald documents "four acoustic stereotypes," namely the sharp, flat, hollow, and robust voice that reflect personality traits (Ostwald, 1963a, ch. 6). Pathological communication is often characterized by unnatural vocal qualities that are the result of particular muscular actions that affect the voice (Chevrie-Muller et al., 1978). Sudden switches in vocal quality reflect different aspects of personality "taking over," and documented cases of multiple personality always refer to the switches being accompanied by different vocal and linguistic qualities.

Because much of what is loosely termed "voice quality" depends on the resonant cavity of the mouth (shaped by the position of the tongue, lips, and jaws), as well as the nasal and sinus cavities and the chest, any change in the condition of these parts of the body is reflected in the timbre of the voice. The cause may be as simple as that of the common cold, or may be a complex set of reactions whereby a person habitually uses, refrains from using, or tenses certain parts of the body for psychological reasons. Just as the physical environment "colors" all sound waves passing through it until the sound reflects the current state of the environment, so the body and the mind color the voice until it is the reflection of the whole person. Whether we are in the position of close friend, casual observer, audience member, or therapist, sensitivity to a person's voice and vocal habits has much to reveal if only we listen.

Voice and Self Image

The cry of the baby is an unmistakable acoustic signal to the mother about its current needs; the loudness and high frequency characteristics of the cry ensure that the message gets through. Abnormalities in the cry have been shown to reveal internal problems that may not have been diagnosed by other means (Ostwald & Peltzman, 1974). But the child with normal hearing quickly discovers that soundmaking produces an immediate aural feedback, and frequently a reaction from other people as well. Language does not develop naturally with the congenitally deaf, and learning to speak becomes a painful and difficult experience. That we take the feedback of vocal sounds for granted can be shown in experiments where speech is delayed by a small amount. The result is a slurring, stuttering, or even a cessation of speech when the normal feedback process is altered (Yates, 1963).

A simpler modification of the feedback process occurs with either earplugs or headphone listening, one producing the reverse effect of the other. With headphones that enclose the ears, one's own voice sounds less loud, and therefore one raises the voice level in compensation. In the case of earplugs, the input level to the auditory canal is lessened, and the phenomenon of bone conduction becomes much more prominent. That is, more of the sound one hears comes directly through the bones of the skull (with characteristic low frequency emphasis), and the voice actually sounds *louder*. The result is that one compensates in the other direction by lowering the voice. To return the voice to a normal level, one must *feel* the muscular force required for speech production and not rely on aural feedback. This skill can be learned fairly easily, but it is clearly not the usual means for regulating voice level.

The voice, as well as other forms of soundmaking, is part of a feedback mechanism with broader implications than simply acoustic control. As referred to earlier, unlike the passive quality of "being seen," to "be heard" requires an active gesture, one which is a strong manifestation of self and contributor to self image. And unlike our inability to see ourselves without external aids, we cannot help hearing ourselves in a way in which no one else is able. Paradoxically, the self we see in a mirror is not the image others see (it is the reversed "mirror image"), and similarly, the self we hear is not the voice others hear—it is colored by bone conduction and head resonances (Sundberg, 1980). Therefore, just as a person often says that a photograph "doesn't look like me" (and won't unless the photographer is astute enough to print the image backwards so that it is the same as what the person sees in a mirror), so too one is usually shocked to hear one's own voice on a tape recording for the first time. This reaction occurs not only because the imagined faults in the voice seem exaggerated when heard objectively, but also because the reproduced voice can never have the same timbral qualities as that heard internally. One has to learn to understand "images" of oneself; the personal experience of self is essentially private and uncommunicable.

In Western society, most people regard "talking to yourself" as a somewhat childish activity, presumably because it occurs naturally in childhood, up to about the age of 7. Piaget and other observers of child development have noted that the majority of the child's speech from the ages of three to seven is egocentric in nature, and only gradually does it become increasingly socially directed towards others. Vygotsky (1962) convincingly argues that egocentric speech in childhood (i.e., speech for and to oneself) is an important link between vocal and inner speech, and that its disappearance around the age of 7 is the result of it being completely internalized as "inner speech, which serves both autistic and logical thinking" (Vygotsky, 1962, p. 19). Thus we see that the earliest stages of soundmaking in which the self is communicating to and about itself, evolve with mental development, and become the vehicle for thought processes in terms of inner speech. Its later use as a rehearsal for speech and inner thought transmute the role of soundmaking as a "testing out" of the external environment, and the relation of self to it, to the testing out of the inner environment.

If words can be internalized as "inner sounds," then so can other sounds. The close relationship of inner speech and thought has led many observers to assume that thought (i.e., logical thinking) cannot exist without language. However, as we shall argue in the next chapter, other "logical" forms of organized sound exist, most notably music, and therefore we should understand that "thinking in sound" represents a wide range of thought processes. Everyone can "replay" silently in the mind some tune, or even a complex orchestral arrangement. What the improvising musician is doing with an instrument, or a composer is doing in an electroacoustic studio, when verbally silent and acoustically expressive, can only be described as externalized thought, the former producing the result in real time, the latter not.

Besides speech, soundmaking for oneself has traditionally taken many forms, most notably music, to amuse, console, and simply pass the time. So much has been made of the social role of music, that often it is forgotten that it is also a private activity of long tradition—a form of external communication with the self that expresses what cannot be put into words, and in that sense, it is a form of autistic thought. It can also become internalized and self-conscious (i.e., composition), or it can serve the purpose of rehearsal for later social benefit, but in its purest form, musicmaking and soundmaking are closely linked as self-referential activity. On a recording of the music of Northern Swedish mountain shepherdesses who spend long hours alone with their charges, one can hear every form of soundmaking—speech, nonverbal noises, and music—linked together with none of the arbitrary divisions that the descriptive labels just used imply. Sounds flow together in an outpouring of sound made simply for oneself. True, some patterns are specifically intended for signalling the individual animals or a friend across the valley, but much of it seems to reflect the space, the loneliness, and the inner thought of the person.

The sound of the self is ultimately intertwined with the environment. In this chapter, we have deliberately concentrated on the various roles of self-communication, but earlier we have emphasized that *every* natural sound comes to our ears colored by its interactions with the environment. Even our own voice comes back to us with the properties of the immediate environment embedded within it. A good exercise to illustrate this effect is to record one's voice in a variety of environments and acoustic spaces. First of all, one hears how, almost involuntarily, one modifies the style and quality of speech to "match" the environment. Secondly, and usually very dramatically, one hears how each space absorbs certain frequencies, reflects others, adds reverberation or echo, and thereby changes the timbre and envelope of the voice. It is not accidental that many religious meditative practices involve chanting or sustaining tones that resonate within a given space, and that are *in tune* with the natural resonances of that space. The experience (which can be readily imitated in any resonant stairwell or shower stall) is that of a coincidence of the inner and outer environments, since each is vibrating directly and sympathetically with the other. The listener cannot tell if the voice is activating the space, or if the vibration of the space is activating the resonances of the body. In such a situation, sound mediates a *unity* between self and environment. Language creates a division between the two concepts; acoustic experience in which the human sound is reflected back to the listener imbued with the image of the environment unites them.

Paralanguage

It is evident to most everyone that the difference between transcriptions of spoken language and the original speech contains essential information for understanding the meaning of the utterance. Any sentence, or phrase for that matter, can be delivered in a variety of ways with meanings that sometimes contradict each other. Even the simple response "Oh" can be said in ways to mean just about anything. People usually refer to this aspect of spoken language by such terms as "voice quality" or "tone of voice," or simply "it's not what you say, but how you say it." Most researchers agree that voice quality influences the listener's perception of the speaker (Pearce & Conklin, 1971). Sometimes it is called the "musical" aspect of speech, because it involves inflection (pitch contours), rhythm, phrasing, emphasis (or accent), punctuation, timbre (or sound quality), silence (rests), and even cadences—exactly those variables which are used to describe a single voice melody.

Linguists, who have researched the phonemic and syntactical aspects of language to death, have done little more than attach some names to these features that everyone agrees are essential for meaning, such as "prosodic" or "supra-segmental" features (Bolinger, 1972; Crystal, 1969, 1975; Waugh & van Schooneveld, 1980). The latter term suggests that after the elements of language have been dissected, there is something missing that held all of them together. But less is known about such features, it seems, than about any single vowel. Those who study interpersonal communication lump such features together with all other forms of nonverbal communication and call them "paralanguage." However, empirical research in this area has not proceeded much beyond the level of determining that utterances expressing hate are loud and quick, and those of love are the opposite (Costanzo et al., 1969). Not surprisingly, "inter-rater reliability" has been shown to be quite good on such tasks (Markel, 1965).

From the point of view of acoustic communication, the acoustic structure of spoken language is of paramount importance and does much to reveal the intentions of the speaker (Pittenger et al., 1960). We will generalize this concept in the next chapter, and for now will attempt to understand the role such features play in soundmaking situations where communication with others is intended.

The relation of *how* something is said to *what* is said is clearly a relationship of form to content. Artifacts are generally said to be well designed when there is a match or equilibrium between form and content. Bateson (1972) and Watzlawick, et al., (1967) have pointed out that any communication *about* a communication can be called "metacommunication." It is of a higher logical type because it is information about how to interpret the message. The traditional example is often a self-referential statement such as "This is a sentence." However, in interpersonal communication, the acoustic manner in which something is said or an accompanying gesture is regarded as metacommunication, such as when a critical or unpleasant word is accompanied by a smile or wink. Because *all* macro-structural acoustic attributes of language clarify a message and put it into context, we can regard them as forms of metacommunication.

Such forms often have an "analog" character, by comparison to words which are "digital" units. All of the acoustic or musical parameters mentioned above have such an analog quality (e.g., higher or lower pitch, more or less stress, longer or shorter pauses, and so on). Whereas in digital forms of communication, statements can be self-referential and even paradoxical ("This statement is not true"), and can implement logical relationships such as negation and the conditional, analog forms cannot. A digital message may refer to an analog component ("That statement's inflection rises at the end as in a question"), even paradoxically ("I am NOT shouting!"), but the reverse cannot happen—an analog element cannot refer to a digital one.

However, an analog component may contradict the digital message; for instance when a usually friendly greeting is delivered in a rough manner. The recordist of the Swedish mountain music referred to earlier tells the story of the woman calling across the valley for her sister to come and meet the visitor. The call was so musically beautiful that he asked her to repeat it once he got ready to record, but she said that she couldn't because then her sister would disregard the message and think she was practising (since the "message" consisted purely of a tonal pattern with no words). The analog message could not clarify its real meaning—it could not be about the message ("This message does not cancel the previous one").

An important type of communication where form negates content is in play and ritual. As Bateson (1972, p. 177ff) has demonstrated with animal communication, playful actions are coded so they are understood not to stand for what they normally mean, particularly when violent. Similarly, human utterances that are intended to "tease" a person (often including highly offensive comments if taken literally) are delivered with a lightness of tone that reveals the true intent which is not to hurt. Of course, the communication can be misunderstood if the "code" is not interpreted correctly. Ritual verbal violence, highly orchestrated and controlled, characterizes peacemaking ceremonies in various traditional societies, and the contemporary sports match sees much ritual sparring between teams and their supporters. The energy thus channelled is a useful, socially acceptable means of "letting off steam" that prevents real violence. However, there is a fine line between the two, and people in a highly emotional state can get sufficiently out of touch with reality to mistake play for the real thing.

In many cases, the paralinguistic component communicates information that is more significant than the simple linguistic content. Typical greetings and standard phrases uttered between people on meeting have little inherent meaning ("How are you?" being answered literally is the subject of many jokes). Instead, the "tone of voice" and other nonverbal manifestations support a reiteration of the relationship between the people involved—the message is something like: "Yes, I recognize you, we are friends, and I want to reassure you of my goodwill." A curt greeting may signify "Don't bother me, I'm busy," or reinforce a rank differential ("I see you've arrived for work, now get busy!"). Even animals can recognize patterns of inflection and other paralinguistic elements sufficiently to give people (particularly pet owners) the impression that they "understand" what is being said.

Patterns of stress and inflection are peculiar to each language, and their use or absence distinguishes a native speaker from a foreigner. These components are learned by the child imitating its parents and other speakers, and any non-native who is learning the language is well advised to imitate its "melodic lines" as well as the correct pronunciation of individual words. Paralinguistic components are also the most resistant to distortion because they depend on factors like pitch which the auditory system is adept at distinguishing, and because they represent macro-level patterns stretching across many phonemic units (and hence are redundant). For instance, when speech is fairly incomprehensible due to the presence of noise, it is still possible to hear inflection and stress patterns and even identify the language being spoken. When speech is synthesized with a gradual increase of detail, or is gradually distorted or modulated, the paralinguistic features are the first to be recognized and the last to be destroyed.

In other cases, the paralinguistic component communicates things that the speaker may not be aware of revealing. Ostwald characterizes the sharp voice as an unconscious "cry for help" (Ostwald, 1963a, p. 59).

Guarded language, carefully controlled pitch range, and absolute rigidity of tempo and dynamics in a speaker may make us skeptical of what the person says. We "read between the lines" that the person is self-protective and anxious to avoid personal involvement, particularly that of an emotional nature. Bureaucrats in particular perfect this style of voice when repeating the "official" policy of others to avoid taking responsibility. The avoidance of using the natural range and resonances of the voice, that is, denying the full integration of the voice within the body and hence within the person's psyche, suggests that the person is avoiding personal commitment on other levels as well. The lack of sincerity may result in the listener's disbelief in the content of what is being said.

People often adopt and switch between different vocal styles in order to act out various aspects of their personality in a more or less unconscious attempt to tell the listener how to interpret what is being said. A typical case might be where a person switches between a light, high-pitched, rapid form of speech with many accents, wide ranges of pitch and dynamics (suggesting innocence or an immaturity that disclaims responsibility), and essentially the opposite—a slow, measured, serious, low-pitched voice with its corresponding mature image. Other polarities between masculine and feminine, young and old, crude and sophisticated may similarly be set up. One can only interpret the meaning of such vocal behavior by knowing the full psychological context of the speaker. In general, though, one can say that when the vocal form matches the verbal content, the communication is coherent and appropriate. People with problems generally communicate in a manner where these levels are mismatched, even when the content denies or avoids the problem area. The sensitive listener hears the way in which things are said as pointers to deeper meanings.

Ostwald's work, referred to already, deals with the same subject from the point of view of the communication of emotion and provides some objective evidence of physical correlates for the speech of people under emotional stress. He has also categorized baby sounds and argues that the later use of such sounds in adult life occurs at times of emotional stress (Ostwald, 1963a, pp. 16–19). Otherwise they are socially curtailed, either by outright prohibition or by their careful control (such as with laughter, hissing, applause, and "raspberries" at public gatherings). He observes the increased use of nonverbal noises in patients showing "disturbed" communication patterns. The communication of emotion is clearly a powerful role for soundmaking, and an excellent example of the mediating role of sound between the person and environment.

Soundmaking in Pairs and Groups

The acoustic structure of dialogue and conversation reflects the relationships of the people involved (Feldstein, 1972; Jaffe & Feldstein, 1970). If paralinguistic components in an individual's speech are messages about how to interpret content, then in conversation, they are also messages about the relationship of the speakers. To extend the musical terminology used to describe speech qualities, we may refer to the "counterpoint" between voices. The traditional rules of melodic counterpoint ensure that two or more musical voices go together in a balanced manner that allows each to be heard clearly. Such rules can also be thought of as ways to control the flow of information so that it is spread out evenly and thus more readily comprehended. The simplest musical rule is that when one voice pauses or holds a tone, the other is free to be active. Another common technique is the statement–response pattern where a figure in one voice is repeated, perhaps with variations, or even inverted in the other (opposite but complementary). If both voices are active simultaneously, then their mutual content should be entirely consonant.

Such guidelines, though presented here in simplified form, roughly characterize the rules of a well-balanced conversation between *equal* partners. Each voice complements the other with variations (exact repetition is too simple-minded except when developed in the stylized art of the canon), and the two blend together in a harmonious whole. The simultaneous feedback between the two speakers and their willingness to express cooperation through balanced acoustic behavior ensures the "harmony" of the result. The opposite, an argument where neither side is listening to the other, breaks all the rules of counterpoint, and communicates nothing other than mutual hostility—on a level that would be apparent even to someone not knowing the language being used.

Matching vocal styles within the limits of personal identity is a necessary skill for anyone who wants to deal effectively with others. An interviewer needs to match the speed and level of complexity of the interview subject, not only as part of establishing a "rapport," but also to allow the person to speak freely and naturally. Such accommodation almost never occurs on radio where "time is money," and thus voices must either conform to the expected format or be left out. The unequal partnership of the "talk show" is evident from the voices alone, where the host, close to the mike, and in full control of who speaks for how long, is in "conversation" with a telephone voice (a boosted low-level signal with restricted bandwidth which will be described further in part II). Because the two signal levels are unequal (the host's being the dominant one), compression techniques ensure that the higher one can always cancel the weaker. The usual turn-taking of normal conversation is distorted; the "two-way flow" of this form of radio turns out to have powerful one-way gates!

When soundmaking occurs in groups, the rules for organizing it always reflect the structure of the group, whether such rules are implicit or explicit. Such procedures as taking turns, leader-group interaction, rules of order, and so on, control patterns of soundmaking as much as they reflect social structure and restrict behavior. Such rules regulate not only the counterpoint of soundmaking, but the types of sound that are acceptable as well. Orderly soundmaking reflects an implicit agreement of cooperation, or at least a submission to authority. Those challenging the social order often do so by using sounds that are normally proscribed, or by making them at an improper time. Just as there is a time for making sound in a group, there is a time to be silent. Mutual silence, however, is one of the few acoustic forms in which everyone participates simultaneously on an equal basis; hence, communal moments of silence most effectively balance the need for both individual and group expression (Bruneau, 1973; Dauenhauer, 1973).

We have already referred to the controlled outlets for ritualized acoustic aggression provided in Western society, most typically through sporting events. The team members themselves often shout encouragement to their fellows with short, "punchy" phrases, sometimes repeated quickly and rhythmically to be more stimulating. Such vocalization stimulates the individual player, promotes "team spirit" and supports the ritualized aggression felt towards the opposing team. The crowd too has ample opportunity to add to the ritual and achieve both a personal emotional outlet and the sense of being part of a larger social unit. The religious forms of group soundmaking extend from traditional leader–congregation patterns of interaction to "speaking in tongues", or glossolalia (Goodman, 1972). One of the most famous communal rituals that has a similar effect is the Balinese Ketjak chanting or "monkey chant." Most of the male members of the community are involved in highly energetic, rhythmic chanting that is designed to get everyone into an ecstatic emotional state. It should be noted that Bali is a small, rather densely populated island with a strong communal social life, and such ceremonies are needed points of release for emotional tension.

Alan Lomax has suggested that ritualized musicmaking in most traditional cultures takes a form that reflects the social organization of the culture (Lomax, 1962). For instance, he describes the "bardic tradition" of many authoritarian, despotic societies in which the solo singer displays a virtuosity within the bounds of a highly formalized musical system. In communal cultures, such as that of the African pygmy, group soundmaking is the norm, with complex musical textures being built up from independent interlocking elements, at least one of which any member of the group is capable of performing. The cooperative style of the musicmaking reflects the sense of cooperation found in their culture. The Western European folk song tradition is often characterized by a virtuosic soloist and a passive audience, a model of "exclusive authority" which he relates to social conduct in other spheres. If we apply this approach to the modern rock concert, we would have to describe the monolithic acoustic power of its heavy amplification, controlled by a small group of performers (backed by powerful commercial interests) and capable of acoustically annihilating the usually passive audience, and ask what type of social structure it reflects.

Acoustic Persuasion

When group communication involves a single individual addressing a mass audience, one usually observes what may be called a stylized form of soundmaking. We are generally familiar with the unique vocal style of the politician, the preacher, the auctioneer, the disk jockey, and the salesman. Rhetorical skills in public speaking have been practised for centuries, and their successful practitioners have achieved some measure of worldly power through their ability to control acoustic power as a persuasive force. Amplification and mass distribution channels have only added to the arsenal of such persuaders. Most everyone, under the right conditions, is vulnerable to the tactics used, and there is a fine line between the politician and the demagogue, the preacher and the religious fanatic, the skillful salesperson and the cunning manipulator, the teacher and the brainwasher. We will examine a few of the techniques of acoustic persuasion.

Probably the oldest and most common technique used in stylized forms of communication is the intonation of the voice, that is, sustaining a phoneme, usually a vowel, on a sung pitch. Intoned speech has the advantage of dissipating air from the lungs more slowly, thereby allowing the sound to last longer and travel farther. More energy can be put into the volume of sound produced without shortening the duration of speech possible (as does raising the speaking voice). In religious ceremonies, intoned speech also gives the congregation a tonal center for unison response. In the virtuosic vocal display of the auctioneer, intoning the voice (usually on a high pitch with variations up and down to a secondary one) allows the rapid "patter" to be sustained for a longer time, thereby attracting attention by the sheer excitement of the voice and sustaining audience interest by not breaking the pattern until needed (e.g., at a critical sales juncture). Anything that sustains vocal effort allows the voice to dominate the audience's attention.

Secondly, the enlargement of the ambitus or range of any vocal parameter increases its expressive power, sustains interest, and promotes excitement or tension. The pitch range of the voice, about half an octave in normal speech, may expand to nearly two octaves in dramatic speech, particularly if the person uses "head voice" (i.e., falsetto). Similarly, dynamic range can be enlarged from the always effective "stage whisper" to the peak vocal capacity. Unnatural stress on a particular word gives it an unexpected "punch," especially if the stress is placed on a percussive consonant (e.g., "Power!"). The tempo of speech may suddenly change dramatically from slow to fast, racing on to an exciting cadence, or it may slow to a point where every word is isolated by silence, to be savored and absorbed. Changing the timbre of the voice from harsh to soothing, from somber to brilliant, or the imitation of accents, dialects or speech mannerisms, are also effective. The wider the range of any of these variables, the more it deviates from normal speech and thereby commands attention. The more dramatic the alteration, the more emotional the response by the audience. Leonard Meyer has generalized this relationship by stating that the change in any expected progression produces an *involuntary* emotional response (Meyer, 1956). The stronger the emotional response on the part of the listeners, the more power the speaker has over them.

Finally, the use of rhythmic devices is one of the most powerful tools available to the speaker. In a large space, particularly when amplification is being used, a normal speech tempo usually results in much of it being incomprehensible because of masking by the reverberation in the space. Effective speakers always slow down their rate of speech, articulate more clearly, and pause after important words (to allow them to be repeated in the listener's memory), or before them (to create anticipatory interest). Such techniques ensure comprehension and also minimize masking effects. As is well known by designers of background music, the body responds *involuntarily* to the tempo of speech or music by increasing heart and respiration rates and releasing adrenalin into the system. Therefore, rhythmic speech not only produces a psychological union between speaker and listener (a kind of mental "foot tapping"), but can also change the listener's physiological state (Clynes, 1978). A slow, steady beat may be hypnotic, and a fast tempo exhilarating; and acceleration causes an upward surge of emotional response which must culminate in a cadence, since the tempo cannot continue to increase indefinitely.

William Sargant, in his fascinating book on the "physiology of conversion and brainwashing," *The Battle for the Mind,* shows that:

> If a complete sudden collapse can be produced by prolonging or intensifying emotional stress, the brain slate may be wiped clear temporarily of its more recently implanted patterns of behaviour, perhaps allowing others to be substituted for them more easily. (Sargant, 1959, p. 128)

From the examples he gives, it is clear that auditory stimulation through voice, music, and other noises can be an important tool for reaching this kind of state, but that it is usually accompanied by other forms of physical and emotional stress that break down the person's normal patterns of functioning. For instance, he describes Voodoo drumming and a religious snake-handling cult where "the preacher used the tempo and volume of singing and hand-clapping to intensify the religious enthusiasm" (Sargant, 1959, p. 93). The effects may be used for political, religious, or ideological purposes to change and control the beliefs of people. Although Sargant's work is 25 years old, the phenomena to which he refers are still prevalent, and in the case of religious "cults," seem to be on the increase.

The "power" inherent in language that is rooted in human soundmaking—the ability to refer to and in a sense manipulate reality—gives the individual control over the external world. Children sense this power from the time they realize as babies that soundmaking can attract attention, and later that words are tools for creating their own reality, whether fanciful, imaginary, or "false" by adult standards. Aldous Huxley refers to this power of language in *Crome Yellow* when one of his characters says:

> Words are man's first and most grandiose invention. With language he created a whole new universe; what wonder if he loved words and attributed power to them![1]

But this ability, by which we express ourselves the most intimately, and by which we reach out to touch others with our voices, is a power that like all power can be abused and distorted for the control and manipulation of others. It is a power to be conserved and respected like any natural resource in danger of pollution or extinction.

---

[1]Aldous Huxley, *Crome Yellow*, New York: Harper, 1922, p. 216 (Penguin edition, pp. 120–121).

4

Systems of Acoustic Communication: Speech, Music, and Soundscape

Our approach in this book is to step back from the conventional, specialized, and disciplinary perspectives that categorize acoustic studies, and attempt to understand basic processes by which sound functions. It is with this end in mind that we use the term "acoustic communication" to embrace all manifestations of sound. The approach is intended to be both naive, in the sense of looking to first principles, and metadisciplinary, in the sense of trying to bridge the gaps between specialized approaches and finding a level on which all of them can be understood as related. However, at a certain point one must acknowledge that there are specialized areas in which the role of sound has become so developed that they merit the individual, intensive study they have received. Two such areas are speech and music which are well known for expert scholarship, a vast literature and their often abstruse concepts. The study of environmental sound is less unified, and generally more recent, perhaps because it lacks the essential feature of the others, namely the humanness of their communicative roles. In this chapter we shall bring together the three areas as *systems of acoustic communication,* mindful of their differences, but alert to their commonalities and points of intersection.

Bringing together highly developed disciplines, as has been popular in the last two decades, is fraught with obvious pitfalls. Too easy comparison, superficial similarities, or wholesale importation of concepts from one discipline to another usually lead to confusion, unless handled circumspectly. Experts in one field become annoyed when they see "their" working models being applied out of context in another field, and the borrowers, inspired perhaps by the generalist's muse or impressed by an apt analogy, find it easy to go past the point where the comparison applies and extrapolate indefinitely. Such problems characterize many of the recent attempts to apply linguistic theory to music, for instance. After some insight has been gained, one ultimately realizes that there are more differences than similarities, and one is better off in the safety of one's own neighborhood, at least until enticed again by an attractive development across the fence.

However, speech, music, and the sonic environment can be linked most simply and effectively on their common basis as sound, which is certain, and as "organized sound," a concept that needs clarification. If one is tempted to ask what other "worldview" is possible, one only has to recall the "quadrivium" of the Medieval world in which music was linked to arithmetic, geometry, and astronomy, presumably on the basis of its quantitative features. If we think of the sonic environment as merely a physical artifact, then it cannot be the equal of the two "relatives" we are proposing, because the only basis of comparison would be the level of physical acoustic behavior which, although relevant in speech and music, does not entirely account for their communicative importance to people. However, once we substitute the notion of "soundscape" to emphasize the way in which the sonic environment is *understood*, it emerges as an important system of human communication that is comparable to the others. Moreover, the orderliness that underlies the natural soundscape (even if its collection of sound seems random to the casual observer), and the degrees of order and disorder that characterize human soundscapes, may be reflected by the *mental* processes that organize them. There are not three brains, one to process each of these different kinds of soundmaking, even though there may be two parts to the brain which perform particular strategies in analyzing sound, as we will discuss later. At the level of our processes of understanding the world, there is a continuum between the systems of organized acoustic communication.

The Continuum

It is useful to order the three major systems of acoustic communication as follows:

Speech–Music–Soundscape

We place music between speech and the soundscape in this continuum because it is a *human* form of communication which is based (until recently) entirely on "abstract" sounds derived from the environment, except for the voice itself (Ihde, 1976, ch. 13). Musical instruments refine the sounds of nature into a powerful form of human expression. But music communicates on the basis of its organization of sound which is the product of human thought processes (Minsky, 1981). In order to understand the systems of acoustic communication better, we need to look at their basic organizational features and compare them as they are situated along the continuum.

There are various senses in which the placing of the three systems in the above order may be justified. First, there is the extent of the sound repertoire of each. As we move left to right, there is a corresponding increase in the size of the acoustic repertoire, from the relatively small number of phonemic units in language (approximately 40 in English), through the wider variety of musical sounds (increasingly wide in the present century), to the enormous range of sound possible in the acoustic environment.

Secondly, speaking *very* generally, there is a decreasing strictness of syntactical structure as we move left to right. The combinatorial rules by which sounds, syllables, and words may be correctly combined within natural language are quite strict, and the native speaker understands, or fails to understand, an oral communication as a meaningful act by first of all judging the combination of sounds as legal or not. Although the syntactic rules governing the combination of sound within a given musical "language" may not be as well understood as with natural language, the listener who is familiar with the "style" of a piece of music can immediately tell when a mistake has occurred. Therefore, the listener implicitly understands that music obeys some rules of organization, and it is generally true that such rules are looser than in language.

One of the many problems of generalizing about music in this way is that there are styles of music where the "rules" seem fairly strict, as in Gregorian chant or classical fugue, whereas in contemporary music it often seems that any combination of sounds "goes." Also, musical rules are not of the same type as linguistic ones, so the comparison is only by analogy. In Western music particularly, rules are often in a state of flux as composers find new combinations of sound that make sense but which involve relationships that previously have been proscribed. However, this inability to define the sum of the musical rules for any given system of organization (e.g., modal, tonal, atonal) supports the kind of relative looseness suggested within the continuum model.

Thirdly, there is a decreasing temporal density of information as we move to the right along the continuum. The elements of spoken language are fairly densely packed (e.g., phonemes are produced with an average of about 5 per second), by comparison to music, at least if we consider only a single line of each. A virtuoso performer may be able to produce more notes per second than in speech, but the information about musical structure is always spread out over a longer period of time. Compare what can be understood or inferred from 2 seconds of speech, compared with the same duration of music (assuming we are not dealing with a known excerpt from which the listener can infer the rest from memory). With music, one might only hear a single chord or a handful of notes, or if the sample were random, perhaps just a silence. How much "meaning," by any definition of what that may be, could be gleaned from such a fragment? By comparison, we could probably identify quite a few characteristics of the speaker from a short verbal excerpt and obtain at least one complete reference from a few words or a phrase. With a sound environment, 2 seconds would give only the grossest impression of its character, whether loud or quiet, dense or sparse. Whatever is communicated by an environment takes a longer period of exposure to become evident. A better way to make the point is to say that as we move from speech to music to soundscape, we rely on longer-term relationships more than short-term ones for complete understanding.

Finally, as a result of the three tendencies already mentioned as characterizing the left to right movement along the continuum (viz., increasing sound repertoire, decreasing tightness of syntactic structure, and density of information), there is a corresponding effect in terms of meaning, i.e., the semantic level. Although language is notoriously ambiguous, the meaning(s) of any utterance can be quite specific, particularly within a given context. Words, in contrast to musical sounds, have specific referential meanings. Musical "meaning" eludes easy linguistic formulation and some philosophers, such as Susanne Langer, suggest that for that very reason, music best expresses the emotions (Langer, 1951). Others contend that music expresses only itself, its own structure as "organized sound." In any case, it is clear that the *specificity* of meaning decreases from speech to music. Laske has suggested that aesthetic artifacts communicate by means of "analogous understanding," i.e., that what the listener understands in hearing music cannot be the "same" in any sense as what was in the mind of the composer (Laske, 1974b). However, musical meaning can be analogous between composer and listener, whether it is an emotion or an image created by a particular set of acoustic relationships.

In the previous chapter we referred to the dual analog and digital nature of spoken language, and pointed out that the referential meaning of the digital units (words) is interpretable through the analog cues (tone of voice, inflection, rhythm, and timbre) that accompany them. Although digital elements are found in all systems of acoustic communication (e.g., the word, musical note, and sound signal), we find as we move to the right along the continuum that meaning depends more and more on the relationship between elements, and between the elements and the whole. As discussed in chapter 2, the environmental sound signal (e.g., a footstep, a bell, the wind, a car), whether foreground or background in perception, *only* acquires meaning through its context, that is, its complete relationship to the environment. The spoken word can be stripped of its acoustic form in print, taken out of context, and still mean something, however incomplete. Whether an environmental sound has meaning or not (i.e., whether it is "just" a noise) depends entirely on its context and how it is understood. The "sound object" (an environmental sound isolated on tape from its context) cannot *mean* anything except itself as an aural sensation. The spoken word can only be as stripped of meaning as the sound object when it is repeated over and over, until it is *reduced* to mere sound. It is the "sound event" (sound + context) that communicates, depending on our ability to interpret it.

The point of introducing the continuum concept is not to force everything unnaturally into a single system, particularly not when the components are as varied and multi-levelled as those dealt with here. The continuum is only a useful and greatly simplified model that allows comparisons to be made and relationships clarified. It also allows us to understand the three systems in any of their particular manifestations as "points" along the continuum that display tendencies of a certain "direction" towards other points. For instance, we have referred to various forms of linguistic communication as relying to various degrees on musical elements. Poetry has always incorporated linguistic and musical elements in a delicate balance, and the contemporary sound poetry movement, with its return to vocal performance as distinct from writing as its focus, enlarges the repertoire of sounds used, loosens its syntax, and may even drop all referential meaning in a move to the right, at least along our continuum.

In this century, contemporary music has moved towards environment with its use of an increased repertoire of sounds, first by extending the orchestra, particularly in the percussion department, and then through technological means that incorporate *any* environmental sound or its transformation (Cogan & Escot, 1976; Erickson, 1975). Having already included the "universal soundscape" within the realm of music, contemporary technology extends the repertoire further to include whatever sound can be synthesized, and thereby it encompasses the imaginary soundscape as well. Besides using this expanded repertoire of sound, contemporary music also tends to model the characteristics of environmental sound organization, such as foreground, background, ambience, texture and spatiality, with results that often reflect the contemporary soundscape, including even its negative aspects. The stylized imitation of natural sounds so common to the Baroque era (e.g., Vivaldi's *Seasons* or the endless "echo concerti") and the psychological portrayal of environment found in 19th-century music (through opera, program music, and literary association), are all examples of environmental phenomena that were transformed into musical material within an existing style. In this century, we see the style and structure of music itself, as well as some of the actual sounds, being derived from the environment (e.g., Ives's *Central Park in the Dark*). R. Murray Schafer (1973) has suggested that the environment be listened to as a composition ("the music of the environment"), that is, as a more or less well-balanced combination of similar and contrasting elements. We will return to the related concept of the "soundscape composition" in chapter 13.

Although speech and music have always been part of the human soundscape (and we have never known any other), these forms developed as "special cases" of environmental sound simply because they were of human origin. Their presence did not substantially change the way in which the natural soundscape functions. But just as technology has progressively altered the shape and character of the soundscape in terms of the introduction of machine sounds, so too, electronic technology has profoundly changed the role of speech and music within the soundscape through the ubiquitous presence of the loudspeaker. By detaching speech and music from their source, as we shall discuss in part II, the loudspeaker changes the character and structure of the soundscape by rendering these sounds *environmental* and not strictly human. They may be of human origin, but they are not produced by human energy. Hence they become as much environmental artifacts as the wind and rain, except with vastly different connotations for the mind which, although able to relegate them to background levels of perception, cannot entirely escape understanding them as simultaneously environmental *and* linguistic/musical.

Finally, the continuum concept can remind us of one important and ultimate fact about acoustic communication—its destructibility. As Jonathan Schell points out in his profoundly moving book *The Fate of the Earth,*[1] extinction of the human species as the result of a nuclear holocaust would not only be the extinction of the race and the unborn generations, but it would also be the end of human values and purpose. Needless to say, it would also be the end of acoustic communication, not only of the obviously human forms, but of the soundscape as well. The *entire* continuum would disappear. Perhaps the proverbial tree would still fall in the forest, should any still exist, but if there were any atmosphere left to transmit the physical vibration, it would not fall on human ears. Such vibration (it could no longer be termed "sound" because it could no longer be heard) would be reduced to the status of any other inanimate form of energy. We are reminded that all parts of the continuum of acoustic communication need each other and are inextricably related; they cannot exist in isolation. The health and survival of any one part depends on that of all the others. The continuum is both a human artifact *and* a human responsibility.

The Model

Now that we have placed the various systems of acoustic communication in relationship to each other, we can ask if, in spite of their obvious differences, there is a model that is general enough to describe a basic feature of all of them. We have hinted at it already when we considered the way in which meaning arises within each system. At the most basic level of each system we find that sound is in some way "organized," and that through the structure of this organization, meaning can be inferred. Therefore, structure has a mediating role between sound and meaning. This relationship can be shown as follows:

$$\text{Sound} \xleftrightarrow{\text{Structure}} \text{Meaning}$$

Jakobson (1978) has described the linguistic relation of sound to meaning on the phonemic level in terms of Saussure's concept of the sign

[1]Jonathan Schell, *The Fate of the Earth,* New York: Avon, 1982.

through which the signifier and the signified are linked (Saussure, 1966). In language, we more commonly refer to syntax than to structure to denote the larger-scale ordering of language units, but the more general term can include paralinguistic structure as well. In music, structure may be expressed through compositional rules that describe the "law-like" behavior of a music. In the soundscape, structure includes not only the elements of the sound environment and their relationships, but also the pragmatic level of the context within which all of it occurs, and without which it cannot be interpreted. In fact, what is missing from the above diagram is the pragmatic "environment" within which the sound-meaning process occurs. Our model is closely related to that proposed by Morris where the elements are termed "sonic," "syntactic," "semantic," and "pragmatic" (Morris, 1938, 1955). Although originating in the theory of signs, these terms and the model within which they function are useful for describing how sound communicates.

The reader may still wonder in what sense the soundscape is a system of "organized sound." The question resembles that of whether a soundscape is "designed" or not. We argue here that design and structure are not restricted to human artifacts, just as form is not. We do not have to resort to teleological concepts for an explanation (e.g., a divinely guided order). The model of an ecological system where all elements are in balance is a familiar one, and we have no trouble admiring the beauty of its working as showing good "design" features. There is similarly an *acoustic ecology* in the natural environment where its sounds and those of the various species are balanced by many of the same physical and biological forces that create a stable environmental ecology. We will return to this concept in the next chapter in the context of the "acoustic community."

When we introduce the concept of "soundscape" and shift the emphasis to the way in which the sonic environment is understood, we may ask whether the structure of the environment is "in" it, or "in" the mind? With speech and music, the problem does not seem to arise, because there are clearly mental processes whose strategies for the *production* of these artifacts correlate with those for their *reception*. That does not mean there has to be an equivalence between the two (e.g., we don't have to think in sentences to be able to produce them). However, there must be some cognitive level at which thought processes are translated into externalized performance in speech and music. Chomsky has proposed the terms "competence" and "performance" to describe two interrelated forms of linguistic knowledge (Chomsky, 1965). These concepts clarify the problem of structure and may be applied to all systems of acoustic communication.

Competence and Performance

Linguistic competence is defined as the tacit knowledge which a native speaker has about a language, and performance refers to the strategies which can be employed in various contexts to exercise that knowledge. In a certain sense, competence refers to knowledge at rest, performance to knowledge in motion. One implication of the distinction is that, by separating the two, we can understand why faults in performance do not necessarily reflect flaws in competence. More importantly, the notion of competence shows that knowledge about language is a form of metaknowledge—knowledge about what constitutes structurally correct communication, even when the communication has never been experienced before! Human memory is not large enough to store all of the sentences that can easily be recognized and understood by a speaker; nor could a child ever learn all of the possible sentences that can be produced in a language. Therefore, what is stored in memory are not the instances of the language, but the *structural relationships* which represent knowledge about the language.

For instance, any native speaker can instantly recognize that the sentence "He is a sound" is not complete; the word "sound" does not make sense as a noun, and as an adjective it demands completion. If the "sentence" were heard and the inflection did not drop at the end, the paralinguistic structure would indicate that the speaker was not finished, and therefore the listener would most likely not respond unless some expected ending (e.g., "sleeper") was not forthcoming. On the other hand, the statement "He is a soundscaper" might elicit the response "And *what* is a soundscaper?" because even though the sentence had never been heard before, it seems plausibly syntactically correct if the last word can be interpreted as a noun. Linguistic competence is the knowledge about such structural features of language that permits us to understand it.

Similarly, we may postulate a "musical competence," following Laske (1975a, 1977), that is the tacit knowledge a musician has about musical structure. A similar example to the above sentences could be constructed by playing a melody that implies a cadence, but either stops short of it, moves to an unexpected but "legal" note (e.g., the deceptive cadence), or jumps to a totally unrelated note that could not possibly "belong" to the melody, given the expectations its previous behavior has already set up. One's knowledge about musical structure would dictate the response in each case as to whether the melody is well formed (Laske, 1980). Composers working with new musical material or forms are typically not understood, or are often misunderstood, by the public because of the latter's unfamiliarity with the structural "rules" the composer is using to achieve meaning. The listener may respond with the same kind of frustration that is experienced if language is used in ways that don't "make sense." But a generation later, exactly the same piece may make perfect sense to a great number of listeners (and even later it may qualify as a "potboiler").[2] Therefore, musical competence may be seen to evolve and expand, both in the individual, where music education

---

[2]Nicolas Slonimsky, *Lexicon of Musical Invective*, 2nd. ed., Seattle: University of Washington Press, 1965.

is of great importance, and in a culture as a whole, where composers are charged with finding new ways of "making sense" with whatever materials are inherited or may be invented. Paradoxically, new musical sense inevitably reflects the culture, even if it remains opaque to most of those within it.

We can postulate that there is a "soundscape competence" within each person that functions analogously to the notions of linguistic and musical competence. It is tacit knowledge that people have about the structure of environmental sound, knowledge that manifests itself in behavior that interprets such sound and acts upon it. For instance, we are at home and hear a car drive up, stop close by, its door slam, footsteps get louder, climbing the stair. We set up in our minds a simple, logical series of expectations about what might happen next based on our analysis of the sound. Our response will be different if nothing else happens (we might eventually open the door or, in certain circumstances, call the police), if we hear a knock, or if suddenly we hear a clatter of pots and pans outside the door. The knock seems as logical and predictable as the expected musical cadence or the expected completion of a sentence, the pots and pans not, though it might if we were expecting their return by a clumsy borrower! Although this example is simple-minded and rather facetious, it illustrates the point that our lifelong exposure to environmental sound gives us a complex body of knowledge about how to recognize and interpret the structure of environmental sound in order to obtain information that we can use. Soundscape competence permits us to understand environmental sound as meaningful. Like musical competence, it is knowledge that can be neglected or fostered, and therefore there is a social responsibility involved in its education.

There is a great deal of literature dealing with linguistic and conceptual development in the child (i.e., ontogenetic development). Similar knowledge for music has been slow to emerge, generally because of the lack of conceptual development as to what constitutes "musical thinking," as opposed to what constitutes proper performance skills. Music education is dominated by a concern for teaching performance skills, and although such skills are obviously important, the particular emphasis is on performance that re-creates the written music of the past, and not on performance as the outward manifestation of musical thinking and as an important aspect of cognitive development. However, over the last 15 years or so, efforts have been made to introduce some degree of creativity into music curricula (Bamberger, 1973), and at the theoretical level to study the nature of musical cognitive development (Laske, 1975b, 1976). A similar approach for soundscape awareness has been suggested as part of music education (Schafer, 1976), but its general implementation is sadly lacking.

In conclusion, we will use our simplified model to sketch out the basis of how acoustic competence develops in the child (Eiamas, 1975; Eisenberg, 1976). In general, we may say that the ontogenetic development of auditory competence involves the progressive ability *to separate sound and sense into identifiable meanings.*[3] At the very beginning, in the womb, sound and sensation are inextricably linked; although the ear is well developed, sound is not airborne but rather comes to the fetus as vibration of the entire body. At birth, the child can both make sounds and respond to them, but in a reflex manner. Within the first few months soundmaking activity begins to diversify. In terms of listening, the baby watches the speaker's eyes and mouth and can react specifically to the mother's voice. When babbling begins at around 4 months with consonant chains ("baba-baba"), the elements of language are beginning to become differentiated (including inflection and interjectional types of structure). The child is also able to turn the head and search for hidden sounds, and to associate sounds with inanimate objects.

All of this behavior is prototypical of the general process of the communication of meaningful information based on perception of the structural properties of sound. It is quite possible that at birth the beginning stages of auditory competence function independently of the kind of sound that is heard. As the child's development progresses, the recognition of increasingly complex sound patterns permits specialized meanings (linguistic, musical, and environmental) to emerge in parallel with, and in support of, all other cognitive development. At maturity, auditory competence seems to have subdivided into quite distinct areas to deal with speech, music, and soundscape, but at their basis, all three systems of acoustic communication have in common the mental processes that make sense out of sound structures.

The Brain

Auditory phenomena are restricted to the biosphere; there are no galactic dimensions to acoustical forms of sound except on the transcendent level of electromagnetic radiation where all waves travel with the speed of light. The "astronomical" dimensions of sound, whether the "music of the spheres" or the mysteries of wave motion, work at the level of metaphor and therefore bring our focus back to the human mind. The "last frontier" in the study of acoustic communication is the mind itself. Through this chapter we have stressed the importance of mental processes in the understanding of auditory phenomena, whether speech, music, or the soundscape. In fact, we have suggested that the structure of such phenomena corresponds closely in our understanding of them to cognitive structures, or competence models, within the mind. This emphasis is characteristic of recent developments in many acoustic-related fields.

For instance, psycholinguistics is a relatively new discipline that acts at

---

[3]O. E. Laske, "Some Postulations Concerning a Sonological Theory of Perception," in Laske, 1975a.

the interface of psychology and linguistics in order to understand how the mind develops and uses language structures (Markel, 1969; Miller, 1967). Psychoacoustics, however, is not a completely parallel discipline in the sense that its field of study centers on the brain's processing of auditory artifacts (whether pseudomusical or test stimuli). It only touches peripherally on the question of syntactic and semantic relationships that function in communicational contexts. However, psychoacoustics is becoming increasingly important for understanding the basis of musical perception and is closely associated with computer music research which provides a fertile ground for testing and direct connection to experimental music (Deutsch, 1982).

Laske (1977) has proposed the discipline of psychomusicology as an appropriate framework for understanding musical processes (by contrast to musicology which studies musical artifacts, usually scores, and historical musical styles). His work clearly points to the need for a unified theory of musical understanding that will account for, and show the relationships between, various performance activities such as listening, composing, performing, conducting, and so on. An equivalent approach to the sound environment has been slow to emerge, except within the concept of the soundscape. Similar developments in what is called "cognitive geography," for instance, are concerned with mental "images of place" (Goodey, 1974) in relation to the physical and social forces which determine the structure of the environment.

The relationship between our concept of "mind" and the neurological level of the brain is a fascinating one. It has increasingly come into public awareness through the brain behavior research of the last 20 years that has shed new light on the role of the two hemispheres of the brain. Knowledge gained from patients with brain lesions about the "centers" of various brain functions dates back to the 19th century. Recent work, for instance with "split brain" patients (those whose connection between the two hemispheres, the "corpus callosum," has been surgically severed to control epiletic seizures), has suggested new insight into the processing of sensory input by the brain (Gazzaniga, 1972). In fact, the role of the so-called "dominant" hemisphere (usually the left one) in language processing and sequential, logical processes such as mathematics, has been sharply contrasted with that of the right hemisphere which is thought to engage in holistic, synthetic operations such as spatial relationships and facial recognition.

However, the right hemisphere has also had ascribed to it artistic, symbolic, intuitive, creative, and even emotional behavior. The simplicity of such a basic duality, particularly when it appears to be represented physiologically, leads people to extrapolate wildly from fairly restricted data until every human polarity is ascribed to hemispheric differences. The concept has even entered popular mythology as a descriptor of a cultural worldview ("the dominant hemisphere of a culture"), suggesting that both as individuals and as a culture, we have given more emphasis to the rational, analytic left hemisphere, and not enough to the (psychologically more attractive) operations of the right hemisphere.

Music has been drawn into this extended metaphor by being placed squarely in the right hemisphere, if only to counterbalance the undisputed dominance of language functions in the left. At a moment in which the *interrelationship* of speech and music might have become clearer, they have suddenly found themselves split into two distinct areas with "opposing," instead of at least complementary, characteristics. Unfortunately, the soundscape gets left out of this model, and out of the research, perhaps because there is no third hemisphere in which to locate it. However, once we get past the superficial level of easy dichotomies, the overemphasis of "place" in the brain (rather than pathways), and test results of brains and individuals in isolation, there is a great deal to be learned from a careful appraisal of the research evidence. Roederer (1975) gives a good, albeit brief, introduction to the research as it impinges on the psychoacoustics of music; a more recent survey is contained in Clynes (1982). We will discuss aspects that are relevant to the general model of acoustic communication systems presented in this chapter.

Auditory Processing and the Hemispheres

First, we should note that, unlike other modes of sensory input, auditory information from each ear goes to *both* hemispheres, with perhaps a 60/40 emphasis to the contralateral (i.e., opposite) side. Smell, for instance, is ipsilateral (i.e., it goes to the same side of the brain as the nostril); control of bodily movement is contralateral, and the visual field in each cornea is projected contralaterally (though it should be remembered that the image on the retina is already inverted). The lack of strict laterality in the auditory field means that it is problematic in certain kinds of research; for instance, a split brain subject holding a known object in the left hand, out of sight, cannot identify the object verbally because the tactile information is only available to the right hemisphere, but if some characteristic sound is made with the object, the auditory information reaches the left hemisphere with its speech functions.

In normal subjects, Kimura (1964, 1973) found a contralateral preference for speech and music when samples of each were presented separately, but simultaneously, to each ear (i.e., the "dichotic" situation where separate information is fed to each ear via headphones). Speech fragments were better identified by the right ear, music by the left. However, one cannot generalize from this evidence that *all* musical operations are performed by the right hemisphere. Kimura's subjects were musically untrained, and the music that was presented (solo Baroque woodwind melodies) was probably unfamiliar to the subjects. The level of listening can be assumed to be fairly general, since the given task was identification and not detailed analysis.

Bever and Chiarello (1974) refined the dichotic listening task by introducing the factor of musical training and by examining more analytical listening tasks. In their results, the musically trained subjects performed better when the tone sequences were presented to the right ear than to the left, whereas the musically untrained subjects did proportionately better with the left ear. The conclusion drawn is that analytical strategies performed by the *left* hemisphere (i.e., that responsible for speech) were available to the musically trained and could be used in listening tasks that demanded a greater level of discrimination. Such evidence is consistent with the model of listening and the interrelation of speech and music tasks presented here. That is, listening can occur at different levels of attention and discrimination. In the listening-in-search mode (or in analytic listening as discussed in chapter 10), pattern-recognition strategies that involve feature detection and sequential analysis are required—whether the subject matter is speech, music, or soundscape. The dominant hemisphere is specialized for such tasks, but because speech always involves short-term analysis of linearly organized features, the *strategy* can easily be confused with its *content*. Therefore, when language functions are "placed" in the dominant hemisphere it should be remembered that non-linguistic tasks can equally employ the same strategies when the task requires them.

Similarly, we have emphasized the role of the analog, or musical, aspect of speech as an indicator of meaning. Therefore, when such aspects require the synthetic operations of the right hemisphere (because they involve recognition of a global pattern, similar to recognizing a face as a complete image), we can understand how the parallel and complementary strategies of both hemispheres combine to achieve the total communicational result. Similar studies show that sung words are activated by the right hemisphere even when speech functions have been damaged, and therefore it can be seen that words in singing, and presumably poetry as well, may be incorporated within the strategies of the right hemisphere. Roederer further suggests that a spatial representation is inherent in the analysis of spectral energy which leads to timbre and tone recognition:

> the incoming sound pattern (in time) is "projected" as pattern in space on the basilar membrane—the result is a *spatial* image, much like the spatial image projected on the retina. (emphasis in original) (Roederer, 1975, p. 168)

The idea that frequency analysis results in a "gestalt" form of recognition performed by the right hemisphere is consistent with current psychoacoustic opinion which understands timbre recognition as the matching of the pattern of spectral energy distribution against similar patterns stored in the brain. Analysis of individual partials is involved, but these are only heard consciously when attention is directed towards them (a process which takes much longer than the recognition stage). Detailed analysis shows that every tone from an instrument has many minute differences, even when on the same pitch; however, the brain immediately recognizes them as the same (Roederer, 1975, pp. 133–142).

Moreover, even vaguely similar timbral patterns are frequently heard by listeners as having instrumental or speech characteristics because of their resemblance at the level of *pattern* (e.g., the sighing or whistling of the wind, or Louis Armstrong's famous "talking" trumpet where the formant patterns were close enough to those of vowels to resemble speech). It is clear that listeners use human sounds as a norm and are quick to ascribe human characteristics even to inanimate sounds whose patterns (of pitch contour, timbre, or rhythm) closely resemble those of the human repertoire. Conversely, people immediately feel "alienated" by machine sounds which bear no resemblance as auditory images to human sounds, unless a suitable analogy can be found (e.g., the "iron horse" whose pantings and wheezings resembled familiar patterns, and whose corresponding image still provokes nostalgia in people who associate it with a "more human" era).

The levels of listening discussed in chapter 2 with respect to environmental sounds all depend on strategies found in both hemispheres and moreover, on the *integration* of the information produced by each. Hemispheric specialization should not obscure the fact that the coordination of the information from each hemisphere is just as important as the function of each independently. We can speak of the relative proportions of analytic/synthetic strategies that are needed for any task (using these terms as simplifications of hemisphere activity), and in that sense, we can understand listening tasks as context dependent. In the case of listening-in-readiness, the listener's background activity scans incoming patterns (right hemisphere), seeking a match with one deemed to be of significance. If a close enough match is found, the listener's attention is redirected to the sound and a closer analysis is made (left hemisphere) to determine its "fine structure" as an indicator of specific information (e.g., is that really the friend's footsteps, and what details indicate the person's mood or purpose?).

The phenomenon of background listening, particularly in the case of the keynote sound, is interesting because it would appear that over time the "gestalt" image of the sound pattern is built up without necessarily ever undergoing detailed scrutiny. Perhaps that is why one seldom notices when such a sound disappears or changes. However, the holistic pattern that is formed in the mind must include the surrounding context as a figure-ground relationship. Hence the entire pattern is stored; a later event or situation may remind one of it on the basis of characteristics that are often undefinable (in linguistic terms). Such patterns, having never been scanned by the dominant hemisphere, seem beyond words and therefore more closely allied to emotions or feelings. They are the stuff on which the poet and the composer play, but increasingly in the modern commercial world, they are also the product of the advertiser and the image-maker. These people are constantly busy reinforcing values and the long-term associations of their products, both in listening and other forms of communication. The long-term effects of noise, which have hitherto been understood only in terms of physiological stress, hearing loss, and interference with task performance, can be seen within the present model as the *obscuring* of auditory images that define the listener's long-term relationships to the environment. Or rather, the *meaninglessness* of noise becomes the long-term auditory image that pervades the psyche of the individual, and ultimately the society. It is these images which have no outer voice but only their own private language that are most in need of rehabilitation and protection in the modern world.

5

The Acoustic Community

Thus far we have concentrated on a model of acoustic communication from the perspective of the listener in which listening is understood as the primary acoustic interface between the individual and the environment. However, the flow of communication goes both ways since the listener is also a sound-maker, and therefore it is the entire *system* of the listener plus environment which constitutes the "soundscape." When the system is well balanced (what we have loosely referred to as a "hi-fi" environment), there is a high degree of information exchange between its elements and the listener is involved in an interactive relationship with the environment. Conversely, an unbalanced (or "lo-fi") environment is characterized by a high degree of redundancy and low amount of information exchange; the listener becomes isolated and alienated from the environment.

A different, but complementary, perspective on these systems may be gained by treating them on a macro level, that is, from their behavior as a whole in which the listener is but one part. The natural soundscape, for instance, may be heard and analyzed as a system of interrelated parts whose "acoustic ecology" reflects the natural ecological balance. In order to study such systems, one must experience them and therefore even the natural soundscape must include a listener within it. However, this distinction is largely theoretical, since it is clear that few, if any, "pristine" soundscapes exist today. Also, natural soundscapes, or close approximations to them, usually include human artifacts which may or may not integrate well within them. One of the lessons of ecology is that when we see ourselves as "different" from nature and not as an integral part of it, we are more likely to violate its balance, ultimately at our own peril. Therefore, acoustic ecology understands natural soundscapes as being part of human soundscapes, as well as providing a model from which much can be learned.

Of particular interest is the soundscape whose coherent identity allows it to be defined as an "acoustic community." A great deal of social science literature has attempted to find a general definition of the concept of "community" that applies equally to those that are geographically, culturally, socially, linguistically (or by any other means) defined. Many, if not all, of these types of communities are supported in their definition by the role which sound plays within them. The *acoustic community* may be defined as any soundscape in which acoustic information plays a pervasive role in the lives of the inhabitants (no matter how the commonality of such people is understood). Therefore, the boundary of the community is arbitrary and may be as small as a room of people, a home or building, or as large as an urban community, a broadcast area, or any other system of electroacoustic communication. In short, it is any system within which acoustic information is exchanged.

Characteristics of the Acoustic Community

Before examining actual instances of acoustic communities, let us discuss some of their most general characteristics. First of all, it should be clear that we are most interested in communities where sound creates a *positive* definition and not a negative one, as occurs when the community is heavily impacted by noise. In fact, noise is the chief enemy of the acoustic community, and we will turn our attention to its effects in the next chapter.

Our definition of the acoustic community means that acoustic cues and signals constantly keep the community in touch with what is going on from day to day within it. Such a system is "information rich" in terms of sound, and therefore sound plays a significant role in defining the community spatially, temporally in terms of daily and seasonal cycles, as well as socially and culturally in terms of shared activities, rituals and dominant institutions. The community is linked and defined by its sounds. To an outsider they may appear exotic or go unnoticed, but to the inhabitants they convey useful information about both individual and community life.

Acoustic Definition and Sound Signals

A community has good acoustic definition when sounds are heard clearly within it, when they reflect community life, and when they have distinctive and varied acoustic features. Good definition means that sounds are easily recognized and identified, and the subtleties of meaning they convey are readily available to the listener. Certain types of sounds have special roles in the environment that contribute to its definition, and the most important of these may be termed *sound signals*.

Sound signals are those sounds which stand out clearly against the ambient noise background (ambience being the aggregate of all, usually low-level sounds heard as a background texture and not as distinct, individual components). The most prominent sound signals in a community are those which are intentionally designed to communicate information, such as whistles, bells, horns, sirens, guns, and so on. However, other seemingly random sounds may convey useful information to those familiar with the situation, e.g., a door closing, voices, sounds of work and play, or even natural sounds such as the wind or rain. In an acoustically well-defined community, all such sounds (and their patterns) convey meaningful information about both regular and unique events.

Sound signals are the most striking components of the acoustic community, and often such sounds are unique and of historical importance; if so, their special status allows them to be regarded as community *soundmarks* (by analogy to landmarks). Because of the strong associations attached to the soundmark, often built up over many years, such sounds are worthy of preservation, like any historical artifact. Sometimes these sounds are also "keynote" sounds and the subject of background listening (as described in chapter 2), but their special ability to become associated with long-term memories means that they create an extremely important continuity with the past. This link may be even more personal and deep-seated than with other artifacts.

Sound signals assist in defining the community, first of all, through the spatial characteristics of the sound's behavior. Each signal has its own *acoustic profile* which is the area over which it may be heard (Fig. 5). Assuming such sounds are the loudest in the community, their collective profiles essen-

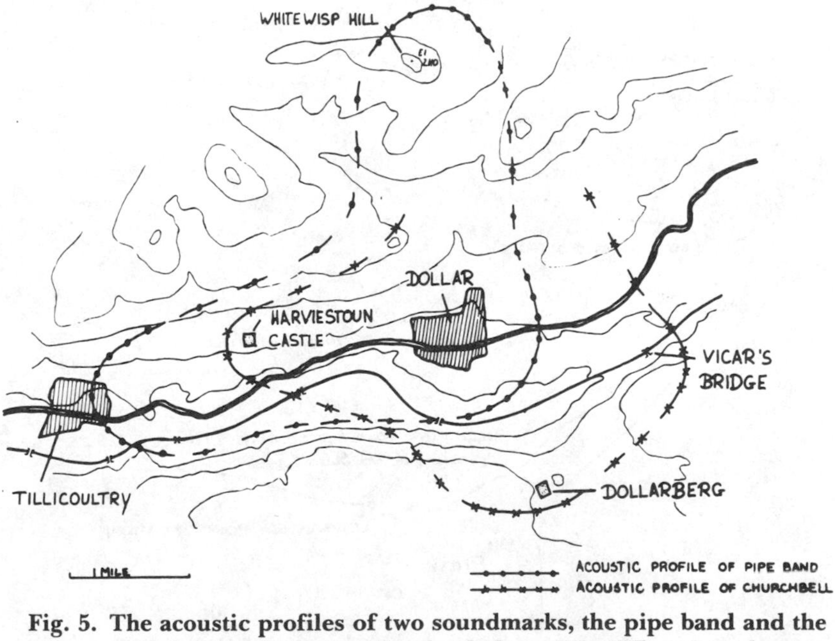

Fig. 5. The acoustic profiles of two soundmarks, the pipe band and the church bells, in Dollar, Scotland (from *Five Village Soundscapes*, R. M. Schafer, ed., Vancouver, British Columbia, A.R.C. Publications, 1977).

tially define the acoustic boundaries of the community, since all within these profiles have the *shared experience* of hearing them, and nearly any definition of community will include some element of a shared commonality. Furthermore, sound signals form an acoustic link to other communities when their profiles intersect. The meaning of the signal for members of the neighboring community may be less an indicator of time, events or institutions, than it is a reminder of particular links between the communities, personal or otherwise. We may speak of the *acoustic horizon* as comprising the most distant sounds which may be heard in a soundscape (Fig. 6); if the acoustic horizon of a community includes sounds which originate outside it, they act as a reminder of such links to the outside world.

If the community in question is a town or village, then the signals not only mark out its acoustic boundaries, but also define it temporally in terms of the regular intervals at which they sound (hourly, daily, weekly, or even

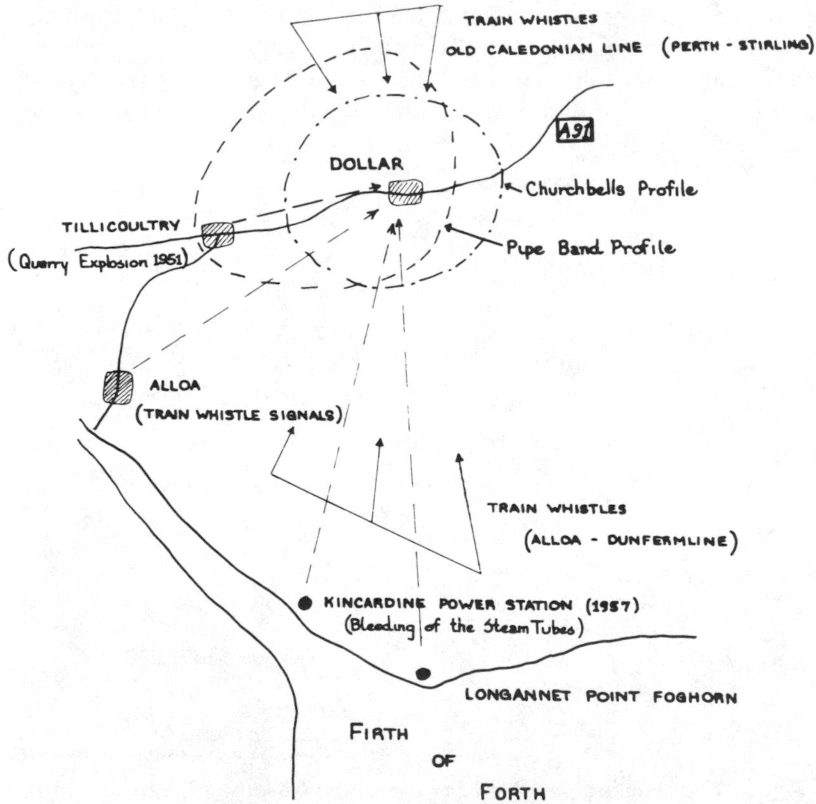

Fig. 6. Incoming sounds constituting the acoustic horizon of Dollar, Scotland (from *Five Village Soundscapes*, R. M. Schafer, ed., Vancouver, British Columbia, A.R.C. Publications, 1977).

seasonally). Such sounds may not even be fixed but may travel through the community, such as trains that sound their whistles at railway crossings at predictable times. Signals are always reminders of the dominant institutions of the community and reflective of its social and economic base. Therefore the shift whistle of a factory may mark the time to go to work for an employee, but it may simply be a subtle reminder of an important economic institution in the community for someone with no other connection to it. Signals also take on some aspect of the environmental character, not only because they are heard over the "ground" of the keynote sounds (e.g., boat horns against the sound of waves in a port), but also because their sound is reflected from buildings, hills, or mountains and comes to the listener "colored" by such acoustic interactions. Moreover, atmospheric conditions subtly change the character of each signalling event and provide additional weather information to those who can detect the differences. In short, the sound signal contains information about its source, its context, and its environment.

Sound signals, and the information they convey, bind the community together and contribute to its character. Whether the force of their action is "centripetal" in calling people together, or "centrifugal" in warning them to stay clear of danger, their psychological power is a positive reinforcement to the community. Those that are repetitive or occur at regular intervals may remain in the background of listeners' attention but still acquire their power precisely because of such repetition. Others, by signalling "differences" or unique situations, perhaps even danger, attract foreground attention and may become indelibly lodged in the memory in association with particular events in the life of the person and the community. Because of the need for such sounds to be designed (for efficient energy transfer), they are usually acoustically rich and may even have musical value, and therefore they acquire their significance in the soundscape through their ability to make a strong imprint on the mind, an imprint that embodies the entire context of the community. It is the relationship between acoustic richness and functionality within the community that seems to account for the significance and longevity of sound signals.

Environmental Character

Much of the behavior of sounds in a given situation can be accounted for through the physical layout of the environment. No geographical or atmospheric feature fails to affect the propagation of sound, whether it is the topography, the presence or absence of vegetation, prevailing winds and climate, or if indoors, the reverberant quality of the space, the style of building, and the amount of insulation between rooms. Further, the materials used in the environment or building affect how much sound energy is reflected, absorbed or transmitted with each interaction. The so-called "canyon effect" is a striking modern example of how the highly reflective materials used in tall buildings, and their symmetrical placement in long corridors, creates an acoustic situation where all sounds are "trapped" through multiple reflection. The result is a "diffuse sound field" of such uniformly high ambient level that a lo-fi situation is immediately created, and only the most powerful sound signals can rise above the noise. The effect on the listener is a kind of aural claustrophobia.

Acoustical engineering is the discipline that studies sound propagation in various environments and the principles for its control. Architectural acoustics does the same, but with the emphasis on the design of indoor spaces in which good acoustics are needed, such as auditoria (Doelle, 1972). The techniques of such disciplines are extremely important for community and environmental design. However, criteria for their use need to be derived from a clear idea of the goal to be attained. In specialized cases, such as a theater, where standards for speech intelligibility or the quality of musical acoustics are generally agreed upon, the goal can be pursued without question, though not without great skill. We lack an equivalent communicational model that suggests appropriate goals for other environments.

Therefore, one purpose of our model of the acoustic community is to define the environmental characteristics that promote effective communication within any environment under study. The criterion of that "which the occupants find satisfactory" (used in Beranek's Preferred Noise Criterion [Beranek et al., 1971]) defines the goal somewhat negatively, i.e., as the average background noise level which the occupants do not find overly disruptive or annoying. Moreover, such criteria depend on listeners' toleration of background noise which itself has been conditioned by frequent exposure to such conditions. Although a first goal in an acoustically oppressive environment may simply be to reduce sound levels to the point where negative effects are eliminated, one needs a model of a positively functioning environment to be able to proceed with a thorough design that is guided by an idea of what benefits might be achieved.

We therefore are faced with the problem of finding a balance between objective physical data in the analysis of any environment, and its subjective interpretation within a pattern of communication in the system. Techniques are well understood for the former, but not for the latter. Sound level measurements, such as decibels measured on the A or C scales (dBA, dBC), or the Equivalent Energy Level (Leq), or the host of other noise measurement systems that have been devised (Truax, 1978), are useful as part of any analysis. However, they provide only a physical measurement of the total sound intensity level, weighted in a certain manner, and cannot distinguish between different sounds that have their own communicative value. We will return to noise measurement per se in the next chapter, but let us indicate here some of the ways in which such objective measurements can be effectively used in environmental analysis.

Ambient (or background) levels, average levels, and peak levels establish the dynamic range of sound within an environment, and when these levels are high they can be correlated with known physiological, psychological, and communicational effects. Such levels can be documented over time (as will be discussed in the next section), or over space where they may be portrayed by the *isobel map*, such as in Fig. 7. Just as the geographer documents terrain on a map by connecting points of equal altitude, or the meteorologist draws up a weather map showing points of equal atmospheric

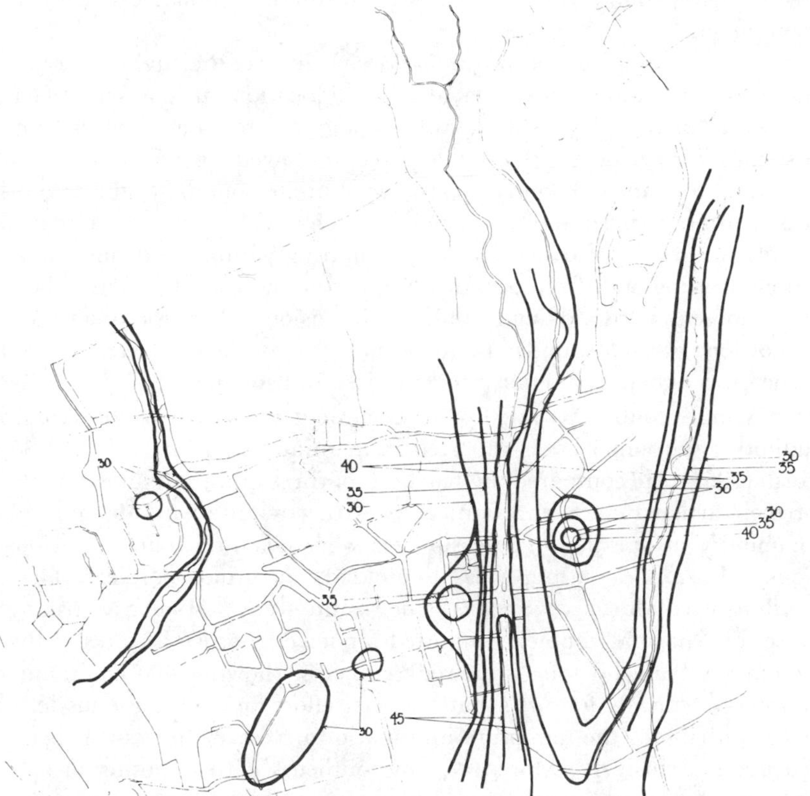

Fig. 7. Isobel map of Dollar, Scotland, constructed from ambient sound levels taken in the late evening. The sound of a small creek accounts for the higher level down the center of the map. Other prominent sounds, creating circles of higher intensity, are an electrical hum, voices, and amplified music (from *Five Village Soundscapes,* R. M. Schafer, ed., Vancouver, British Columbia, A.R.C. Publications, 1977).

pressure (isobars), the isobel map joins points of equal sound level (e.g., in units of dBA). If such a map is constructed from data taken at night, or during the relative absence of foreground activity, the map shows the "base line" of sound that is always present, assuming the sound sources are constant. Such sounds are keynotes (but keep in mind that foreground sounds may also function in this way). Isobel maps taken at various times during the day identify the highest level sound sources in the community and some extent of their influence (though their psychological influence may stem from other factors). A comparison of dBA and dBC levels indicates the presence of low frequency sound which is usually the result of technological factors in the environment.

A better indicator of the *qualitative* character of the environment can be derived from sound counts taken at selected locations at representative times of day, or during a "soundwalk" around a given area. Each sound (or group of sounds if they constitute a single perceptual event) is noted and classified according to standard source types, e.g., human sounds, traffic (motorized and non-motorized), natural sounds, mechanical sounds, electroacoustic sounds, and so on. Further, sounds originating within the defined area and those intruding on it from outside are noted to indicate the balance between local indigenous sounds and non-local intrusions. Both the quantities and proportions of such sounds are good indicators of the character of a soundscape (and obtaining them a good exercise in listening!).

A more ambitious attempt to document the *quality* of the visual and auditory environment was reported in a unique study by Michael Southworth (1969). He compared the reactions of three groups of subjects, selected for their articulateness and familiarity with environmental design and the community in question. These subjects were taken on tours of various regions of Boston; one group was blindfolded, one group wore earmuffs, and the third used all sensory modes. The results were particularly striking because the "normal" subjects reported far fewer sensory features of the environments than did the "impaired" subjects, showing that environmental awareness typically follows a path of least effort for each sense mode. Each mode contributes the minimum information necessary unless it is being relied upon exclusively. Moreover, environments with opposing visual and auditory character became quickly evident, as sighted subjects would respond enthusiastically to an environment which was acoustically oppressive (a situation typically found in cities). Southworth concluded that:

> memorable sound settings communicated more about spatial and activity character and were also unique with respect to other settings in the sequence. Most settings were sonically uninformative in terms of both spatial and activity form, and consequently lacked identity; they also changed greatly over time. The

diversity of sounds perceived was narrow. In addition to being unique and informative, preferred settings were responsive. Least preferred settings were uninformative, redundant, and usually very stressful, having sounds of high frequency and intensity, and thus distracted from other interests. (Southworth, 1969, pp. 63–64)

Southworth attempted to document the results in terms of what might be called "soundscape character" on the map in Fig. 8. using such terms as strong or weak visual/sonic identity, temporal continuity, sounds that are distracting, uninformative or undifferentiated, and spaces which are responsive and allow sonic involvement. Unfortunately, his suggested solutions tend toward *imposing* sound artifacts (e.g., "sonic signs," sound sculptures, etc.) onto sonically dull environments, and thus he betrays a visual bias with such "beautification" approaches to design. However, his study is significant in that (perhaps for the first time) perceptual and cognitive "images of place" were studied to yield criteria for design, instead of objective measures being recorded that could not possibly account for listeners' reactions. Except for some cognitive approaches in geography and environmental preference studies (Anderson et al., 1983), it appears his work has not been followed up.

Rhythm and Cycles

Above all, sounds exist in time, and to a large extent, they create and influence our sense of time. Therefore it is not surprising that our sense of the character or coherence of an environment is closely tied to the temporal relationships exhibited by sound. These relationships include both the sounds' internal evolution over time and their patterns on different time scales, from those at the short-term memory level to the largest circadian and seasonal variations. Because we normally pass through environments, we seldom become aware of the larger rhythms and cycles they exhibit. Nothing is more revealing to the soundscape analyst than to monitor the changes in an acoustically rich environment over some lengthy period of time. And no feature of the acoustically oppressive environment becomes more quickly evident than its utter sameness and meaninglessness even over a short period of time!

The rhythmic patterns found in the natural soundscape and the products of human energy show a remarkable interplay of regularity and variation. Just as the auditory system is quick to identify a periodicity at the micro level of the waveform, and hence to ascribe the phenomenon of pitch sensation, so too a perceived regularity at the macro level of event-to-event durations is a strongly compelling feature. Many writers have ascribed this "sense of rhythm" to corporeal regularity found in the bodily functions of the

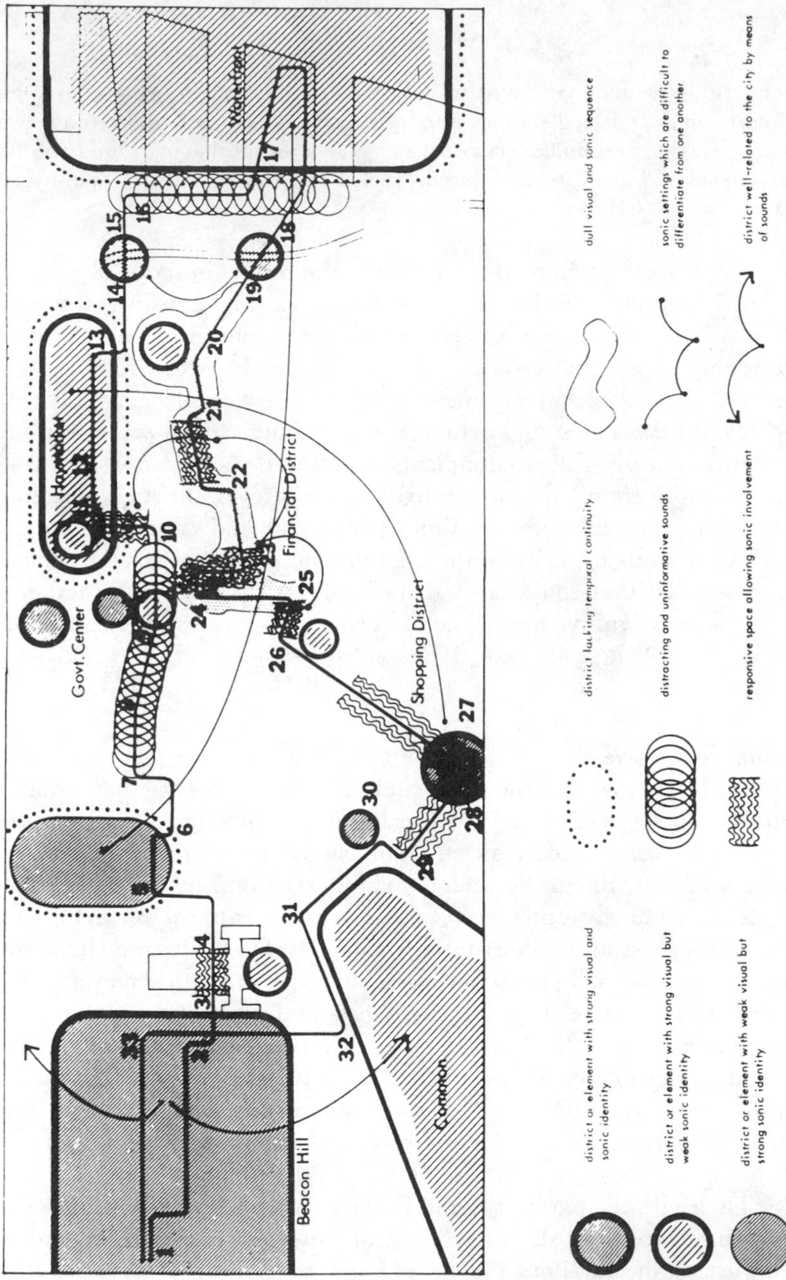

Fig. 8. Evaluation of part of the Boston soundscape (from M. Southworth, "The Sonic Environment of Cities," *Environment and Behavior,* Vol. 1, No. 1, 1969, p. 66. Copyright © 1969 by copyright holder. Reprinted by permission of Sage Publications, Inc., Beverly Hills, CA).

heartbeat, breathing, and bodily movement of the hands and feet.[1] The ability to mark off regular units of time seems to be universal, and the "unison" effect of synchronized bodily movement is easy for any group to create. Such phenomena are fundamental to music, as well as to speech and the sound environment. Moreover, the stimulating effect of rhythm on the body is known to be involuntarily experienced, whether in "foot tapping" music or the planned stimulation curves of the tempi of background music. However, just as remarkable as the phenomenon of the regular beat is the inevitable degree of variation (small deviations from precise regularity) that is found in all natural and human sounds.

In fact, *absolute* precision in rhythm is generally associated only with machinery, and any human attempt to simulate it, such as in military drill, although admired for machine-like efficiency, is thought to be unnatural and potentially inhuman. The periodicities involved in repeating phenomena are judged according to their human equivalents (e.g., waves at 6 to 8 seconds per cycle that evoke a slow, relaxed breathing rate, or the "andante" of a relaxed walking rate, or the excitement of a running tempo). Likewise, variations from the precisely regular are regarded as essentially human indicators. Regularity in such motor rhythms as hammering a nail, or pumping water from a well, signify an efficiency in energy use (only a novice hammers irregularly). But small deviations, such as hesitations or speed-ups, betray the human capacity of using feedback from the result of an action to control the execution of the next; small adjustments are made in compensation. Simple machines which do not use the principle of feedback must standardize the environment to the point where "blind" (and deaf) repetition is guaranteed success. If machines were to simulate human activity more closely, their rhythms would show more variation. However, automation proves more advantageous when it *exceeds* human limits of speed and precision, and therefore the sounds of the machine age speed up to the point where rhythmic events fuse into the drone or "flat line" of continuous sound.

Therefore, the internal rhythm of a sound brings with it strong psychological implications for the way it is understood. On a larger scale of time relations, the temporal sequencing and overlay of sounds in a soundscape (their "counterpoint" to use the musical term) is crucial for their comprehension. In a coherent environment, sounds obviously can't all "talk at once," and therefore rhythm is a key factor in the balance or imbalance of a soundscape. Community sound traditionally follows cyclic patterns, but (just as at the micro level) with room left for meaningful variation. In tribal society or the traditional community, daily activities of each of the members

---

[1]Wilfrid Mellers uses the terms "corporeal" and "spiritual" to describe metric and non-metric rhythms respectively. See W. Mellers, *Caliban Reborn*, New York: Harper & Row, 1967, p. 3 ff.

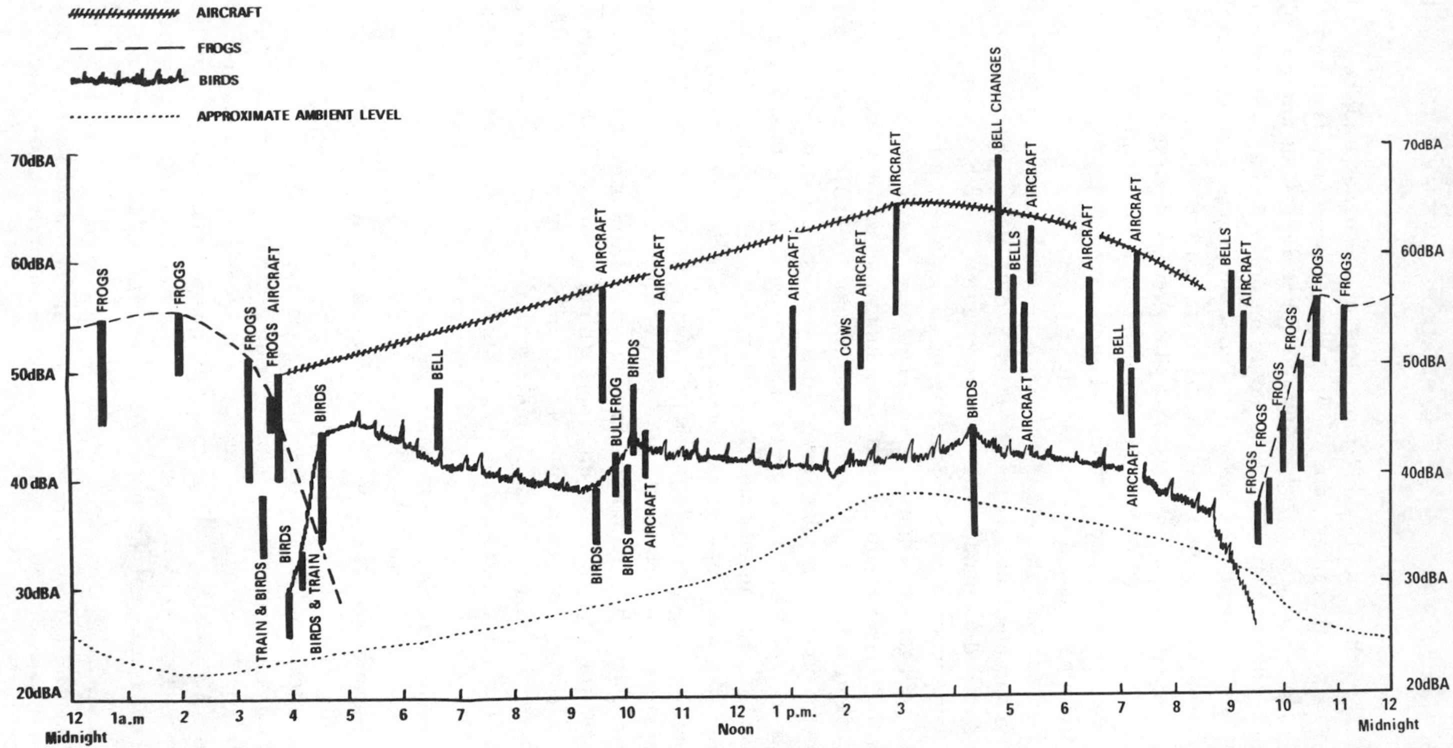

Fig. 9. Daily pattern of sound levels and sound sources based on a 24-hour recording in the countryside on summer solstice, 1974 (from *Handbook for Acoustic Ecology*, B. Truax, ed., Vancouver, British Columbia, A.R.C. Publications, 1978).

follow predictable patterns, and hence a strong circadian rhythm can be observed in the resulting soundscape. Of equal importance to the periods of activity are the periods of rest, most typically at midday or during the afternoon heat in many climates, as well as during hours of sleep. Religious and social customs traditionally enforce a day of rest and longer periods at specific times of year. The corresponding "low points" in soundscape activity ensure a rhythmic, as well as a psychological, point of repose. The homogenization of time through shift work in industrial societies, and the progressive obliteration of Sunday as a day of rest in Western culture, affect the uniformity of the urban soundscape as much as the prevalence of low-information sounds and constant ambient levels.

The norms for circadian and seasonal rhythms come from the natural soundscape, and therefore are deeply rooted within the human psyche. The diagrams in Figs. 9 and 10 give a schematic representation of two such patterns, one for a single day, the other for a year, as documented by the World Soundscape Project. Although a full account of acoustic communication in the animal world is beyond the scope of this book, these diagrams are a reminder of the traditional wisdom that "to everything there is a season." The human scale of soundmaking and rhythm intersects the natural scale at certain crucial points. But above all, what the natural soundscape presents is a model of a balanced acoustic "community" where form and function are in equilibrium.

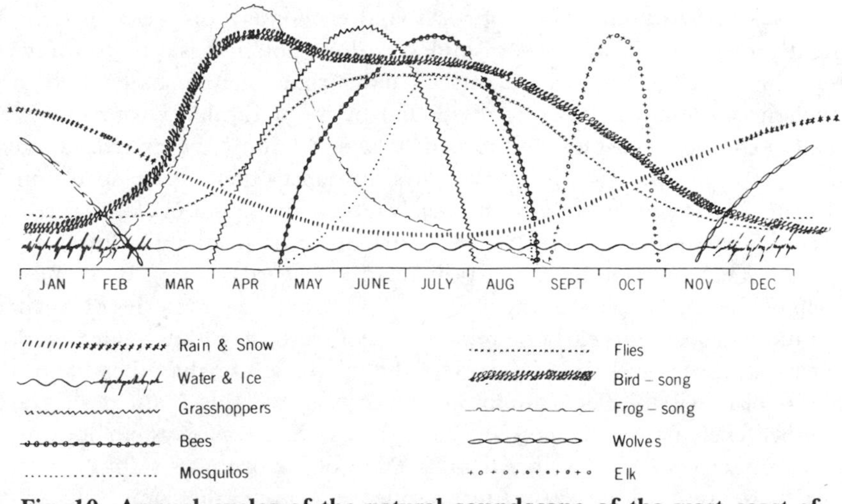

Fig. 10. Annual cycles of the natural soundscape of the west coast of British Columbia by relative volume of sounds (no scale) (from *Handbook for Acoustic Ecology*, B. Truax, ed., Vancouver, British Columbia, A.R.C. Publications, 1978).

Variety, Complexity and Balance

On the basis of the characteristics of the acoustic community which we have described, we can present a model of its behavior that will also lead to criteria for acoustic design. Throughout this discussion we have treated the acoustic community as a system within which acoustic information is exchanged. When such a system is observed to be functioning successfully, it will have the following three characteristics:

1. A *variety* of different kinds of sound, and variations of particular types of sound, are present and clearly heard. Such sounds may be said to be "rich" in acoustic information.
2. A *complexity* exists within the sounds themselves and in the types and levels of information they communicate. Listeners who are familiar with the environment are able to decode and interpret subtleties in the sound that the novice does not recognize.
3. A functional *balance* operates within the environment as a result of spatial, temporal, social, and cultural constraints on the system. That is, variety and complexity are constrained by balancing forces which keep the system in a functional equilibrium. However, the system is limited in its ability to reorganize itself when threatened by perturbations and change at the organizational or structural level.

Contrary to our notion of social and economic "progress" leading to greater complexity, acoustic complexity does not necessarily continue to increase with such developments as industrialization, urbanization, and modern communication systems. Sound in the natural environment is already extremely complex and varied. It is never static, never redundant, it never repeats, and usually every physical aspect of it, from spectrum to rhythm, is complex and not easily analyzable. One might even interpret the myths surrounding the creation or "gift" of music in many cultures as reflecting a natural wonderment at the relative *simplicity* and purity of musical sound. The perfect periodicity of musical pitch and the mysteries of harmonic ratios suggested to early peoples a level of truth that transcended worldly events and mirrored the structure of the universe. On the other hand, the ability of music to affect human emotions in an edifying manner suggested another level of awesome power. Complexity in music as a system of communication derives from its organization and not just from its sound material, and therefore music in early times seemed to channel the complexity of the natural acoustic world, and the supernatural power people ascribed to it, into an ordered and purely human form.

Similarly, the sounds of preindustrialized society are varied and complex simply because they have not become standardized in the sense that materials and goods are not mass-produced. Moreover, few high intensity or continuous sounds exist in the preindustrialized world. Therefore, more "smaller" sounds can be heard, more detail can be discerned in those that are heard, and sounds coming from a greater distance form a significant part of the soundscape. In terms of acoustic ecology, one might say that more "populations" of sound exist, and fewer "species" are threatened with extinction.

The complexity of information communicated to people by such sounds may be inferred from the three "earwitness" quotes of chapter 2 that exemplify three modes of listening in the traditional soundscape. In the listening-in-search mode, the ear is alert to every possible subtlety of information in the environment, and in the listening-in-readiness mode, the auditory system scans all incoming sounds to obtain a match to one that is familiar and recognizable. The complexities involved in ascribing meaning to such sound sequences suggests that environmental sound can function as a "language" within a soundscape. The essential difference is that such languages are quite localized, even idiosyncratic, and that the encoding of information is not in discrete digital units such as words, but in terms of a holistic image that can be recognized as a "gestalt" or analyzed for some particular qualitative feature. The difficulty of putting such information into words should not obscure our recognition that an effective and complex system of communication exists within the soundscape.

The notion of complexity is being used here to refer simultaneously to aspects of the sounds of an environment and to the information processing they undergo in the mind. In the last chapter we discussed this dual role of structure in terms of a competence and performance model, and suggested that "soundscape competence" is the tacit knowledge listeners have about the structure of environmental sound. Such knowledge is a representation of the "rules" which are understood to operate in complex sound input to make it meaningful. However, this model does not imply any storage of the sound itself, since even the brain is not large enough to store all possible sound patterns. The pattern of a familiar sound, through repetition, does enter long-term memory in terms of the features that have been used to decode it *combined with* the environmental context in which it is typically heard. The reader may verify this assertion by remembering any particular sound and noting the environmental context that accompanies the remembered image. What we are referring to here are not only the stored patterns, but also the performance strategies which allow the decoding of any input and its comparison to memory. Complexity in the acoustic community therefore refers both to the quality of the sounds it includes and to the level of information processing performed by the inhabitants in recognizing and using such sounds.

The Sound Symbol and Metaphor

Although we have implied that every sound event in the acoustic community is unique in the information it conveys, it is also true that such occurrences are not random. Over countless repetitions, the images created in people's minds by such sounds and their contexts build up coherent patterns that may be called *sound symbolisms.* Sound symbols function analogously to Jung's archetypes (which are strongly visual)[2] in that they are mental and cultural images of great suggestive power. The experience of a specific instance of a sound may take on special significance when it touches or evokes such symbolic imagery. Even a common sound may seem symbolic; in depicting a burial scene, Flaubert reports that "the stones striking the wood of the coffin made that awesome sound that seems to us the very voice of eternity."[3] Because sound in our model mediates the relationship of the person to the environment, it is only a simple additional step for it to come to symbolize that relationship. And when such symbolisms function for countless people over the centuries in many different contexts, the symbol acquires the richness and abstractness of the archetype, with its power to find expression in countless specific instances.

A simpler form of symbolic behavior exhibited by sound comes when it functions metaphorically. The pattern recognized in an aural image can often be compared to other patterns which it can then come to represent. The sound of flowing water, with its intricately detailed texture and yet its overall continuity, is a powerful metaphor for life processes and has been used as such by many writers. The strong clear voice of the trumpet or other sound signal, cutting through the soundscape with an assertive message, is a suitable metaphor for effective human communication.[4] In contrast, perhaps the best known Biblical acoustic metaphor, in which St. Paul suggests that without love, one becomes as "sounding brass, or a tinkling cymbal,"[5] is based on the purposelessness of sound that finds no meaning for the listener. And the acoustic, as well as physical, comparison of the sound of beating on a tree trunk and evoking its rich internal resonances, to that of hitting the human chest is a sound metaphor that finds expression in many tribal societies. These illustrations (which could be multiplied indefinitely) suggest the layers of meaning that sound can have within the acoustic community. In 20th-century communities, which rely on acoustic information less and less, it is hard to find positive acoustic metaphors in contemporary writers—

---

[2]C. G. Jung, *Man and His Symbols,* New York: Doubleday, 1964.

[3]G. Flaubert, *Madame Bovary,* F. Steegmuller, trans., New York: Random House, 1957, p. 383.

[4]I Corinthians 14:8.

[5]I Corinthians 13:1.

sound increasingly seems to be a negative reflection of modern society, if it reflects anything at all.

Balance and Equilibrium

Finally, we referred above to the *balancing* forces that operate within the acoustic community to keep it in a functional equilibrium. Without constraining forces, acoustic complexity turns against itself and prevents effective communication through sensory overload. Acoustic sounds (as distinct from electroacoustic phenomena which we shall treat in part II) are constrained by their own physical characteristics. Acoustic energy can only last so long before it is dissipated, travel so far, and occupy different frequency ranges in certain amounts. Such constraints are traditionally sufficient to prevent sound from occupying too much physical space too much of the time, or from masking too many other sounds. In other words, the physical properties of sound are the basis of its natural ecological balance.

Some additional information may be necessary to clarify the balancing principle related to masking, or the sharing of spectral "space." As described in chapter 2, incoming sounds are analyzed according to frequency along the length of the basilar membrane in the inner ear. The spectrum, or frequency content, of all natural sounds is spread out over some band of frequencies in the audible range (20 to 20,000 Hz). The energy is analyzed in terms of what falls into small parts of that range, namely the "critical bands" (which are approximately one-third of an octave wide). The different component frequencies of a sound, from low to high, can be individually distinguished because they are analyzed separately in terms of such bands. For instance, the lower harmonics in a complex tone can be heard separately, if the tone lasts long enough, up to the point where they are too closely spaced, i.e., less than a critical bandwidth apart. Therefore, a sound whose energy is predominantly in one part of the audible spectrum can mask, or cover up, a more diminutive sound whose energy is also in the same range. Conversely, however, if the two sounds have energy in quite distinct ranges, then both may be heard clearly, even if there is a considerable difference in their respective intensity levels (e.g., traffic and bird sounds).

There is, however, a secondary aspect of masking in that a given frequency band tends to mask upwards more than it does downwards (i.e., it covers not only other sounds in the same range, but to some extent those in the immediately adjacent higher bands as well). Therefore, low frequency and mid-range sounds, and certainly broad-band sounds, are more likely to create masking effects than purely high frequency sounds.

From these psychoacoustic considerations, we learn that a *minimal* criterion to ensure a balance between various sounds is that their spectral energy is distributed over different parts of the audible frequency range. If all the sounds of an environment are in the low frequency range, they are hopelessly jumbled, even though a single bird can be heard clearly over top of them. A mix of spectra in different ranges, reinforced by contrasing envelopes, rhythmic patterns, and spatial characteristics, provides the basis for a meaningful soundscape.

In the traditional (pre-industrial) community, the balancing forces are the spatial geography of the community where buildings and other obstructions keep sounds somewhat localized (unless perched on bell towers), and the social organization that leads to distinct rhythms of community life and determines "who does what when." Potential noise problems are solved by the "qualitative" by-law approach of proscribing specific sounds and activities, or by limiting the times of day when they can occur. Appeals to the "good citizenship" of the community members are generally sufficient to enforce the desired norm. The social hierarchy perpetuated by the dominant institutions keeps everyone "in their place," but also it holds the soundscape in check.

Although the acoustic community can easily accommodate change at the level of sound populations (i.e., any sound may be replaced by a similar one), it is extremely vulnerable to changes that affect the balancing forces. Industrialization (and later electrification) challenges the natural acoustic constraints by creating sounds that are louder than those in the natural environment, that are continuous (i.e., powered by the constant addition of energy so they do not die away), that travel farther, and that have broadband spectra. As a result, both the character of the soundscape changes and also its functional ecology. There is no natural mechanism which can restore the equilibrium, except through individual and collective action to impose new constraints on the system. The "annoyance" factor of noise acts as a catalyst for such change, but it also produces a lack of desire to listen, simply because there is less meaningful information to motivate it. One characteristic of system behavior is that when feedback is amplified instead of being counter-checked, the result is an instability of the system (or what is commonly called the "vicious circle"). Such a situation occurs when noise leads to human adaptation and a desensitization to it that permits more noise to occur unheeded. Deafness is the only ultimate constraint on an acoustic community. But prior to the point of physical breakdown, many stages of psychological and social disruption occur which we shall examine in the next chapter.

Therefore, the concept of the acoustic community and the forces that serve to keep it in balance leads to our understanding of the need for *acoustic design* as a conscious and informed attempt to restore equilibrium to malfunctioning soundscapes. Natural balancing forces cannot accommodate the profound changes in the soundscape brought about in the modern world (just as it is questionable whether the environment in general can survive). However, the systemic basis of the soundscape permits not only the "vicious circle" syndrome created by noise, but also the means for positive action. A change at any point in the system for the better can also be "amplified" throughout it. If the soundscape were only a physical "effluent" of society, then objective, physical control would be sufficient, and objective standards could be agreed upon and enforced. However, the soundscape by its very definition depends on people and their listening habits. Therefore, design can begin with the individual (including listening habits) as much as with the environment. In fact, if the individual is *not* included (as is the case in most noise control programs), the results will be superficial. Profound change in restoring some measure of functionality to the acoustic environment must include all elements within the soundscape, from the individual to the entire community. We will return to this basis for acoustic design in chapter 7.

Some Case Studies

From what anthropologists tell us about soundmaking in other cultures, it seems that all traditional communities have a strong acoustic orientation (Merriam, 1964). Listening is a valued skill that plays an important part in the lives of the individual and the community. In the rituals of the Navaho, for instance, silence is strictly enforced and the participants must be prepared to repeat the lines of the chanter with great exactitude for hours on end.[6] Likewise, in the Hopi villages there is a strong injunction against unnecessary soundmaking indoors because it might interfere with critical acoustic information coming from the equivalent of the "town crier" or from the distant fields. Listening in these communities is a vital channel of communication that must not become cluttered, and many of the social rituals ensure that its skills are well practised. Survival may depend on it (for instance, the Navaho must be able to hear the warning sounds of rattlesnakes), just as the community as a whole depends on sound to keep it functioning smoothly and its inhabitants coordinated.

Much of the groundwork for the model of the acoustic community which is presented in this chapter was laid through the field studies conducted by the World Soundscape Project at Simon Fraser University from 1972 to 1976[7] (Truax, 1974, 1977). The work included a detailed study of the Vancouver soundscape, a cross-Canada field recording tour, a detailed study of five villages in Europe, and the beginning stages of a similar study of a small community in British Columbia. In the Vancouver study, the relative youth

---

[6]C. Kluckhohn & O. Leighton, *The Navaho,* Cambridge: Harvard University Press, 1960; David P. McAllester, "Enemy Way Music (A Study of Social and Esthetic Values as Seen in Navaho Music)," *Peabody Music Papers*, Cambridge, Vol. 41, No. 3, 1954.

[7]Published project documents from these studies are listed under World Soundscape Project in the Bibliography.

of the city allowed some of the history of its soundscape to be documented through archival search and unstructured interviews with "oldtimers" (three of the "earwitness" accounts from this study appear in chapter 2). What was striking about the reminiscences of such people was the accuracy of detail about acoustic events that were far in the past. A catalogue of such memories produced essentially an "acoustic map" of the early city and indicated that in those days, the community was defined geographically in at least some people's minds by its sounds. The present-day features of the soundscape were found to include many prominent sound signals and soundmarks, some with a rich history, but the profiles of none of them covered the city to any extent. In fact, the only "shared" sound experiences in the community today seem to be the ubiquitous traffic and aircraft sounds. Vancouver, like most urban environments, has become increasingly defined by the common noise element, and acoustic communication patterns have largely been replaced by electroacoustic links and other media.

After the Vancouver study, the question remained whether *any* communities still existed which preserved a strong sense of acoustic definition. Some were found in Europe in the form of small villages which, although obviously affected by the forces of industrialization, still retained an acoustic character. Ambient levels were generally low (32–37 dBA), and in one of them, a small Italian mountain village (Cembra), nonmotorized traffic (i.e., pedestrians, bikes, etc.) still constituted the main traffic movement at the center of the village, and was the main type of sound heard in the residential areas along with other human sounds. The community was still defined by sound on a human scale.

Each village in the study had striking acoustic features and characteristic rhythms in its soundscape. In the Swedish village (Skruv), the profiles of the whistles of the glassworks, brewery, and passing trains extended over the quiet community and defined its boundaries, as did the keynote sounds of the factory hums. An interesting interplay emerged between the actual profile of the signals and their psychological profile (i.e., how far villagers *thought* they could be heard). When the villagers were asked to estimate the profiles of the whistles in comparison to the churchbells located a few kilometers outside the community, that of the latter was estimated as being larger, even though the sound was weaker acoustically. This paradox suggests a direction for further research in acoustic community definition—is the psychological profile of a sound indicative of its social importance?

In the German village (Bissingen), churchbells rang every 15 minutes and thereby constituted a keynote sound in the community. Interviews with older residents attempted to ascertain the profile of the bells earlier in the century, in terms of whether they could be heard in neighboring communities, and similarly, whether bells in those communities were within the acoustic horizon of Bissingen. It appears that both the bell profile and the acoustic horizon have shrunk, presumably as a result of rising ambient noise levels. In fact, ambient levels were highest in this village and had a large low frequency component caused by industry and aircraft whose sounds were trapped in the bowl-shaped valley in which the community is located. Acoustic links between neighboring communities seem to have diminished over the years, and possibly this fact indicates that other types of links have changed as well.

An acoustic horizon that functioned differently was found to operate in a small French fishing village (Lesconil) as a result of the "solar wind" cycle, an offshore–onshore cycle of wind that rotates its direction throughout the day and corresponds to the pattern of the fishboats leaving before dawn and returning to port in the afternoon (Fig. 11). The winds result in a shifting

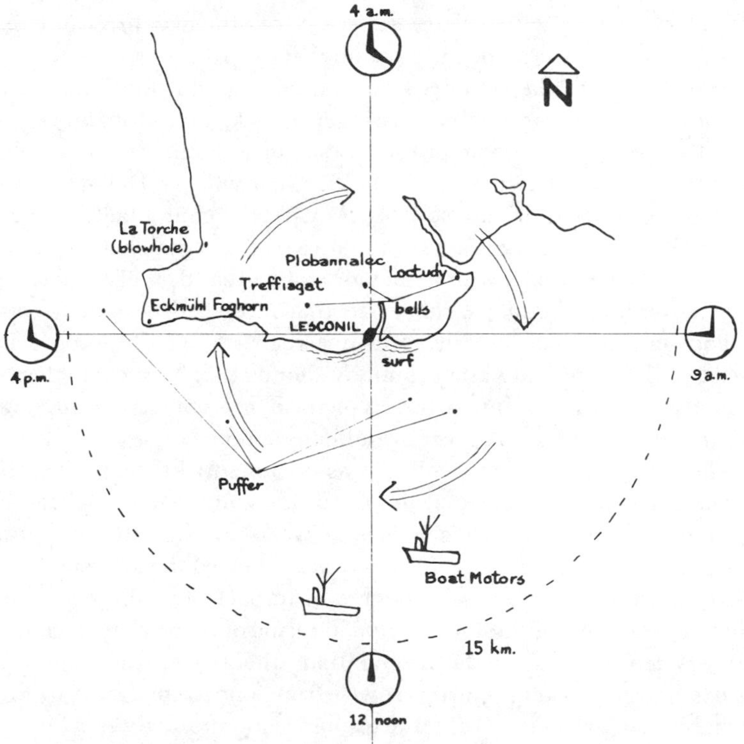

Fig. 11 Daily pattern of the solar wind cycle in Lesconil, France, showing the sound sources brought by the winds to the community throughout the day (from *Five Village Soundscapes*, R. M. Schafer, ed., Vancouver, British Columbia, A.R.C. Publications, 1977).

acoustic horizon that is highly dependent on atmospheric conditions. Sounds from different directions are heard in the community at different times of day. Although the fishing fleet is now motorized and no longer depends on the winds directly, the acoustic pattern still provides weather information to the inhabitants, and a unique soundscape character to the village.

A characteristic part of the acoustic definition of Cembra, particularly during the period of its greatest prosperity, was an annual cycle of seasonal rituals, festivals, and events that incorporated many types of soundmaking. Bells, bugles, ratchets, cannons, drumming, singing, and general noisemaking were all incorporated into these events which marked off the seasons, the church year, and major events in the life of the community. However, with the decline of the village's self-sufficiency and population, the number of events fell off, as did their acoustic complexity. Church rituals still occur regularly, but their counterpoint is now the jukebox of the local "albergo" that plays incessantly with a characteristic low frequency throb and forms an electroacoustic link to the outside commercial world.

Several of the villages suffer from intrusive sounds that blur the acoustic definition of the community. Bissingen is near an autobahn, as well as Stuttgart airport; sonic booms from low-flying military jets were heard at least once a day in the village. In the Scottish village (Dollar), where the pipe band of the local private school vies with the churchbells as the dominant soundmark of the community, the presence of a major highway cutting through the village brings with it the noise of a great deal of nonlocal traffic. Interviews with the populace suggested that most had become accustomed to it, and only the most aurally sensitive realized that the progressive increase of traffic noise had obscured many sounds that once characterized the community. *Denial* of the intrusiveness of noise through passive acceptance is one of the most common aspects of public reaction to noise.

The soundscape of each village was documented through field recordings, sound level measurements, hourly traffic counts at the village center, and sound counts taken during half-hour walks through the community at specified times. The latter two types of counts showed the acoustic rhythm of the daily pattern of activity, the degree of impact of traffic noise, and the qualitative character of the soundscape in terms of the variety of community sounds. When normalized for population, the traffic and sound counts showed a fairly constant linear growth from one community to another, presumably on account of differences in economic activity. The rate of growth was 1:4, that is, one new residential traffic sound for every four additional traffic movements at the center (traffic being both motorized and nonmotorized human types). However, the *total* number of community sounds did not grow at an equivalent rate, and this observation (though tentative given the small number of communities studied) suggested that:

> increased motorized traffic, producing high intensity, low information sounds, tends to desensitize the populace and result in less social interaction, as indicated by fewer resultant sounds. It is not merely a question that many quieter sounds are masked; this is true to some extent, but since only a small rise in ambience is involved, this is not the only factor. We contend that the fundamental social changes taking place result in a soundscape of reduced character and variety, and that this leads to a reduced interaction between community members and the environment. (WSP, 1977b, p. 77)

The balancing forces described above were found to operate in all of the communities studied. The physical layout of the village and its vulnerability to nonlocal noise sources were important variables. In Cembra, the labyrinthine streets of this mountainside community contained the remarkable variety of community sounds and added a reverberant quality to most of them. The rhythm of the daily cycles, except in Bissingen where the factory operates continuously, contributed to the balance of each soundscape by alternating peaks of activity with periods of rest. The social patterns of the villages involved different times and activities for the men, women and children, and the dominant institutions had characteristic forms of soundmaking (whether the daily fish auction in Lesconil or the church services in Cembra). All of these factors aided acoustic definition and balance. However, none of these forces was sufficient to restore balance to a soundscape imperilled by noise or economic and social change.

Lack of time, as well as language barriers, limited the amount of information that was gleaned from the populace—a key part of any soundscape analysis. Unstructured interviews were carried out with many of the locals, and in Dollar, one particular interview subject with a keen aural sense and accurate memory was found who contributed greatly to our knowledge of the soundscape history of that community. However, the methodological problem remains of how to balance the statistical level of a large population sample (which of necessity includes many people whose reactions to sound are so habitual they can be expressed only with great difficulty), with the vivid and accurate memories of the minority of the population who are truly sensitive to their acoustic environment. The dominant social survey methodology is entirely geared towards statistical reactions to specific sources of annoyance, such as traffic and aircraft, and does not concern itself with broader questions of how sound functions in the community.

A Social Survey Approach

The sole exception to this norm, as far as I know, is a study of ten English villages carried out by the Institute of Sound and Vibration Research of the University of Southampton (Hawkins, 1980). The study is unique in several ways: first of all because it dealt with low-noise rural environments, and secondly because it developed a questionnaire which allowed people to express both positive and negative feelings about sound. In addition, it attempted to ascertain a few of the actual types of information which people glean from their acoustical surroundings. The authors were well aware of the radical departure from the conventional study which theirs represented, even though exploratory in nature. They stated:

> The conventional methodology, looked at critically, may be regarded as both negative and restricted. Negative in the sense that all sounds are referred to as noise and rating scales usually provide no scope for a positive response. Restricted, since usually the social survey concentrates predominantly on one sound. . . . The conventional approach may be considered satisfactory when studying the degenerate and relatively simple acoustical environments occurring when one sound (e.g. transportation) dominates to such an extent that the effects of other sounds are swamped. But when studying other more rich, complex and subtle acoustical environments comprised of many and varied types of sound, the paucity of information and understanding that the conventional methodology would reveal is obvious. A more comprehensive approach is required if many of the important distinctions and measures of subjective response are not to be distorted or entirely overlooked. (Hawkins, 1980, pp. 69, 76)

Although the study represents a laudable departure from the norm, the majority of the questions put to residents were of the "like/dislike/no feelings" sort which reflect certain community attitudes but do not reveal any of the subtler levels of information processing. For instance, churchbells were liked by upwards of two-thirds of the respondents. The percentages increased with the age of the people and according to the importance which the church had in their lives. Also, wild birds were reported as a sound that was liked by nearly everyone. Sounds with pleasant or at least positive associations are understandably reported as being liked, and conversely for those with negative associations. But many other community sounds, even when reported as being heard by the majority of respondents, often provoked a "no feelings" response. Feelings of like or dislike have little to do with sounds conveying information to the listener and establishing an acoustic orientation to community life. How then are we to interpret a "no feelings" response?

The study looked further for correlations between likes and dislikes with such background variables as outdoor noise level, sex, age, age education finished, occupation of head of household, time spent in garden, and so on. Possible significant relationships on the "dislike" side were typically found for male subjects with more years of education and in professional jobs; such people were often more active in disliking particular sounds. By way of explanation one might suggest that, given the social status conferred on such persons, they were simply readier to complain and assert their rights, as it were. Or, given that a significant part of their "world" existed outside the immediate home environment, they felt less "connected" to the latter and were therefore more likely to regard its sounds as intrusions on their privacy.

However, the study also asked a few questions that attempted to establish whether the people "were aware of and interpreted various amounts of information implicit in their acoustical surroundings" (Hawkins, 1980, p. 141). The questions asked whether the type of event signified by churchbells could be distinguished, or if a neighbor's car could be recognized from sound alone, or if there were sounds that denoted time of day and weather. Positive responses were obtained from 51% of the respondents for churchbells, 33% for neighbors' cars, 48% for early morning sounds, 39% for sounds at special times of day, and 42% for weather indicators (the latter three included a fairly wide range of different sounds). These findings suggest that at least one-third to one-half the respondents in these villages have an acoustic component to their orientation towards the environment and the community. A similar study in an urban area, including different styles of residential housing, would be valuable for understanding whether this acoustic orientation remains significant or not in the city.

The Indoor Community

The emphasis on larger scale communities should not keep us from applying the model to smaller scale environments as well. In fact, the natural acoustic boundaries created by building structures make them amenable to conceiving an indoor environment as a "community" within which acoustic information is exchanged. The acoustic principles that dictate the behavior of sound in enclosed spaces are well known, as are the practical options for controlling its propagation (Wetherill, 1975; White, 1975). Background noise levels that permit adequate speech comprehension (e.g., the Speech Interference Level [SIL]) are also known (Webster, 1969, 1974), as are the effects of higher levels in requiring a raised voice or shouting. The Preferred Noise Criterion establishes "acceptable" ambient levels for various types of working environments (Beranek et al., 1971). In environments with high sound levels, where sound is a menace and not a channel of communication, Damage-Risk Criteria are established by the Worker's Compensation Board and public health officials as a guide for permissible noise exposure (Guignard & Johnson, 1975; Truax, 1978). These criteria, plus the known effects of noise (Miller, 1974; White, 1975), are suitable reference points for the acoustic assessment of an environment, but they are also limited in their usefulness.

As we shall discuss in the next chapter, many cases and noise phenomena are inadequately covered by existing criteria. Moreover, the negative quality of such criteria strongly implies a concept of design that is simply a matter of reducing levels to the point where negative effects are presumably eliminated. They do *not* provide guidelines for creating a positively functioning acoustic environment. It is a case where "not negative" does not necessarily equal "positive." More seriously, however, the criteria are such that even when their recommended levels are adhered to, they guarantee only *minimal* protection and acceptability for a *certain percentage* of the exposed population. Such criteria simply reflect what the majority can adapt to, and as such they serve to maintain a precariously balanced status quo.

How does a communicational approach to similar environments differ? In general, one analyzes the environment as a *system* of communication within which many factors, and many levels of influence, are at work. Once noise factors are assessed, one can ask what positive role sound plays, or could play, in the lives of those living or working in the environment, and how the given acoustic situation is facilitating or inhibiting such a relationship. Interviews with the individuals involved are important, but people cannot be expected to be consciously aware of the aural component in their behavior, and in the case of noise, they may react typically by actively denying the problem, rationalizing its existence, or internalizing it by blaming themselves. Therefore, it is important for the analyst to function as a careful *observer* of the entire acoustic system on the qualitative level as well as on the quantitative.

For instance, consider two different daycare settings (the following descriptive account is based on an actual study done by a student at Simon Fraser University, British Columbia). The first is located in a large old house with the activities spread out in several rooms on two floors. Because of the house's sturdy construction and its distance from outside noise sources, sound is reasonably well isolated between the different areas, each of which is devoted to children of a different age group and different activities, such as playing, sleeping, and eating. The ambient level is 40 dBA and activity levels are 50–60 dBA; staff attitudes to their work are good and the children seem happy. The staff report that they are able to "stay in touch" with what is going on in all the various areas, i.e., they can easily spot potential trouble with a child. According to our model, their state of listening-in-readiness is functioning well, i.e., the ambient levels and the amount of sound in any one area does not exclude sound coming in from another area at a level of easy audibility, not as an intrusion. Note that complete acoustic isolation of one area from another is *not* desirable in this case because such sound functions positively. The variety of soundmaking activities (and the complexity of their interpretation by the staff) is balanced by favorable acoustics and the spatial spread of activities in acoustically absorbant sub-areas, as well as by the cycle of times for each activity and the organizational principles adopted by the staff.

The other daycare setting is located in a church basement with highly reflective walls and no acoustic isolation: there are two rooms, one of which is a gymnasium-style play area. The excessive reverberation in the other room allows the sound from any activity group which is noisier to dominate all of the others. Although the ambient level is around 40 dBA in the main area, the levels of most activities are higher than 60 dBA, and often reach 78 dBA; as a result, the staff have to strain to hear what is going on in one group from even a short distance. The children soon learn that attempts to make their needs known will go unheard and unheeded. Tempers of the staff are short, and the children are hyperactive. To cope with the situation, the staff allow th children to "run wild" in the gym area for a period of time, but the reflective acoustics amplify the sound (from 80–90 dBA) such that it overstimulates the children and they begin to scream. The smaller ones get knocked around as they cannot cope with the hyperactivity of the older ones. The staff is demoralized, tense, and defensive about the situation. They blame the government for lack of funds and rationalize the situation by saying "there's nothing to be done" or "you get used to it." The situation is a system that is typically out of control: a vicious circle of an acoustically oppressive environment leads to hyperactivity in the children; they produce more noise and increase the tension of the staff, who then cannot deal with the children appropriately and instead, let them "run wild," and aggravate the situation even more.

Admittedly, environmental situations exist which are victims of a lack of economic and social support. However, the people involved in this daycare seem so caught up within the situation that they do not see or hear the effects of the immediate environment on their own behavior. They blame outsiders or themselves before understanding the dynamics involved. Simple acoustic measures (which needn't be expensive) that absorb more sound between areas might start to reverse the cycle by reducing noise levels to the point where sound stops being an oppressive factor and regains its role as an important communication channel. But first, the people have to step outside the situation, start listening, admit the problem and their victimization by it, and make a conscious effort towards a solution with whatever support they can find. Change does not happen immediately, and profound change in an acoustically malfunctioning community requires structural (re-)design and cooperative community involvement—but it can be done!

6

Noise and the Urban Soundscape

For people living in a technologized society, noise becomes a "fact of life," something one either puts up with (i.e., desensitizes oneself to) or complains about in the hope that some small relief may be obtained. But in either case, most people feel that noise is another environmental force that is beyond their control—an inevitable, if unpleasant, accompaniment to progress (Schafer, 1970). As early as the 1890s, popular journals in England and North America contained articles and editorials on noise as one of the perils of the modern world, and the level and character of public debate has not changed much since. In fact, noise has accompanied urbanization and been regarded as a problem for some time. The *Oxford English Dictionary* contains references to noise as unwanted sound that date back to 1225. And in *The Epic of Gilgamesh,* from the 3rd millennium B.C., we read in the Sumerian account of the flood that:

> In those days the world teemed, the people multiplied, the world bellowed like a wild bull, and the great god was aroused by the clamour. Enlil heard the clamour and he said to the gods in council, "The uproar of mankind is intolerable and sleep is no longer possible by reason of the babel." So the gods in their hearts were moved to let loose the deluge.[1]

But it has remained for the 20th century to elevate the study of noise to the level of an applied science and a commercial business. After several millennia we now know how and why sleep is disturbed by noise, though our solutions in removing the irritant tend to be less effective that those of the Sumerian deities!

In response to the "noise problem" in our own age, government feels it should regulate, scientists and sociologists want to measure, health officials try to protect, business doesn't spend more than it must to keep everyone in a

[1] *The Epic of Gilgamesh,* N. K. Sandars, trans., Harmondsworth, England: Penguin, 1964, p. 105.

compliant mood, architects leave the matter to the engineers (being more absorbed by "aesthetic" aspects of design), and the acoustical engineers busy themselves with band-aid solutions to rectify everyone's problems! The result of all this activity is an enormous literature so vast that no one could ever read it all (even basic bibliographies have a thousand entries), as well as an array of vested interests that are hopelessly entangled, a noise industry that would collapse if a solution were ever found, and a public that is all too willing to leave the whole matter to the "experts" instead of trusting their own common sense. Noise has become a political problem, an environmental issue, an economic factor, a health hazard, grounds for legal action, a business for consultants, and occasionally even a hot issue for journalists and radio talk shows. Seldom is it ever regarded as a basic *human* problem that is part of any system of acoustic communication. And even more seldom does anyone, particularly the experts who are bent on measuring and visualizing noise levels, actually *listen* to it and think about its implications.

It is beyond the scope of this book even to summarize the effects of noise and the acoustical engineering techniques for its control. Fortunately, the scientific aspects of noise, including the human effects, have been described in several good books on the subject (Bragdon, 1970; Burns, 1968; Duerden, 1970; Kryter, 1970; White, 1975). Although factual knowledge about noise control is absolutely essential for the study and practice of acoustic design, so too is a fresh approach to the entire problem. As indicated in chapter 1, treating noise within a signal processing model presents serious limitations to understanding its effects on listeners. Instead of using such a model, we propose to examine the subject of noise within a communicational framework as an aspect of information processing, and from this analysis we hope to achieve new insight into the principles of acoustic design.

Noise and Acoustic Communication

We have characterized sound as having a mediating effect on, and therefore as creating relationships between, the individual and the environment. Noise seems to be the source of a negative mediation of such relationships, an alienating force that loosens the contact the listener has with the environment, and an irritant that works against effective communication. But what constitutes "noise" in the first place, and when does sound become noise? Since Helmholtz, the physical acoustic definition of noise has been that it is a non-periodic vibration, by comparison to "musical" sound which has a periodicity and therefore pitch. However, non-pitched sounds are also used in music, and even music, when it is heard in an inappropriate setting, can be classified as noise by someone annoyed by it. In communication systems, a similarly dualistic definition is used which treats noise as the opposite of the signal, whether it is an interfering hum (which is periodic) or the random fluctuations of static, hiss, or "snow" on the television screen. Quantitative noise by-laws define noise functionally in terms of the sound's intensity level to determine whether it is acceptable or not. The problem with legislation, of course, is finding the right cutoff point above which a sound is unacceptable enough to be called noise and therefore prohibited. All of these systems, as useful as they may be for certain purposes, treat the criterion for noise as a property of the sound itself. A sound becomes noise because of some property it has or because of its behavior in a given situation (the same traffic sound that was tolerable during the day may be unacceptable at night). The definition is a static labelling of sound, not a reflection of its role in a process.

By contrast to these objective definitions, the generally accepted subjective definition of noise is that it is "unwanted sound." This definition clearly shifts the responsibility for the identification of what is noise to the listener and the level of agreement regarding prohibition to that of majority decision as in the democratic model. (It is interesting that socialist countries, such as China, generally claim that they have no noise problem.) Although the subjective definition may be adequate in some situations, it should be realized that on the larger scale it reflects, supports and encourages the desensitization of the majority at the expense of the reactions and feelings of the minority. Some studies have suggested that the percentage of those in society who are "very sensitive" to sound, and therefore most vulnerable to noise, may be as small as 20–30% (Bryan & Tempest, 1973). The subjective definition of noise, when used as the basis for community standards, supports the adaptive behavior of the majority.

The "vicious circle" of adaptation is that it leads to greater tolerance levels, or conversely, that the levels of sound required as stimulation increase. Similarly, we have argued here that noise is a disturbance within the listener-environment system that is amplified (as in positive feedback) when it promotes less attentive listening simply because there is less meaningful sound to listen to, and that this lack of inclination to listen allows more noise to proliferate unprotested and unnoticed. Robert Baron (1970) refers to the "tyranny of noise" to describe the suffering and damage it inflicts, as well as the difficulty of breaking its domination of the environment.

Throughout this book we have placed the listening process at the center of all systems of acoustic communication, and therefore we should examine the nature of noise within the listening context. In our model of listening, the auditory system is designed to detect differences, with the higher cognitive levels acting to discern what differences are significant, i.e., to extract usable information from the incoming sensory data. Noise can function in at least three ways within this processing system. First, it can refer to sounds that are recognizable and even meaningful, but which have negative associations, whether the purely subjective reactions of like/dislike, or actual physiological stress, annoyance, or disruption of other activity. When such reactions occur at a conscious level of awareness they are amenable to annoyance studies such as the social survey. However, the negative reactions may involve adaptation and habituation at a lower level of awareness. More seriously, conscious awareness of the problem may be inhibited by defense mechanisms such as denial, rationalization, transference of blame, or internalization of the problem. In such cases there is an active denial of the disruptiveness of noise, or even an unawareness of sound as having any effect at all.

Secondly, noise may function as the obscuring of the auditory image, that is, as an agent that lessens the clarity or definition of the acoustic information gleaned from an environment. Whereas the first type of noise reaction receives the most attention because the effect is the most blatant, this second type is the most easily unnoticed, but in the long term, it may bring about the most profound changes in acoustic communication. It is also the most difficult to observe because it does not involve a stimulus/response mechanism whose effects can be measured. Instead, it produces a change in the listener's mental image (of the relationship of self to others and to the environment) which manifests itself in behavior that may not seem directly related to aural experience.

For instance, workers stressed by noise may have trouble communicating with friends and family and feel less satisfied with their jobs. White noise, introduced into open office areas to mask extraneous sound, may reduce the acoustic space perceived by the listener and isolate workers from effective contact with others. In our discussion of the acoustic community, we argued that auditory information is a frequent reminder of the individual's connectedness to the community. If less information becomes available to the listener, through lack of variety or loss of definition, the traditional sense of community involvement is weakened and probably replaced by other ties, mainly via the media. However, the commercial media *redefine* the individual as a consumer and the community as a market. Traditional noise studies are incapable of tracing effects of this kind.

When listening is at its most active, as in listening-in-search, the auditory system has powerful mechanisms for discerning information that is interfered with by conflicting noise elements. One of these mechanisms is called the "cocktail party effect" by analogy to the experience of being able to focus on one conversation or voice in the midst of many. Although one could say that in such a situation the noise is the "unwanted" sound, it is perhaps more accurate to say that the brain is able to identify and give preference to one particular message in the midst of simultaneous, conflicting others which are the "noise" in the system.

In the case of listening-in-readiness, where the auditory system is alert to identify a familiar sound while attention is fixed elsewhere, noise can refer to any factor that obscures incoming information and makes it harder to recognize familiar sounds and extract usable information from them. Even in a background listening situation, noise, in the sense of information that cannot be patterned or is meaningless, reduces the acoustic orientation of the person to the environment. The soundscape that was information rich becomes information poor, and the mediated relationship that was interactive and integrative becomes habitually withdrawn, alienated, and even pathological. In the most extreme case, meaninglessness itself becomes the person's long-term auditory image of the environment, and since relationships are mediated both ways by sound, a lack of meaning in the environment is reflected back to the individual's own self-image which must suffer.

Finally, as pointed out by Bateson (1972) and others, noise in the sense of information that is unpatterned and unordered by the brain, is the only source of new information. The foreign language or musical style that once seemed unintelligible becomes meaningful once the cognitive structures that are required to decode and understand it are in place. People often use the word "noise" in a non-pejorative sense to mean any undefined or unrecognized sound that is *potentially* meaningful. This sense of the word is the farthest removed from that associated with sounds that are psychologically irritating or stressful. Whereas such annoyance reactions seem ingrained and unchangeable in us, noise as a source of new information is open-ended and offers the promise of all that we may possibly experience.

Theoretically, it is information that could exist now and yet go unrecognized (something impossible for noise in the pejorative sense), but if it is beyond our current comprehension it can only act at the level of myth—as the symbol of the future. Mozart could not have heard intimations of Stravinsky in the noise of Salzburg, and even the audience of 1913 that called *The Rite of Spring* noise did not realize that the world reflected in that masterpiece was already the one they lived in but had not yet learned to recognize. Noise in this its most abstract sense is not just the opposing force that is the enemy of information, or the pain that complements our pleasure in sound. It is also the symbol which offers hope for new meaning to be created—assuming that noise on the physical level does not debilitate us in the meantime to the point where we are incapable of achieving such growth!

Interlude: The "Deaf Spots" of Noise

Let us contrast our theoretical discussion of the implications of noise for acoustic communication with the commonly heard rhetoric that surrounds it in public life. We will call these arguments "deaf spots" because they can usually be traced to a lack of sensitive listening combined with an ignorance of fact. Each one also represents a "syndrome" because it includes a variety of symptoms that all derive from the same ideological problem. These syndromes manifest themselves in many forms, and one must be alert to spot them when they reappear in new guises.

"What You Don't Hear Can't Hurt You."

This is the ear versus the body syndrome—the myth that the effects of sound can be measured from simply what enters the ear. It is probably a near relative, if not an actual descendant, of the classical mind/body split syndrome, since the ear seems more related to the mind than to the body for most people. This syndrome ignores the fundamental fact that sound is first and foremost a *physical* vibration that affects the whole body. For instance, the body contains many enclosed spaces or cavities which can resonate sympathetically to vibration, each at its own frequency. In addition, and more importantly, the body reacts to noise as it does to any stressor, an age-old reaction that associates loud noise with potential danger. The result is tension, which manifests itself as a constriction of the blood vessels (vasoconstriction). This form of reaction deprives the extremities of nutrients (including the hair cells in the inner ear itself) and increases blood pressure. Changes in breathing rate, muscle tension, and skin resistance also occur. What the mind may rationalize or deny, the body expresses.

A more subtle institutionalization of this syndrome is in the formal measurement of sound intensity level on various scales that are weighted according to frequency, such as the A-scale and C-scale, indicated as dBA and dBC respectively. Described simply, the sensitivity of the A-scale progressively falls off for frequencies below 500 Hz, whereas the C-scale gives approximately equal weight to lower frequencies as it does to higher ones. Therefore dBC readings include the low frequency component of a sound environment, whereas dBA readings do not. It is the low frequencies and infrasound (i.e., below 20 Hz) that are most likely to cause bodily vibration and resonance of bodily cavities such as the chest and stomach. It is generally known that low frequencies do not cause hearing loss, and only produce dramatic effects (e.g., nausea and blackout) at quite high intensity levels of exposure (Tempest, 1976). However, research has not been done on long-term exposure to lower levels of low frequency sound. What is of concern is the increasing standardization to the use of dBA levels, and many inexpensive meters do not even include the C-scale.

The emphasis on A-scale readings is historically ironic, as the A, B and C scales were originally obtained from the ear's own sensitivity patterns (i.e., the inverse of the equal loudness contours) at low, medium, and high intensity levels respectively. In other words, the A-scale was originally designed to measure low level sounds and the C-scale high level ones. Yet dBA measurements are commonly used for measuring the high intensity levels of industrial and transportation noise. The ostensible justification is that reported human annoyance in empirical studies seems to correlate better with dBA than dBC measurements, even for high intensity sounds such as aircraft (Kryter, 1959). However, could it be that such a correlation exists because of the ear versus the body syndrome—that people simply aren't used to equating the effects of noise with what their body feels, as distinct from what their ears hear? If so, the syndrome will amplify itself; the less that sound is associated with bodily vibration, the more the use of dBA measurements will continue to ignore the rather high amounts of low frequency sound that proliferate in technologized society and seem to go unquestioned.

"If You Can Get Used To It, It Can't Be All That Bad."

The habituation syndrome is probably the most commonly expressed by people in their response to noise (Campbell, 1983). At first they notice an intruding sound, probably find it annoying but too much trouble to do anything about, and before long they grow accustomed to it and accept its presence. Essentially they *deny* its intrusiveness. Habituation in such cases is also a form of desensitization, and as already discussed above, desensitization usually leads to more of the same. It also leads to an acceptance of the status quo, and therefore it is a powerful ally of the noise producers because it minimizes complaints, and they need only outwait the initial opposition. The syndrome also coincides nicely with the prevailing model of Western medicine which is concerned only when there are overt symptoms of toxicity, not when there is adaptation, even if of an ultimately detrimental nature. One goes to the doctor when something's obviously wrong, not when one is able to adapt.

At the physical level, adaptation in the form of auditory threshold shift is a natural protection mechanism against auditory overload, but it is not sufficient to protect hearing from damage. In general, increased exposure to a stimulus promotes increased toleration of it, and when the agent is potentially dangerous, such toleration may not be in our best interests. The problem with the extraordinary human ability to adapt to environmental changes—a significant factor in the success of the human race on this planet—is as René Dubos has remarked that we can adapt to what kills us (Dubos, 1965, ch. 10). The ability to adapt to noise (which is only the option of the majority) is insufficient grounds for its acceptance, much less a guarantee of its harmlessness.

At the social level, "toxic symptoms" take the form of public protest and threats of legal action, as illustrated in chapter 1 with the results of the Community Noise Equivalent Level correlated with public reaction. The message which such noise studies give to government is that if the *increase* in noise levels is kept gradual enough, public protest will be kept under control. In countless community situations one sees the same pattern—in the neighborhood where there is a sudden increase in noise from a particular source, protest erupts, especially if the people expected the area to be quiet when they moved in, and if their class background gives them the feeling they have the right to protest. But in an area such as around an airport where noise has become a daily occurrence, even at high levels, the only protest may be against those who try to change the situation. Those who can't adapt have left, and those who can have rationalized the problem.

"If It's No Worse Than Average, Nothing's Wrong."

Closely related to the habituation syndrome is that of the fallacy of the average. The problem is not only that habituation to the average reflects the level of desensitization of the majority, but also that nothing is to prevent the average from changing. Given that noise studies in North America span only the past 25 years, and that the methodologies of measurement have changed considerably during that time, it is difficult to arrive at reliable evidence as to how much the average noise level of a given city is changing. There are simply too many contributing factors. But from Stevens' 1954 data of background and aircraft noise in communities near airports, Price (1972) has estimated that the noise climate in Vancouver, and that reported by Donley in 1969 for suburban areas in the mid-Atlantic states, shows an increase of 10 dBA over 16 years. Such data give rise to the commonly quoted figure that sound levels have been rising at the rate of about half a decibel per year in North American communities. In the terms of the present argument, this rate of increase can be interpreted as the rate of *desensitization* of the populace.

This syndrome can take a subtle ideological form in the methods of interpretation of a noise survey. If a study concludes that the rate of hearing loss observed in those living near freeways is no worse than the American average, the authors will probably interpret this negative evidence as justification for claiming there is no problem. But the point is that the average American is *highly* exposed to traffic noise! Although such exposure probably doesn't produce hearing loss, it does result in bodily stress and tension, the total effects of which are not known. It is only when the current context is thrown into sharp relief by a striking alternative example that we can judge it correctly.

Such a situation occurred when Samuel Rosen (1962) reported his observations of the Mabaan people who live in a remote area of the Sudan which had been closed to outside contacts until 1956. He reported that the sound level in the villages was generally less than 40 dBC, that the levels associated with some work activities were only 73–74 dB. The only really loud sounds were from musical activities during festivals. The loss of hearing with age (i.e., presbycusis) was found to be slight among the Mabaan, and certainly much less than that normally found in North America. In his autobiography Dr. Rosen describes the results as indicating that "the Mabaans aged fifty to fifty-nine had much better hearing than Americans aged twenty to twenty-nine," and that their hearing of extremely high frequencies (14–18 kHz) declined very slowly with age (Rosen, 1973, p. 211). However, he also discovered that the Mabaans suffered from practically no increase in blood pressure with age, nor from most of the other ailments related to hypertension found in North America. Instead of these results proving that environmental noise is the direct cause of presbycusis, they suggest that healthy living conditions with respect to diet, tension, and noise combine and support each other to reduce many of the effects of aging, including hearing loss. The results also show how much the "average" in any given society is a product of many forces that are specific to it, and that although they may be a norm, such averages are not necessarily proof of a rational or healthy lifestyle.

A subtle variant of the fallacy of the average is the percentile approach to noise abatement which states that, no matter what the average may be, the only pragmatic action that can be taken is to deal with the 10% (or whatever figure) that are the worst cases. The procedure is similar to that involved in determining "peak level" which may be statistically defined as the level exceeded 10% of the time. When consultants recommend acceptable levels, and governments and other institutions attempt to create an enforceable law, they usually resort to a similar line of thinking: find the level exceeded by only 10% of the cases and deal with those. Although a pragmatic solution is better than none, at least some of the time, this approach does not provide any mechanism whereby a progressive program might reduce levels to an acceptable point over a longer period of time. Statements such as "every dB reduction will cost American industry . . . ." scare people away from such approaches, but those making such statements never look at the other side of the cost ledger to estimate the true cost of noise in its broader effects. The 10% solution also implicitly fails to raise public awareness of the problem because it focuses on the small minority of offenders, the "few bad apples" that can be dealt with without much fuss, instead of showing the degree to which everyone is a contributor to the problem.

"It's Got To Be Loud To Be Bad."

The noise-equals-loudness syndrome is another manifestation of the desire to label and categorize things once and for all, and thereby avoid examining the larger context of the situation. The syndrome is supported by all of the methods devised to measure noise levels and by the empirical results showing that reported annoyance tends to rise with increases in such levels. Although that correlation may be true, the converse does *not* hold: noise at lower levels is therefore acceptable. There are many instances in which sound at levels lower than conventional norms for damage risk has proven unacceptable to people. Low frequency and infrasound have already been mentioned as factors that may produce bodily discomfort without contributing to a measured sound level, at least not enough to put it in the danger zone. Modulation, pulsation, and pure tone components may function similarly. One family known to the author fought for years to get relief from the low frequency throb of ventilation fans on a commercial building near their home that totally disrupted their sleep, health, and well-being. The conventionally measured sound levels were not high enough for the danger to be obvious, and such quantitative evidence is generally the only admissible evidence in court. The owner of the building eventually moved the fans at the expense of the family who by that point were willing to do anything to secure relief. The family's suffering in the meantime, however, was never compensated.

The loudness syndrome is ironic because the decibel itself, in its very definition, is a *relative* measurement, not an absolute one. All dB measurements are comparisons (i.e., a ratio) of a given level to some reference level, normally the threshold of hearing. They are not measurements of absolute intensity or pressure. Moreover, our perceived sense of loudness is relative, given the constant adaptation of the auditory system to the environment via threshold shifts. Therefore, when a numerical level is set that does not take into consideration any notion of the ambient context, it is being regarded as an absolute measurement. For instance, if a home in a rural environment is situated next to a gravel crushing operation, it can be exposed to sound levels that are intensely annoying to the occupants, but which fall within the limits set by a local noise by-law (limits which reflect, if not actually copy, those found in urban legislation). The same noise may be acceptable in a city, but in the quieter rural environment, it is not. Some improvement in the use of quantitative levels in by-laws has gradually started to appear in recent years with the inclusion of an alternative specification of the maximum level above ambience, as well as the fixed level.

The opposite of the loudness syndrome occasionally surfaces as well, when sounds that are decidedly below proscribed levels provoke legal action while nearby offenders at higher levels do not. *The Vancouver Soundscape* reports the 1971 conviction of members of the Hari Krishna sect under the local noise by-law (of the older "nuisance" variety) for their street singing, while across the street, the construction noise was measured at over 90 dBA (WSP, 1978a, p. 56). Such occurrences are in fact consistent with the tradition of the qualitative approach to noise by-laws over the centuries. Such laws have been regularly used, not to prevent loud noise, but to control "undesirable" elements in society from being too conspicuous. The opposite, the toleration of high levels (as in public entertainment using heavy amplification), occurs when no vested interests are threatened. It is a particularly difficult problem to combat when it appears that the public chooses (and pays) to be exposed, whether knowingly or not. The only solution seems to be educating the public as to the risks, the need for protection and their right to choose.

Quantitative levels, no matter how they are measured, will never offer complete protection to everyone from harm or annoyance. No damage risk criterion can guarantee "safety" for anything but the majority of those exposed. Individual susceptibility is highly variable and always unpredictable. Moreover, treating noise as a signal in a stimulus-response chain where some parameter of the signal, such as intensity level, "causes" some particular effect (which generally can only be proved in *isolation* from other real-world variables) ignores the broader implications of noise as information in the listener–environment system of communication. The way a sound, or a noise, *functions* within the system depends not only on its objective characteristics but also on the way in which it is understood by listeners and the community. Any design criteria, therefore, must be based on an understanding of communicational functionality.

"You've Got To Have Noise To Have Progress," and Other Social Myths

Perhaps the longest lasting and most deeply ingrained of all of the traits of noise are the myths that surround it and condition our personal and social reactions to it. The noise-equals-progress myth is one of them. It is closely related to the noise-is-power myth which dates back to the dawn of time when supernatural forces were thought to be responsible for the biggest sounds that were experienced. But today such symbolism is applied to mundane things like household appliances which manufacturers deliberately keep noisy to a certain extent because they don't believe they will sell if they're quiet. Is a quiet vacuum cleaner really working? Ironically, noise is the *opposite* of efficiency, because it represents wasted energy. But this logic is lost on the consumer who buys an appliance that adds noise to the home and who rationalizes it by thinking that the noise is an inevitable price for the labor it is saving.

Hand in hand with the equation of noise and power is its equation to outmoded concepts of "manliness," as in the worker that's "tough enough" to take a little noise and shuns all forms of ear protection. Luckily, this myth seems to be on the decline with the fight against sexist stereotyping, and the realization by younger workers that such "machismo" has only resulted in their elders going deaf. Health education in the workplace has improved over the last decade, and the message of how imperative it is to protect one's hearing from irreparable damage is gradually getting through. Gone are the days when earplug boxes were labelled "for swimmers and nervous women"! Everyone has the right to be protected, but unfortunately basic knowledge about the risks involved and the necessity for hearing protection has not reached the classroom to the same extent that it has the workplace. High school students are seldom taught even the basics about noise, and there have been cases where music teachers working long hours in acoustically untreated bandrooms have had to retire early because of hearing loss! If those charged with developing musical sensitivity take no responsibility for disseminating facts on hearing protection, one cannot blame young people for "ruining their hearing"—they are the victims of adult exploitation on the one hand and neglect on the other.

When we define noise as "unwanted sound" we invite the dangers of the psychological myth "it's all in your head." If subjectivity means that ultimately all values are individual and idiosyncratic, then no collective action can ever be taken for mutual protection. Likes and dislikes may be subjective, but the physiological stress of noise affects everyone, and some more than others, whether they are consciously aware of it or not. When the movie "Earthquake" appeared a few years ago, it was accompanied by 5 minutes of exposure to low frequency sound that was measured at 120 dBC. Theaters had to be specially chosen not only for sound reproduction equipment but also for their structural solidity in the face of such vibration. To add insult to injury, the credits contained a disclaimer against responsibility for any "psychological side-effects" that the film might have. The message was that the effects of noise "are all in your mind," and we're not responsible. The building inspector was needed to check out the theater, but where was the public health inspector to protect the audience?

Such occurrences show how deeply ingrained in society are the myths about noise, and how all of them together result in its general acceptance. Together such myths and the attitudes they create support the pollution of the soundscape and its victimization of everyone. Most seriously of all, they support the victimization of those who have the least power to fight back—the young, the elderly, the sick, and the poor. Current legislative and professional practice is inadequate to counteract the problem, much less lay out a blueprint for an alternative approach. How then can change come about and the individual, as well as society at large, regain control?

The Path Toward Change

First of all, I should state that I do not purport to have *the* answer to the problem of noise, In fact, no single answer exists, and those that readily come to mind tend to prove idealistic, too general, or impractical when applied. Many observers see the problem as requiring fundamental social or political change. But understanding noise at that level, as useful as such a perspective may be, tends not to deal with it on its own terms, i.e., as an aspect of acoustic communication, but in concepts which have little to do with acoustic reality. On the other hand, we may be inspired to action by our own experience (perhaps the most effective driving force of all). But if we simply extrapolate our own likes and dislikes, or some aesthetic preference, we are guilty of imposing personal choices onto the environment which may or may not satisfy others.

The suggestions I have to offer take the form of general principles which I perceive to be present in any force for positive change. They are not absolute prescriptions or specific cures. Instead, they attempt to generalize certain properties of the systems of acoustic communication which have been documented in this book and which allow successful intervention for change. As remarked before, the advantage of understanding acoustic communication as a system, instead of as isolated stimulus–response reactions, is that an intervention at any point in the system can cause cascaded effects throughout it, whether for its improvement or even its deterioration and destruction. The other factor, perhaps even the most important, is that the individual is inevitably a part of the system. The soundscape and the phenomenon of noise are not things that are "out there," apart from ourselves. They are inextricably related to us; we create them and they have their effects on us. We therefore have a responsibility toward them, just as we have to ourselves and to others.

We can summarize three factors that can promote change in an acoustic system, particularly one that is malfunctioning: a) listening and critical evaluation; b) preservation and protection; c) design of alternatives.

It should be obvious that nothing is to be gained, except on the short term, from shutting out sound and ignoring it. Listening is our only means of contact with the sound environment, and if it is not practised and kept sensitive, we will lose, both individually and culturally, all of the human benefits it can provide. Careful listening leads to questions about what we hear and an evaluation of its usefulness, interest, and beauty—or lack of the same. In an age where noise is an ever present danger and technology is powerfully used by commercial interests to influence our minds and behavior, critical evaluation of what we hear (as well as what we see and read) is an indispensable ability that needs to be encouraged in everyone, but particularly in the young.

Preservation and protection of all aspects of the soundscape are strategies that recognize its value and integrity and therefore seek to ensure its continued existence, including the well-being of ourselves as listeners. Such strategies concern not only the physical and psychological protection of people from the adverse effects of sound, but the preservation of what constitutes an "aural history" of our culture. The soundmark, historical and disappearing sounds, as well as the memories of those who can recall the soundscapes of the past, are all worthy of preservation and respect. The transience of sound and its swift erasure through change necessitate that a special effort must be made before it is too late.

Preservation of the acoustic quality of the community is a common social concern, particularly when faced with expansion of an airport, industry, or transportation patterns (Baron, 1970; Berland, 1970; Rodda, 1967; Still, 1970). Unfortunately, most such efforts become "anti-noise lobbies" which, besides seeming negative and being easily labelled as "complainers," tend to become isolated as special interest groups, as if everyone didn't have a vested interest in the soundscape! Such lobbies also have to face the mystifying language of the "experts" and the bureaucratic intransigence which is paid to outwait them. However, one must still fight any kind of change that occurs without adequate protection for the people most affected. A broader community base might be gained, though, if the focus of the action were, first of all, more positively oriented as advocating protection of the soundscape (instead of being simply anti-noise), and secondly, more focused on the kind of sound environment we are passing on to our children—the people most likely to be affected by today's changes.

One can also work to preserve variety in the face of standardization, and to protect uniqueness from the onslaught of homogenizing forces. We need to be able to experience alternatives in order to counteract a stultifying sameness. The most powerful action against noise may be the preservation of silence. The "acoustic sanctuary" is an area whose physical characteristics allow it to retain its own acoustic character against intruding forces. It may be a park, a wilderness area, a valley or lake with limited access, or even an old building. In any case, the very fact of its official public designation as an acoustic sanctuary serves not only to protect it, but also to heighten public awareness of the need for alternatives to noisy environments. It also represents a *positive* action that can often gain broad public acceptance and support.

Much of the work that is needed is educational because there are so many gaps in people's awareness, gaps that are scarcely addressed by present school systems. We teach all the language skills except listening! Even at the most elementary level, listening to sounds, making them, recording them, talking about them, and playing with them can be pleasurable, and at the same time begin a lifelong orientation and receptiveness toward sound. In higher grades, sound should not be restricted to a few classes on acoustics in the physics department, learning an instrument in music class, and having the school nurse hold a watch to your ear to test your hearing. Sound is related to every aspect of the curriculum, from the lifting of words off the page into vocal utterance in literature, to the social geography of the soundscape. If the pleasure of sound is valued, the path to controlling noise will be much clearer.

Finally, the design of alternatives involves broadening one's experience and touching the imagination. Traditionally, the arts have functioned with this purpose, but in the current situation of the arts, the composer and the environmental artist cannot be counted upon as designers of the soundscape or as educators of listening. In fact, composers are probably the least significant designers of the environment, compared to the explicit and implicit influence of the media, noise, and Muzak. The composer who uses environmental sound as material for a composition, or the environment as a venue for performance, leaves the environment as it was before, and unless the composition is so directed, does not change the audience's awareness of the soundscape. The aim is aesthetic, not social, and today "environmental art" is more of a label to promote the artist's image than it is an attempt to apply artistic design principles to the environment.

Therefore, it is the responsibility of composers, as well as other professionals dealing with sound, to create the alternative experiences and environments which will put what we now experience into proper perspective by suggesting how it could be different. It may involve the work itself (for instance, a "soundscape composition" as described in chapter 13) which draws attention to the listener's relationship to the environment as part of its compositional design. Or it may involve the composer temporarily abandoning an artistic stance and becoming socially involved in functional acoustic design or public education. The electroacoustic media provide excellent tools and channels of communication for this kind of work, as we shall describe in part II. As for noise, the techniques for its control at any stage of the linear chain of transfers (i.e., source, medium of propagation, and the receiver), are well known. What limits the effectiveness of such techniques is precisely the linearity of its model and the negativity of its orientation. The path to effective change of the soundscape must be guided by an understanding of the broader sense of how sound functions, both positively and negatively, as well as by strategies for protecting acoustic systems of communication, through innovatively designed alternatives and, above all, by sensitive listening.

7

Acoustic Design

The concept of "acoustic design" refers to the analysis of any system of acoustic communication (i.e., soundscape) that attempts to determine how it functions. Criteria for acoustic design are obtained from the analysis of positively functioning soundscapes. Therefore, it is just as appropriate to say that the natural soundscape is well designed acoustically as it is to evaluate the design of a human soundscape. The design of an environment need not be intentional; it may be implicit, or indirect, as with most traffic and aircraft noise when it constitutes a prominent feature of a soundscape. Whether the soundscape is natural or artificial, and its elements intentional or simply by-products of other processes, its quality of design depends on how it functions.

As described in chapter 5, the balanced soundscape is vulnerable to change, just as it is to noise. The forces that preserve balance can accommodate only certain kinds of change, for instance, at the level of sound populations where a sound may be replaced by one that is similar to it without causing disruption. However, changes at the structural or organizational level prevent the system from reorganizing itself and restoring balance. Once started on the road to deterioration, a soundscape seldom reverses the process by itself. Some form of intervention is required. Therefore, acoustic design has a second aspect to it, namely the application of its principles to the improvement of malfunctioning soundscapes.

Deliberate intervention raises the problem of who exercises control, and with whose agreement as to the goal. Is acoustic design only the responsibility of "experts" in the field, or can it be practised by everyone? Ideally, if it were indeed practised by everyone, experts wouldn't be needed. On the other hand, leaving it entirely to those with authority ignores the importance of involving the listener in the process. Those with special sensitivity or expertise are needed to set an example, as well as to instigate public awareness and suggest courses of action, but unless the concepts and skills involved reach everyone, the effects will be limited. However, it is clear that it is not simply a matter for government legislation or professional consultants. A broader base of awareness needs to be found for acoustic design to achieve its goals.

Another fundamental problem associated with the use of the word "design" is the traditional aesthetic conflict between functionalism and beauty. Should our criteria for design be simply what is functional, or should they include subjective evaluations of what is beautiful? According to the Bauhaus principles, beauty is the result of functionality. But according to others, art is art only if it is useless. The problems of aesthetics may discourage us from embracing any subjectivity at all in our design criteria, but if we turn to scientific objectivity instead, we inherit a methodology that can explain *why* sounds behave the way they do but not how they *should* behave, except to avoid negative effects.

Clearly, the old dualisms of science and art, or that of objective and subjective criteria, do not serve us well in attempting to formulate principles of acoustic design. Communications, as an interdiscipline, provides a different approach that is not based on such dualities or on Newtonian models of linear energy transfer. The communicational approach redefines functionalism as the behavior of a system that is adapted to its environment, and understands beauty as a value expressed through people's attitudes. Instead of separating the individual from the environment "out there," the communicational approach focuses on the *relationship* between the individual and the environment as mediated by sound or other elements. The shift is away from artifacts, and causes and effects, towards process. Acoustic design, therefore, represents an understanding of the processes of acoustic communication and seeks to redirect the mediating influence of sound in relationships that are observed to be malfunctioning. Let us examine some of the principles that operate in well-designed systems of acoustic communication.

Variety and Coherence

Throughout the previous chapters we have characterized the listening process as the search for meaningful information in the incoming stream of data provided by the auditory system. The basic unit of information itself can be traced to the perception of a "difference"—a comparison that discovers change between the present state of the environment and previous states. Uniformity in an acoustic artifact or a soundscape desensitizes listening, just as constant sound levels fatigue the hair cells of the inner ear. Higher levels of auditory processing are designed to detect differences, as well as to compare incoming patterns of information with previously experienced ones and to alert other parts of the brain when awareness or action is required.

Variety in the incoming information, however, must be balanced by its being understood as meaningful in order for communication to be effective. Too much information, or information that is unordered and cannot be patterned, is as useless to the brain as too little information. For instance, white noise presents the greatest amount of information to the brain because it consists of random fluctuations of sound pressure whose frequency content is distributed equally over the entire audible range. However, its very randomness results in the information being unpatterned and therefore meaningless. One could say that such sound is all variety and no coherence. Similarly, a constant periodic tone, such as a sine wave with a single frequency, is totally coherent but shows no variety. Both become either boring or annoying.

The white noise example also reminds us that information can be perceived at different hierarchic *levels*. Three levels are commonly distinguished, namely the level of sound pressure variation (the micro level which determines timbre); the "event" level with its specific characteristics such as pitch, loudness, duration, and timbral quality; and finally, the level of longer-term relationships between sounds at various times (the macro level). The information content of white noise is only at the micro level, whereas as a total sound it has a static quality to which the ear adapts, as it does to any drone or stationary sound. Conversely, the sine tone that is totally predictable at the micro level may undergo rapid fluctuations in pitch, envelope or loudness that may make it much more interesting. Early electronic music compositions were frequently composed with sine tones, but in order to be successful, a highly developed structure was required to provide enough information at the event-to-event and long-term levels to keep the listener's attention.

Environmental noise, as we have discussed already, is not only meaningless in itself to the listener, but it also obscures the information of other sounds. Electroacoustic technology, as argued in chapter 9, also tends to reduce the information content of the sounds it produces, unless such sounds are specifically well designed. Much of the degenerate quality of contemporary soundscapes can be traced to the influence of noise and poorly designed technology, both of which attack the balance between variety and coherence for the listener. Natural and human sounds, on the other hand, almost always show an admirable variety of information that is constrained within specific limits. Therefore, it is not surprising that such sounds are preferred by most listeners, and that their particular qualities often serve as reference points in our evaluation of other sounds.

For instance, in chapter 5 we described the interplay in rhythm between the regularity of a pulse and the subtle variations that keep it from becoming monotonous. Because such variations are always found in the sounds of human activity, other sounds on a similar time scale that show a balance between regularity and variation tend to be regarded as having a human character. The corporeality of the regular pulse gives its coherence an intuitively physical quality, whereas subtle variations appeal to the mind, enticing it with information, new possibilities, and flights of the imagination. Binding these two characteristics together into one sound makes it totally satisfying. Waves on a beach, for instance, occur in cycles that show random variations around an average duration, and this sound is well known to be soothing and relaxing.

In music, melodic pitch variations are similarly effective when they are perceived to revolve around a tonal center—a fixed point from which variations may occur. Similarly, a drone can stabilize the "tonic" or tonal center while a second voice is free to weave complex melodic variations above it. In early Western music, the lowest melody or "cantus firmus" was similarly designed to have a cohesive effect on the other parts which were much freer. The later development of tonal harmony, simply put, was structurally useful to give coherence to the forward motion of many simultaneous parts. It is generally agreed that the music of Bach represents an apogee in the balance between vertical harmonic structure and horizontal melodic variation. In 19th-century music, the balance leaned toward the predominance of harmonic structure at the expense of melodic freedom, but new levels of information were added with the exploitation of orchestral coloration and thematic development. The early atonal compositions of Schoenberg and Webern frequently resorted to simplified or even traditional forms once the unifying force of tonality and harmonic structure were lost, and sounds started to exist "on their own" once again as individual units.

The various trends in contemporary music, far too numerous to be described here, can be understood as exploring particular ways in which musical coherence may be maintained in the face of the "free" combination and design of sound material. As a result of the freedom available in such music, it runs the risk of being meaningless if pattern and meaning cannot be perceived. If there is unlimited variety possible in the use of any sound or its technological transformation, and in the infinite possibilities of their combination, what is required are organizational frameworks within which all of this information can become meaningful. Even in so-called "minimal" or repetitive music, where pattern abounds, the level of variation simply shifts to the micro level of phase shifting and timbral nuance.

From this cursory overview of some of the acoustic design features of music, it can be seen that all of them represent techniques for achieving coherence while permitting variety, or more simply, for organizing information into meaningful communication. In spoken language, the structural rules for organizing linguistic information are well known, at least implicitly by language users. In the soundscape, a similar balance is achieved as described in our discussion of the acoustic community. In chapter 5, we referred to variety, complexity, and balance as three characteristics of the way in which sound functions in the acoustic community. The three are closely related, since the complexity of information interpreted in the variety of community sounds cannot exist without the balancing forces which constrain the behavior of the soundscape. Therefore, the practice of acoustic design cannot only be concerned with the elimination of certain sounds, or the design of particularly interesting other ones, because it must also deal with the entire environment as a system of interactions between all elements. A sound sculpture, no matter how sonically enticing, will not "beautify" an urban soundscape that is dominated by traffic noise and populated by people who don't listen. Nor will the installation of white noise generators to mask office sounds automatically produce a better acoustic working environment. Design must proceed from a more effective analysis of an environment as an acoustic system, an analysis that includes the listener in the process.

Stochastic Processes and the Archetype

To conclude our discussion of the dynamic balance between variety and coherence, let us examine how it operates in two quite dissimilar processes involving sound, the stochastic process and the symbolism of archetypes. The stochastic process refers to any time-dependent phenomenon where occurrences of individual events are random, but where the behavior of the entire system follows a particular statistical pattern (Xenakis, 1971). In other words, the process is not predictable at the micro or event level, but only at the macro level. Simple examples such as raindrops falling or insects chirping are familiar instances of such a process. The macro level perception is typically that of the density of events (e.g., how "hard" the rain is falling) or the quality of a texture. The variety produced by randomness at the micro level is balanced by a statistical form of coherence at the macro level.

Many of the natural processes involving discrete random events follow a statistical pattern known as a Poisson distribution. The Poisson curve of probability peaks at a particular density that is the most probable, with densities that are higher or lower becoming less and less probable the farther away they are from the average. In other words, random occurrences still cluster around an average density, as opposed to being totally random such that any value may occur at any time with equal probability. The Poisson distribution, which applies only to discrete events, not continuous textures, represents a process by which variety is accommodated within a global pattern that seems coherent. With rain, for instance, one intuitively knows not to expect a sudden silence or a sudden high density of events unless some external agent interferes with the process. The sound is "designed" to be coherent, yet never boring.

Although it operates on a much different level than the stochastic process, the archetype is similar because it is an abstract image that finds its expression in numerous specific instances which are recognized as having some common basis. The archetype operates at the level of a pattern which it comes to symbolize. Yet it can only be perceived through the various instances of its manifestation to which it gives coherence. The inexplicable "aura" which certain sounds possess perhaps can be attributed to qualities and connotations which link them to other sounds, and even other types of experience. Such sounds seem to be retained better in memory, and their psychological power is more profound. Some level of explanation for their effect exists because there are always comparisons to human features or those of the natural soundscape, with their age-old associations, but ultimately a sound that functions symbolically achieves its power because of its simultaneous uniqueness and universality. Sounds in the contemporary world seldom, and perhaps only coincidentally, achieve this level of acoustic design.

Conclusion

In this first part of the book, I have presented a communicational model of what might be called the traditional systems of acoustic communication. I have dealt with them as they exist without the introduction of electroacoustic technology, that is, the technology that changes sound from a physical vibration into an electrical signal. The purpose and justification for making this division is, first of all, that the introduction of electroacoustic techniques represents a watershed in the development of acoustic systems. It is not just another technological development that changes the soundscape, similar for instance to the Industrial Revolution which profoundly altered both social patterns and the acoustic environment. That kind of change, like those before it, altered the soundscape but not the fundamental rules by which sound behaves, as does electroacoustic technology. Moreover, although industrialization produced a new sound environment that influenced listening habits, it offered few additional possibilities for acoustic design (only more urgency to its need!). Thus, a linear historical approach is apt to link the industrial and electrical revolutions as phases of the same process of technological growth, instead of making a distinction between them. The effects of the latter are profound and far-reaching, as we shall see in part II.

The second purpose for the division is the belief that in order to understand the effects of electroacoustic technology on acoustic communication, one must know how such systems function independent of it, and only then can the full effect be judged and the new potential effectively explored. The love/hate relationship we have to technology, and the belief that it is the frontier for all that is new, means that it is all too easy to focus our attention on it exclusively and ignore the listening environment into which its new discoveries are being introduced. On the other hand, if we think we can be concerned about musical or aural sensitivity without considering the impact of technology on listening habits, we are, in effect, trying to live in the 19th century. Therefore, neither a total preoccupation with technology nor a total ignorance of it can be defended. The approach I am taking suggests that the traditional acoustic systems form a base, or reference point, with respect to which technological change can be evaluated and understood.

Similarly, the study of noise and its effects is limited if such knowledge is not integrated within an understanding of how sound functions positively in the soundscape. The situation is parallel to any study of a disease, such as cancer, which is not accompanied by a model of what constitutes good health. Even the World Health Organization's definition of health makes it clear that health is not simply the absence of disease, and similarly, good acoustic design is not just the absence of noise. Despite such warnings, though, we still think that a solution to the problem of a disease like cancer lies in finding a "cure" for it, and society as a whole seems prepared to support a very large industry devoted to that search and give it a higher priority than many other health care concerns. This kind of thinking tends to work against an understanding of how the health environment functions in general, and what forces within it combine to cause the disease in the first place.

Similarly, the preoccupation with noise as a "disease" that can somehow be "cured" overshadows an understanding of how the healthy soundscape functions. Of course, such a cure would be economically disastrous if it were ever found, just as a cure for cancer would. Although no one is really looking for a cure for noise, a great many earn their livelihood from its measurement and control, and therefore depend on its perpetuation. The ideology of noise is indeed self-perpetuating because noise, as it is currently defined and treated, does *not* have a solution. We know a great deal about the effects of noise, and above what levels damage is statistically likely to occur, and we even know a lot of practical methods by which noise levels could be reduced—everything except *why* it is there in the first place! As long as we treat noise as an environmental pollutant that should be "cleaned up" by the experts, and as long as we have no idea what kind of processes within systems of acoustic communication result in it, noise will continue to be a problem.

In the previous chapter we suggested some general strategies for change that could have a much greater effect on the soundscape than the current one-sided dependence on noise studies and consultants. Earlier we suggested why such strategies might work, and it is time to return to those considerations. Our thesis is that the same processes that amplify deterioration within a system of acoustic communication (leading to noise, as well as to other communicational problems), can be turned around to effect positive change within the system. If sound were not part of a communicational system (for instance, if it were merely an environmental by-product such as wasted energy), we would not be able to treat it as a positive force for change, and then the noise experts could be called in to keep it under control. But the way it functions is not that simple; sound creates and modifies relationships, and therefore, when one relationship changes, so do many others, directly or indirectly.

The simplest strategy for acoustic design is the imperative "Listen!" The way sound functions is not independent of how we listen to it, and many of the problems it creates can be traced to, at least partially, our lack of ability, or willingness to listen. Therefore, acoustic design can be as simple as encouraging listening sensitivity. The effects of increased awareness cascade throughout the system because a listener is not one who passively adapts but a person who reacts and interacts, one who questions and evaluates. Moreover, this simplest form of practical acoustic design avoids the difficulties of imposing solutions, leaving problems to experts, or quibbling over aesthetic preferences. The people who have the most to benefit or lose are the ones making at least some of the most significant decisions. Of course, when noise oppresses the individual to such a degree that listening is not possible, one must first reduce the level of stress to the point where adverse physical and psychological effects are minimized, so that the person can recognize the real problem and think clearly about it. Under strain, a person will more likely impose self-blame or transfer the effects to others, instead of being able to identify the true source of the problem and take action. Removing the block in the system lets it reorganize itself in a new direction.

Awareness of the value of sound within human and social communication, as encouraged by the strategies for preservation and protection outlined in the previous chapter, also leads to positive benefits throughout the system. A person is less likely to sacrifice something unwittingly when its value is recognized. In a society where economics is the "bottom line" for most social practices, people who value good acoustic living and working environments represent a powerful consumer force that cannot be ignored. Business and industry could not afford to neglect acoustic design if that were a significant determinant of market preferences. The role of government to regulate, mediate, and provide incentives on behalf of the public good could serve to encourage private enterprise, as well as to set a good example. Under such favorable conditions, positive effects would snowball throughout the system.

Pessimists and cynics will say that it won't happen, or even that it can't under present conditions. Others will say that change will not happen without social and political upheaval, or without the catalyst of environmental disaster. But the behavior of noise is such that its deteriorating effects lead to desensitization, not outrage, and social or political change will not necessarily change listening habits or consumer appetites. We can only hope that an awareness of the imminent danger, if brought to enough people's attention, may spark a desire for change and eventually create the large-scale shift in values that is required. In the meantime we can begin by examining our own listening habits, and become aware of the kind of relationships which sound mediates in our own lives. Are we satisfied, or are we missing something? Will we accept our victimization, or can we regain control of the soundscape through our own actions? After all, the soundscape is not an alien force but a reflection of ourselves.

II.

Electroacoustics—
The Impact of Technology on Acoustic Communication

8

Electroacoustic Communication: Breaking Constraints

We began part I with a brief account of the traditional energy transfer model that is the basis of the formal study of sound, and suggested that the impact of electronic technology in this century, in creating the concepts of the audio signal and signal processing, has been based on a parallel model, namely that of signal transfer. The basis of electroacoustics, as reflected in the term itself, is the transfer of sound energy from its physical form, i.e., the sound wave, into an electrical form, the audio signal. This signal is intended to be exactly analogous to the sound wave and can be converted back into it via a loudspeaker. The points of conversion are called transduction processes, and everything that happens to the audio signal from the time it is created until it is transferred back to acoustic form comes under the heading of signal processing, e.g., storage, transmission, manipulation, mixing, and so on.

However, we also pointed out that signal processing operates on the implicit basis of what we called a "black box" model, that is, a model of neutrality. In theory, at least, audio processing is intended to reproduce the original signal with perfect "fidelity," and all methods of evaluating the result, or any intermediate stage, depend on measuring the quality of the signal according to common standards. As long as the result is "faithful" to the original, the impact of the process is neutralized, and no responsibility has to be taken for the content of the signal or the implications of the way it is used.

Much of the debate surrounding modern technology centers on the conflict between the "neutrality" of the scientific method and the profound implications of its use. Since engineering is traditionally given the task of applying "pure" science, the claim of neutrality is all the more controversial when it arises there. It is sometimes said that technology itself is neutral, but that its organization is not. Exactly who is responsible for the organization of technology, and who controls its development, is not a simple matter of identification. For the public, technology becomes a "fact of life" with strong psychological implications, as well as a pragmatic necessity. It cannot be neutral; it represents too many things—progress, automation, a way of life, the threat of forces getting out of control, the novelty of the latest toy or technical marvel. We indulge in its innovations or resist them with the same psychological attitudes that were once reserved for decisions of a moral nature, with or without the appropriate feelings of guilt or virtue. Like the problem of noise, audio technology is a highly visible aspect of technology in general and seems to represent another force in the world whose dynamics we do not understand.

The impact of technology on acoustic communication is so profound that our discussion of it here occupies an equal part of the book. However, our goal is to understand the changes that technology brings about from the perspective we have built up in part I about traditional acoustic patterns of communication. Once we understand how the system of sound-listener-environment works traditionally, we can examine the types of changes that the introduction of technology brings to the system. And with such an understanding we hope to be able to control technology better and use it as the tool that it is, i.e., as an extension of human capabilities, for the design of effective forms of communication.

The New Tools: Extensions or Transformations?

In all of the traditional situations in which sound functions, it is constrained by its own physical characteristics and limitations. Acoustic power is relatively small on the scale of energies that are available—its "power" has always derived from its ability to affect the mind, not from its absolute physical power. However, acoustic energy can only travel so far, sustain itself for so long, and distribute its energy in certain ways over the audible spectrum. All acoustic technologies that have been invented to produce or control sound (e.g., instruments, machines, architectural designs, etc.), as fascinating and diverse as they are, operate within the same physical constraints as sound does in the natural environment. These technologies simply shape the sound to be more interesting, more functional or more artistic, but they do not *change* the rules by which the sound functions—they merely refine its behavior.

For instance, the horn and bell are louder than the human voice, they can communicate over a larger distance and travel faster than a person can, at least before the supersonic era. The architectural features of the Greek amphitheater, the mosque, or the cathedral allow reflections of acoustic energy that permit sounds to last longer than in an open space and to be heard farther and more clearly. The ingenious devices of the mechanical instrument maker allow sounds to be produced automatically with their hidden control devices. And, of course, the art of the musical instrument builder over the centuries has been directed at producing sounds of purity, harmonicity, and beauty that surpass those found in the natural environment.

From the perspective of physics, we may say that all of these inventions are constrained by the rules of vibratory motion and energy conservation. Within these rules, endless variation is possible, but the system remains bounded by physical constraints. Consider the phenomenon of "amplification" for instance. The term is used in physical acoustics without any contradiction to the law of energy conservation because in all acoustic systems, no additional energy is *added* to the system through natural acoustic methods of amplification. Instead, the acoustical energy within the system is made more efficient in its transfer. If the physical sound source is damped, its energy is dissipated quickly, whereas if it is attached to a resonator, the energy transfer is improved (i.e., it sounds louder, or amplified) and the sound lasts longer. Since both resonance and reverberation prolong sound energy, they are often confused in everyday speech. Though the way in which they work is different, both result in a slower dissipation of energy. But no matter what the situation, all physical acoustic systems have a relatively short lifetime for producing sound. The beauty of sound is in its transience, and hence in its inevitable relation to silence. The "eternal sound" is a powerful symbol for the mind, a Platonic ideal whose purity can only be approached in the acoustical world through repetition.

The electroacoustic process changes the groundrules for acoustic behavior, first of all, by changing the *form* of the sound's energy from physical and mechanical to electrical, and secondly, by *adding* energy to it. The resultant audio signal, representing patterns of voltage in time, takes on the characteristics of electricity, for instance, the ability to travel with the speed of light, nearly a million times faster than sound! Moreover, the adding of energy to the signal produces a new sense of the term "amplification," one that allows the actual physical magnitude to increase beyond its original level by nearly any amount. With the constant addition of electrical energy, a sound (particularly a synthesized one) may have any loudness and may even be prolonged indefinitely to achieve an "immortality" that is impossible within the physical, acoustic world!

Therefore, we can see that at its very basis, the electroacoustic process is not merely a simple extension of the capabilities of sound, but rather a fundamental *transformation* of how it works. The change is not only quantitative, in the sense of extending the range of a variable by some amount, but is also qualitative in the way that it permits totally new concepts to operate. It is little wonder that such fundamental change has had a profound impact on society, and that its arrival was greeted with wonderment at the magical or supernatural power it suggested. In Francis Bacon's famous "sound-houses" quotation from 1600, such marvels were to be found in the utopian *New Atlantis* of the future:

> We represent small sounds as great and deep; likewise great sounds, extenuate and sharp; we make divers tremblings and warblings of sounds, which in their nature are entire. . . . We have also divers strange and artificial echoes, reflecting the voice many times, and as it were tossing it; and some that give back the voice louder than it came, some shriller and some deeper; yea, some rendering the voice, differing in the letters or articulate sounds from that they receive. We have also means to convey sounds in trunks and pipes, in strange lines and distances.[1]

Space and Loudness

Before the advent of electroacoustic technology, every sound was closely bound to its source and limited to a relatively small area over which it could be heard, an area we will call its "profile." The ability of a signal to be heard over some distance made it a useful means of communication. Unless there are substantial obstacles, sounds of medium to high frequency tend to be heard better over long distances, and therefore the raised voice, a high-pitched horn, bells, whistles, and other devices were commonly used historically for signalling. However, sound propagates in all directions simultaneously unless funnelled in a particular one, and therefore it encompasses an area. The fact that everyone within that area can hear the same sound provides the basis of a sense of community for those people.

The church parish has traditionally been defined in relation to the acoustic profile of its bells. In Fig. 12 we see the profile of the Holy Rosary Cathedral bells in Vancouver, as quoted in *The Vancouver Soundscape*. The profile today extends only for a few city blocks, whereas the reports of those recalling its sound from 50 years ago indicate that it could be clearly heard 10 to 15 miles away. This shrinkage, which can only be accounted for by the rise in ambient noise level and the presence of newer buildings acting as obstacles, reminds us that the acoustic profile, and hence the communicative power of a sound, is extremely vulnerable to noise and environmental change. The only solution, one which has been followed by emergency warning signals, is a continual increase in sound level in order to keep a favorable signal-to-noise ratio within the environment.

---

[1]F. Bacon, *New Atlantis,* London: Oxford University Press, 1906, pp. 294–295; Oxford, England: Clarendon Press, 1974, p. 244.

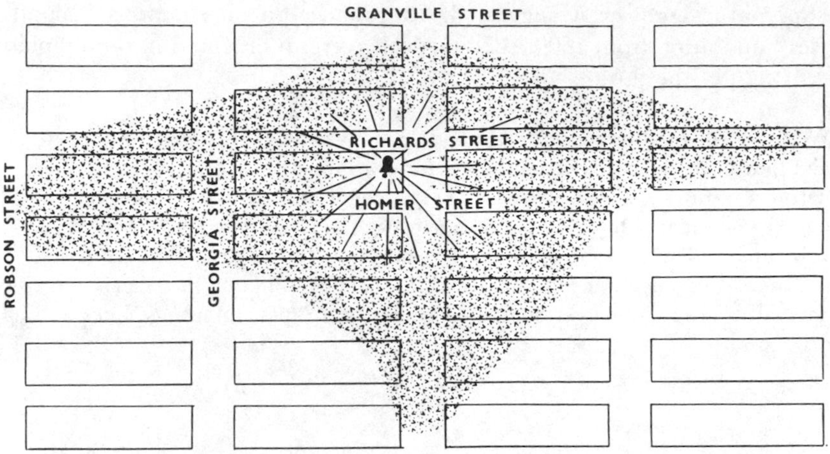

Fig. 12. Acoustic profile of the Holy Rosary Cathedral bells, Vancouver, British Columbia, made June 16, 1973 by the World Soundscape Project (from *The Vancouver Soundscape*, R.M. Schafer, ed., Vancouver, British Columbia, A.R.C. Publications, 1978).

In contrast, the *electroacoustic* profile for the contemporary radio station, examples of which are shown in Fig. 13, is on the order of magnitude of hundreds of kilometers, and is obviously not affected by acoustic forms of noise. The change, as with all electroacoustic phenomena, is so dramatic that it generates a new concept—the mass audience. For commercial purposes, the "community" within the radio profile becomes a mass market. When we consider cable and satellite transmission as well, we see that the bounds have reached such proportions that space can hardly be called a constraint. Access to receiving equipment, not distance from the source, is the key requirement.

The telegraph, dating from 1838, was the first instance in which sound, or at least audible clicks, could be heard over a distance larger than that possible acoustically. But it remained until the telephone and wireless radio made the transmission of voice a reality that the true impact of the phenomenon was felt. Hearing a disembodied voice coming from a great distance—a phenomenon previously available only to mystics and saints—was the experience that generated the most wonderment. Only sounds of apocalyptic dimensions or supernatural origin had ever been heard over such distances, so even the voice of a mortal took on a special aura when heard electroacoustically, an aura of authority that even today has not entirely disappeared with familiarity. The image of a nation with its attention fixed to the voice (and picture) of a man on the moon still captures some of the awe associated with the conquering of distance. Later unmanned missions to more distant planets have been impressive, but silent.

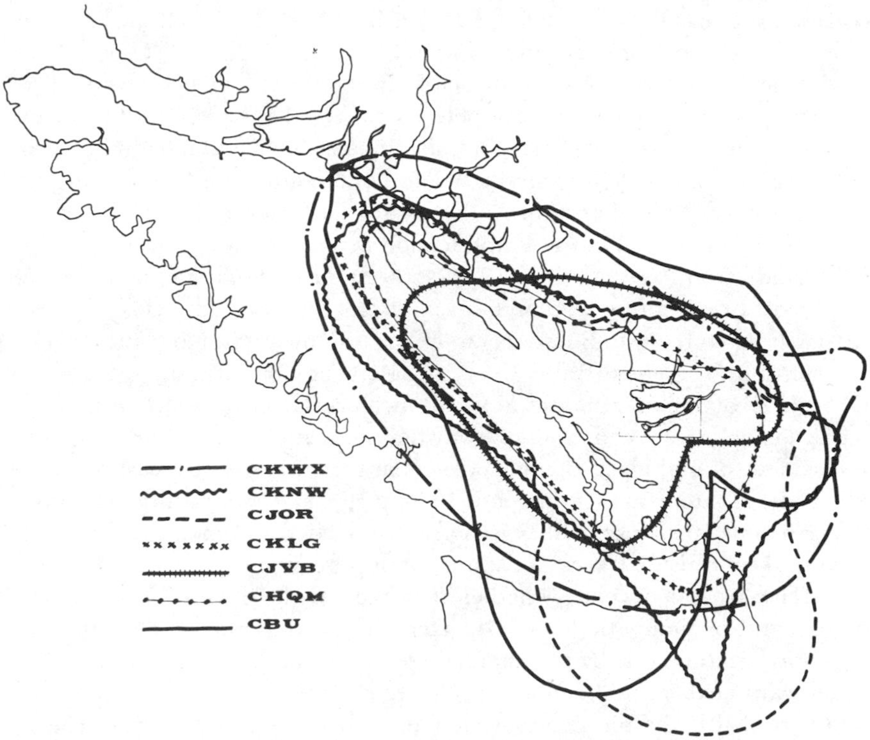

Fig. 13. Electroacoustic profiles of seven AM radio stations, Vancouver, British Columbia (from *The Vancouver Soundscape,* R.M. Schafer, ed., Vancouver, British Columbia, A.R.C. Publications, 1978).

The control of spatial communication, as H. A. Innis (1972) has made us aware, is essential to centralized power and domination. Therefore, acoustic power, amplified through the loudspeaker, or in the form of any loud sound, is linked to the domination of space. The loudest sounds have always been associated with the most powerful forces in the world, whether they represented physical or political power. Because of the extreme amount of physical energy required to produce low frequency sound in great quantities, the natural elements at their most violent were the source of the most powerful sounds for primitive society, e.g., thunder, earthquakes, typhoons, hurricanes, and fire. The *psychological* power associated with low frequency sound remains with us today. Like Prometheus, urban man "stole" noise from the gods, and ever since, the most powerful institutions have produced the most powerful sounds. R. M. Schafer (1977) has termed those that are immune from social proscription as "sacred noise."

Electroacoustic power represents the ultimate democratization of acoustic power—anyone can compete on the decibel scale. Manufacturers even capitalize on the aggressive implications of their portable audio products by giving them such names as "The Loudmouth," and in current parlance, a certain style of portable radio is called a "ghetto blaster" or "boom box." The commercial use of amplification is not recent, however. The first noise study from New York in 1929–1930 reported home radios to be the third most prevalent noise complaint, and those used commercially (broadcasting from stores onto the street) to be the fifth most common, after trucks, car horns, and elevated trains (Noise Abatement Commission, 1930, p.27). Over 12% of the complaints arose from electroacoustic sources, in comparison to deliveries, construction, whistles, bells, and vocal sounds which all ranked less. Sound levels of loudspeakers in the streets were measured at 79 dB (Noise Abatement Commission, 1930, p.36), and as a result, a city ordinance banned their use. Other early noise by-laws also mention the use of loudspeakers outside stores as targets for suppression.

The amplified voice, whether it is that of the advertiser, politician, demagogue, or simply that of the speaker who has the floor, carries with it an authority unattainable by the unaided voice. Part of that power is the ability to be heard farther and by more people (an extension of the spatial concept), and part of it is the physical power that is always associated with acoustic energy. However, other factors specific to the type of voice and the image it projects may be important. Most public address systems tend to emphasize the low frequencies of the voice which are normally stronger in an enclosed space anyway because of room resonances. Hence, the speaker may seem to have a richer, more resonant voice than normal (assuming nervousness has not resulted in a poor timbre to start with). In addition, the dynamic range of the voice that is possible is enlarged with amplification. The smallest whisper or dropping of voice level is audible and dramatic. A whispered sound, close to a mike, conveys a paradoxical intimacy at a distance that can be very effective. The raised voice, more distant from the mike, combined with traditional rhetorical skills, is a formidable weapon for persuasion. The power of the voice can be greatly enhanced through amplification, just as its faults will become more conspicuous.

Time and Repetition

Once it was realized that the pattern of a sound wave could be stored in a physical medium, an idea that lagged several decades behind the invention of photography, the constraint of a sound being fixed in time was broken. No sound had ever been heard twice exactly the same. The brain's processes developed on the basis of detecting slight differences that reflect variations even in repetitions, but now a sound could be repeated *exactly*. Because of the extreme transience of aural phenomena, the "freezing" of sound and its preservation seems of far greater significance than that of visual images which at least have other kinds of representations.

The stored sound immediately becomes historical. It is an artifact as soon as it is recorded, and therefore it creates the possibility of an "aural history" preserved on tape. No other culture has had access to the actual sounds of the past. Repeated performance of stories, music, poetry, and drama have been required to keep them alive for people to experience. Does our present ability to document something for all time contribute or detract from the experience of tradition? Does not all of the recorded past simply become part of the present?

The concept of linear, historical time is denied, if not actually eliminated, by the electroacoustic media. If a particular sound can be preserved and embedded within that originating from any other time, the concept of a linear flow of time becomes an anachronism. Our experience of the present may operate in the same way, no matter when the sound we are hearing originated, but often we know that what we are experiencing *in* the present is not *of* the present. We may refer to this arbitrariness of time sequences as the "embedding" of time. It occurs even in such a common media event as the news. We assume that the person reporting the news is doing so live, and that various "parentheses" can be opened whereby we step into some past event ("here is a report from. . . . ") whose commentator can lead into still another past event ("here is an interview made yesterday. . . . "), and so on. As long as the parentheses of these various time segments close again in reverse order, the entire sequence seems logical to us, assuming we know how to interpret its punctuation.

Occasionally, our notions of linear cause and effect in time can get mixed up. The Canadian Broadcasting Corporation operates a series of delayed signals across the various time zones of the country, so that each program seems to be occurring live, and so that announcements of time are accurate. However, only the news items are actually done live on the network. In one instance, the news report that a certain decision had been announced was followed by a delayed program segment that discussed the possible outcomes of the same decision which was still in the future. It is the attempt of the medium to create the illusion of a linear time flow that results in such paradoxes.

The possibility of exact repetitions of a sound event makes information processing simpler for the brain in the sense that it is easier to make a match with a stored pattern. There are few complicating differences between sounds (except those that depend on the coloration by the immediate acoustic environment, and it is easy for the brain to ignore this information if it is not needed). Instead of detecting differences, the main aspect of the processing is matching a pattern. The type of listening we have described in part I as occurring in response to repeated patterns is background listening, such as that which operates with keynote sounds. Electroacoustic repetition encourages this kind of listening, and in fact makes it easy for the brain to adopt a background listening attitude. What may be of concern is that mental energy is not being devoted to active evaluation of the environment and the formation of new concepts, but to template matching.

The templates of listening—patterns with stencil-like repetitions—can clearly be exploited for the commercial purpose of "brand loyalty." One simply has to fix a pattern in the mind of the listener and reinforce it with enough repetitions for the brain to recognize it quickly and link it to whatever (presumably positive) associations always surround it. From this point of view, the supposed "complexity" of modern life is in fact reduced to the relative simplicity of pattern matching. The opening bars of a popular music tune are the most critical for its success, because they must fix in the mind to identify the song. At a live concert, the group need only sound the first chord or two of a hit song before the audience identifies it and bursts into an applause of recognition. Because repetition of the pleasurable quickly becomes the motivating force in this kind of listening, the audience will be dissatisfied if the group cannot produce live what they have come to expect through countless repetitions of the original recording. The sophistication of modern recording studio techniques cannot, in fact, be easily reproduced live; hence, the frequent dissatisfaction when the live experience cannot match the prerecorded one which the listener has come to prefer, and perhaps idealize as well.

The concept of musical theme or "leitmotif" (a short musical pattern that can easily be remembered) has been transformed into the commercial jingle. But whereas the musical theme was the basis for variation, and the ease of remembering it was to make its transformation and counterpoint with other themes more evident (i.e., to permit complexity and sustain coherence), the commercial version is *never* varied, and the result is deliberately kept simple. In the 1930s, products began to be advertised in radio commercials with accompanying short motifs (the aural equivalent of the trademark). Typically, these first ones were associated with the product name, in fact, quite literally. *Lifebuoy* soap had a descending pitch motif produced by a foghorn-like sound that represented the two syllables of its name, and played on the aural pun of the "life-buoy." *Jello* used an ascending pitch pattern to spell its name: J E LL—O, which I am sure that most readers can easily recall if they say the letters with the correct rhythm. These literal, musical interpretations reinforced the brand name as a word, and were supported by corresponding visual patterns on the packages. Later, once product names were established, advertisements moved to a concern for the image surrounding the product, but we will leave this development to be picked up in chapter 11.

The breaking of the time constraint has profoundly changed the nature of acoustic communication. We have almost come half circle from the time in which every sound was an original to the point where we probably expect it to be a repetition. As with Kuhn's scientific paradigms[2] we have to be jolted by blatant inconsistency before we note differences between sound-alikes. The very experience of time becomes a paradox. We have access to sounds of the past, but all of them seem to be part of the present in some great collage of juxtapositions. And yet, we are emotionally susceptible to the bringing back to life of a sound, perhaps a familiar voice, that has long since been silenced. We understand a picture to be merely that, a representation which we have never experienced until we see it (because there are differences between the way a camera lens "sees" and the way we do). But a recorded sound, even if imperfect in its reproduction, is close enough to our own experience to be capable of bringing back all of the original context and the feelings associated with it. Therefore, to many people, a sound recording seems a more powerful link to the past.

Objectification and Commodity

The process of storage, which we have just discussed from the perspective of breaking the time constraint, is essentially a process that objectifies sound. We transform something that occurs in time to a physical medium—an object in fact—that exists in space. By transforming time into space we make it accessible to visual and tactile inspection. Whether we wind up the spatial representation on a reel, or spiral it into the grooves of a record, we create an equivalence of space and time: inches per second or revolutions per minute.

The implications of this reification are, first of all, that the subject, now an artifact, is available for analysis, i.e., scrutiny outside of time. Such analysis is obviously important for the scientific study of sound and leads to new forms of its visual representation. Earlier forms of notation, whether musical or scientific, were symbolic and mnemonic, that is, a representation of what we hear or can produce. New kinds of analysis, on the other hand, such as the spectrograph, show microscopic details of the internal structure of the sound that are inaccessible to the ear, even if the analysis reflects that performed by the auditory system itself.

For ethnomusicologists and anthropologists, the possibilities presented

---

[2]T. S. Kuhn, *The Structure of Scientific Revolutions*, Chicago: University of Chicago Press, 1962.

by the early cylindrical phonograph to document music in the field were enormously useful (Nettl, 1964, p. 16 ff). The archival potential of such recordings came at a time when many indigenous cultures were already severely threatened, or had already disappeared, ironically as a result of the same Western industrialization that produced the technology used for the documentation. Such ethnomusicological collection dates from the turn of the century, and although the quality of the early recordings is poor by modern standards, the fact remains that the technology provided a literal documentation that surpassed the results of even the most sensitive transcriber. We know, for instance, that many early ethnomusicologists were so conditioned by Western musical practice that they interpreted what they heard and transcribed it according to Western musical notation, ignoring the microtonal variations that can still be heard on original recordings. Therefore, such objective documentation can be said both to preserve the aural artifacts of a culture, and to provide the means whereby its sensibilities and practices may be absorbed through repeated listening. There is no guarantee that one can ever bridge the gaps between cultures, but the perspective of time and familiarity can certainly clear away some of the veils that obscure a culture from us.

The equivalent type of documentation for our own history, as it survives in the memories of living people, only began in earnest after the Second World War, with the oral history project at Columbia University (Shumway, 1970; Waserman, 1975). People who had played an important part in society were interviewed, and these tapes, following the bias of historians to have written documents, were transcribed and sometimes even edited for readability. It was only later that the practice of interviewing anyone with memories of the past (Grele, 1975) and emphasizing the actual sounds on tape—what is called "aural history" to signify that emphasis—became an important part of archival, museum, and broadcasting activities. Today, the possibilities offered by the documentation process are very important, and we will return to them in some detail in chapter 13.

Like most processes, objectification of sound has another side to it. To objectify something makes it a commodity which can be bought and sold. The evanescence of sound previously kept it relatively immune from commerce. One could pay to have the experience of a sound in concert, but one could not actually own the sound itself, only copies of its notation. Therefore, it is not surprising that the advent of the mass-produced sound artifact, cylinders, and records, quickly became part of the "music industry" in the early years of the century.

The stage had been set for such commoditization, however, by the advances in mechanical musical devices up to the end of the 19th century (Buchner, 1959). Mechanical organs date back to the 16th century and music boxes somewhat later, and by the end of the 19th century, some very sophisticated devices that encoded control patterns on paper or metal disks (the predecessors of the phonograph record) could be bought for home entertainment. The sophistication of such mechanical devices as the nickelodeon, the forerunner of the modern juke-box, was amazing. Some metal disks even anticipated stereophonic recordings by providing a double set of playing mechanisms, and the range of sound extended over five octaves. Within a few years of the introduction of the electrical reproduction of live sound—no matter that it was of poorer quality—the mechanical devices became collector items.

The history of recordings as commodities up to the present is long and intricate (Gammond & Horricks, 1980). Novelty and technical innovation have been the key elements. The industry has grown to billion dollar proportions (see chapter 12), and is closely allied with the manufacture of the audio products used for reproducing sound. The word "stereo" has gone from being an adjective to its new status as a noun, an object that one owns and seemingly cannot be without. Likewise, our vocabulary has been enriched by such concepts as the audiophile, the hit single, the LP, the soundtrack, multitrack studios, component systems, direct-to-disk, and the Walkman, not to mention the endless technical terms that have sprung up around the industry. But perhaps more important than the way in which all of it touches our pocketbooks is the way it has changed our listening attitudes. In short, the listener becomes the *consumer* of sound as a commodity. And such consumption, as we will see in chapter 10, is characterized by the same dynamics and economic implications as all other types.

Finally, objectification leads to control, manipulation, and distortion of the sound (Kaegi, 1971). The manner of storage determines the kind of control that can be exercised over it. For instance, the early wire recording could not be easily or effectively spliced, nor could the original disk recordings be edited. The latter, however, could be mixed, albeit laboriously with two turntables of source material and a third for recording. Therefore, editing and the associated techniques of montage had to wait until the invention of tape in the 1930s, and until after the Second World War for it to be commonly available. Among the first attempts to use prerecorded sounds as musical material was John Cage's *Imaginary Landscape No.1* from 1939 which used existing test recordings. The modern period of musical applications begins in 1948 with Pierre Schaeffer's work as a radio producer in Paris (Cross, 1968). He originally worked with disk recordings, and after 1951 with tape when it became available. The work was first termed *musique concrète* because it worked with "found" sounds in a manner reminiscent of Marcel Duchamp's found-object "readymades" and "concrete poetry" experimentation with words and syllables. After that came the concept of "tape music," i.e., music created purely through the manipulation of sound on tape, with the early American work by Cage, simultaneous with Luening and Ussachevsky's experimentation at the Columbia–Princeton Studio. From these beginnings has arisen a rich tradition of what can best be generalized as "electroacoustic music," the possibilities of which we will return to in chapter 13.

Schizophonia

When we discussed the "black box" model of electroacoustics in chapter 1, we contrasted the conventional notion of fidelity—which compares only input and output signals—with a communicational model which shows that the *context* of the original signal is completely different from that of the output signal. The comparison of signals ignores the obvious split in context, and when context is ignored, most of the communicational subtlety of a message is lost. Comparisons based on signal quality alone imply absolute, universal standards which can be applied under any circumstances. Most functional artifacts, on the other hand, are designed with consideration for the environment in which they are to function. A car that is suited for highway driving may be inefficient in urban traffic, for instance. H. A. Simon refers to this matching of artifact and environment as achieving a homeostasis, or equilibrium, between the inner and outer environment (Simon, 1969, p. 9).

A simpler way to define the problem is to refer to the split between an original sound and its electroacoustic reproduction as "schizophonia," a term coined by Schafer (1969) and used by the World Soundscape Project. Use of the Greek "schizo," meaning split or separation, emphasizes the difference in context which characterizes electroacoustic manipulation. Schafer points to the word as being "nervous" and makes a comparison to the psychological aberration of schizophrenia. We have already described in this chapter some implications of the breaking of traditional acoustic constraints, and we will elaborate on these considerations in the following chapters. However, it should be clear that, like most tools, electroacoustic technology is a double-edged sword that provides benefits and conceals dangers. Schizophonia is an inevitable fact of audio technology, but our concern with it will be to understand its implications, not condemn its existence altogether.

The challenge of the schizophonic situation for the listener is to make sense out of the juxtaposition of two different contexts. In many cases, the "sense" becomes conventional acceptance. We come to expect that voices should appear from the walls and ceilings in public places such as airports and train stations to give us information. We think nothing of hearing music (even of a 100-piece orchestra!) emanating from the smallest places. We come to depend on radio and television for information, entertainment, and distraction. However, in other cases, the schizophonic discontinuity may strike us as being inappropriate—the sound of a radio "blaring" in an environment, particularly a natural one, or one in which privacy and concentration are desired, strikes most people as an infringement of their personal space.

In many situations, electroacoustic sound *imposes* its character on an environment because of its ability to dominate, both acoustically and psychologically. Muzak and other forms of programmed background music are specifically designed to impose a mood on an environment and to have predictable effects on the behavior of those within it. Similarly, many individuals prefer some form of background sound in their own personal environments, for reasons that we will go into later. The question of when such practices are simply exercises of free will and when they become public infringements is, of course, both important and controversial. In every case, however, the mood of the environment becomes that imposed by the electroacoustic sound, and therefore mood becomes a designed, artificial construct. Whether one likes or dislikes the effect is not important to the discussion. Instead, we should be concerned about the long-range effects when (and if) most environments that people experience have predictable, perhaps stereotyped moods associated with them. Does "happiness" become what you feel when you shop in an environment with happy music in it? If so, emotion does not arise from within our relationships to people and environments, but instead, is a property *of* the environment and yet another commodity to be experienced, and therefore consumed.

The imposition of one environment on another now includes the "embedding" of an environment within another through use of portable, lightweight headphones—the so-called "Walkman" phenomenon. The schizophonic split between electroacoustic and natural environments becomes nearly complete in this situation. The *choice* of audio environment has the attraction for the listener of being entirely one's own. The psychological "shutting out" of the environment that we described in part I as being typical of the lo-fi environment, now becomes an objective and highly visible reality. Whereas no one seems to be offended by the non-listener's introversion in the lo-fi situation, it is remarkable to note the public outcry against people who blatantly shut themselves off with portable sound systems. People who dislike intrusive noise usually regard headphone listening (for others) with grateful relief ("just as long as they don't bother me"). Society is now faced with the visible evidence that such self-isolation can occur anywhere and at will. The audio advertiser's exhortation to "Shut out the city!" with their stereo products is now being answered by the walk-person's logical response, "Shut out everybody!" It becomes the electroacoustic answer to noise pollution, as well as a psychological listening habit made profitable.

In conclusion, our brief survey of the basic implications of electroacoustic technology on listener–environment relationships shows that fundamental changes are at work. Traditional acoustic patterns of behavior are superseded and replaced with artificial ones mediated by technology. As we come to depend less and less on acoustic information because fewer sounds we experience are meaningful (an alternative definition of noise pollution), electroacoustic technology extends the world of listening possibilities as much as it exploits the listener's habits and creates psychological dependencies. The issues become difficult to discuss objectively because, first of all, everyone is personally involved in the changes. Investigations of listening habits to the media are often treated by people as attacks against their personal lifestyle. It is easy to be subjective and respond by saying, "But I like it," or "You can't stop progress," or "I can do what I want"—responses that are also typical of the public's response to noise. Electroacoustic listening preferences represent psychological investments, and people are often as sensitive about them as they are to what they wear or the way they look. In the face of such personal involvement, it will be our task in the next few chapters to document the behavioral changes we observe in the new environments of electroacoustic communication as carefully and objectively as possible.

9

Electrification: The New Soundscape

We normally think of the technological impact on sound in terms of the audio media. However, the widespread use of electrical power as a source of energy has altered the character of the soundscape as much as audio technology has. All energy forms leave their mark on the sounds they produce, either directly or as a by-product of their processes. Human power, horsepower, mechanical power, steam, internal combustion, and diesel motors—all of these sources of power have acoustic implications in terms of such factors as speed, uniformity, attack characteristics, timbre, and so on. Beyond changes in the sounds themselves are the social and economic changes which new forms of energy bring about, and which inevitably result in differences in community life and patterns of communication. R. M. Schafer (1977) provides a fascinating account of the historical changes in soundscape character in *The Tuning of the World*. Here we will consider the implications of electrification on cognitive and perceptual processes that are involved in acoustic communication systems.

Redundancy and Uniformity

The use of electricity as a means of power provides a nearly unchanging source of energy that allows a machine to be driven at high, uniform speeds. The sounds made by such machines, termed "flatline" sounds by Schafer, have a corresponding uniformity and invariance, both in intensity and spectrum (Fig. 14). We often describe the sound of a machine as a "whir" or "whine"; the former reflects a constant intensity level, perhaps combined with the modulatory grain of a rolled "r" sound, and the latter suggests the presence of high frequency components. The onomatopoeia of such words is not accidental. Both words can be prolonged into a machine-like drone, and "whine" has the added connotation of a human vocal expression that is annoying because of its persistent and irritating high frequency components. The high speed of revolution of electrically powered machines typically produces an unnatural amount of high frequency energy in the region (1–4 kHz)

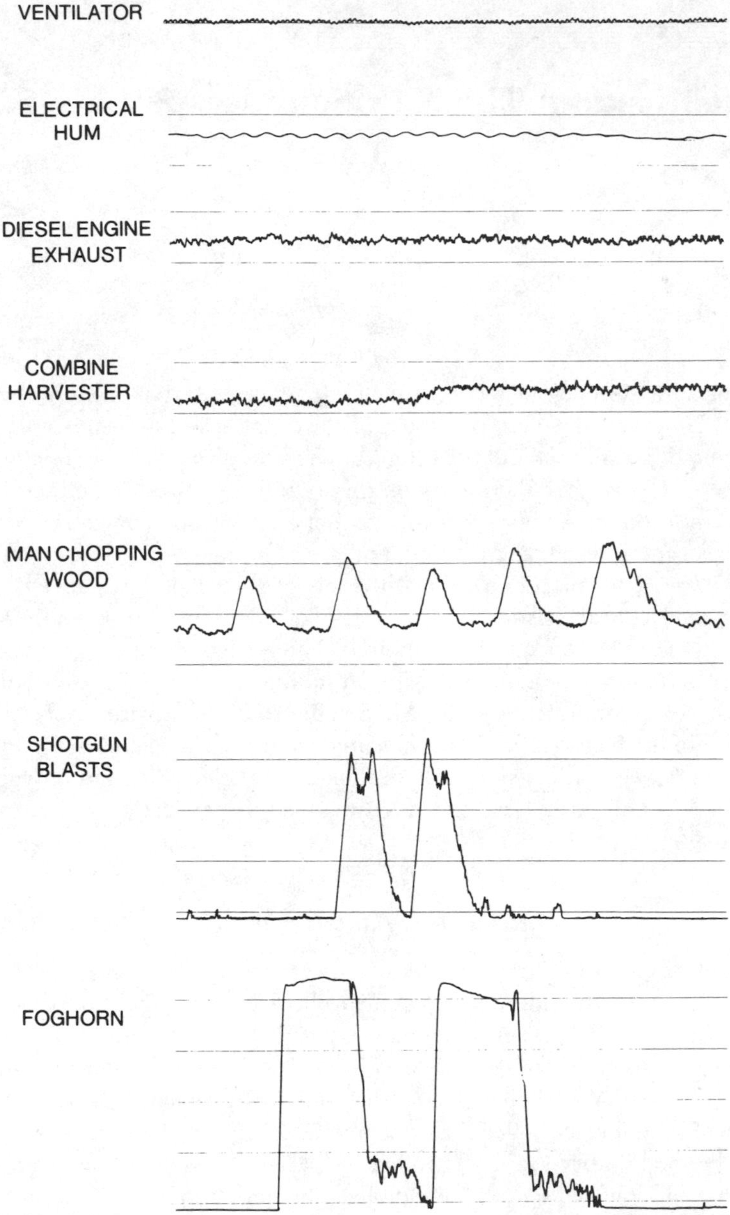

Fig. 14. Graphic level recordings of various environmental sounds recorded by the World Soundscape Project. Typical mechanical and electrical sounds show little amplitude variation over time in comparison to the sounds shown below.

where the auditory system is most sensitive. We can say that such a spectrum is unnatural because few acoustic sounds have a large amount of their energy in that region, and perhaps that is why the ear developed its special sensitivity in that range.

Uniformity and exactness of repetition is desirable in a machine in order to minimize wear on the parts and to maximize precision. However, as we have described it earlier, such uniformity is contrary to the brain's function to detect and interpret *differences* in incoming stimuli. In terms of information theory, we have described such sounds as having a high redundancy and predictability. The brain's reaction to repetitive, low information, constant level stimuli is called habituation, and is characterized by a decreased neural firing rate. In terms of the perceived sense of loudness, the process is called adaptation. A constant level of sound is said to "fatigue" the auditory system and produce a decreased level of sensation, e.g., the loudness of a constant tone falls off with duration.

Of the various types of "flatline" sounds which result from electrical processes, we may distinguish the hum and the drone. Electrical hum occurs when an electrical circuit is not properly grounded. It only occurs because the conventional form of electricity uses the principle of "alternating current" (AC), in contrast to "direct current" (DC). Alternating current oscillates with a certain frequency, 60 Hz in North America and 50 Hz in Europe. Therefore, if this signal leaks into the air through mechanical vibration, or if it is present in the audio signal itself and is converted to sound by a loudspeaker, it produces a low-pitched sound around the musical pitch of *B* natural (for 60 Hz). Frequently, electrical hum is accompanied by its harmonics which, being higher, are usually more prominent. Anything powered by DC, on the other hand, cannot produce a hum because the current does not oscillate; early forms of electrical power were of this type, and today, DC batteries are still frequently used. Electrical drones, on the other hand, may be caused by any portion of a machine which is vibrating fast enough and with sufficient uniformity to produce a constant sound, such as with the motors of household appliances, construction equipment, electric lawnmowers, and so on.

Hums and drones form many of the keynote sounds of contemporary society. Their low level constancy allows them to stay in the background of perception provided they do not interfere too greatly with foreground signals. Still, one is always amazed at hearing a very loud hum in some electrical system and finding that other people are oblivious to it ("What hum?"). The power of the brain to block out even the obvious is truly amazing. If it is easy to ignore such sounds, how can they possibly be an environmental problem? Perhaps it is better not to attract attention to them. Unfortunately, however, constant level sounds, as easy as they are to ignore, have other communicational implications.

Any constant level sound raises the ambient level and masks other more diminutive sounds. Distant sounds are blurred, and therefore we may say that such drones reduce the "acoustic horizon" of an environment. In general, continuous sounds reduce acoustic definition. Sounds are not clearly separated by silences; they are not discrete entities, but part of an overall texture. None of these implications is problematic *by itself.* However, when multiplied across all the environments that people experience, and when fewer situations provide any aural contrast, texture becomes the norm, and listening habits invariably adapt to it. The result is also a kind of aural "crowding"—the distance over which one can communicate is severely reduced, and that space starts to include few other people. The crowded rock concert or discotheque, as exciting as such gatherings may appear to be, are characterized by high sound levels of extreme constancy that give the illusion of "togetherness," but because the individual's aural space is drastically reduced, there is literally no room for interpersonal communication. The experience of being enveloped in quiet is replaced by that of being smothered in sound.

Whereas the dangers of high sound levels for long periods of time are well documented in terms of hearing loss and stress, the long-term effects of low-level constant sounds are not. Given the many other sources of physical and mental stress, the effects of such sounds may remain cognitive, unless the levels involved exceed 50 or 60 dB, as they in fact frequently do. In other words, the effects manifest themselves more at the level of communicational problems than in physical damage. Such "dangers" are usually minimized by people who believe that any degree of subjectivity in one's reaction to a danger renders it harmless. Only objective physical damage is a sufficient criterion for action to be taken (in this prevalent attitude); otherwise it is "caveat auditor"—let the hearer beware! However, when we think of what makes life meaningful, it is usually the things that depend on effective communication that come to mind. The interactive nature of communication within the hi-fi environment—one where hums and drones have not homogenized it into a thick texture—is an essential part of human experience that needs to be protected. There is no assurance that modes of communication other than the aural can replace the information and meaning we derive from that sense.

The Fixed Waveform Oscillator

Another type of redundancy with electrically produced sound occurs at the micro level of sound pressure variation, the level that is usually termed the "waveform." Patterns of sound pressure, or waveforms, are constantly changing in the natural acoustic environment—no sound is ever invariant. Through electrical means such invariance is not only possible, but in the case of alternating current, such uniformity is highly desirable. Variations in electrical power are always to be avoided, hence the perfect form of electricity has an invariant waveform. The uniformity of electrical power is passed on to the machines it powers and the waveforms of the sounds they produce. Therefore their spectra (i.e., frequency content) are also usually characterized by constancy. The problems of the "fixed" waveform become particularly clear in its use in electronic music.

The electronic music synthesizer is based on fixed waveform oscillators which produce a variety of standard waveforms. Unlike all acoustic instruments, these oscillators have waveform patterns which are exactly repetitive. Traditional Fourier analysis of sound tells us that if the waveform is constant, so is the harmonic content. Computer analysis of musical tones reveals a wealth of minute fluctuations in frequency and strength of harmonics in even the simplest tone. Whether all such detail is essential to the brain is not clear, though it has been demonstrated that if straight line envelope segments replace the "wiggly" variations observed in analysis for the strength of each harmonic, the result is indistinguishable to the ear (Moorer, 1977). However, there appears to be a critical level of detail and time variation that the brain requires to find a sound interesting and lively. Experience with fixed waveform oscillators quickly reveals that such sounds appear unnatural to the ear and are potentially boring (and perhaps alienating) to the listener, unless treated with the greatest musical skill.

Typically, the public's reaction to electronic music, at least in the early days, attributed machine-likeness to the sounds used in this music. On the basis of the environmental sound produced by electrical machines, the comparison has some factual basis. However, the reaction probably says more about our psychological attitude to machines, and our inability to realize that they are invested with human knowledge and reflect all of its limitations. If a machine produces a sound we find uninteresting, it is the acoustical model it implements that is inadequate and not the machine itself. The machine is merely a convenient scapegoat to cover our ignorance. The limitations of the traditional Fourier model quickly became apparent once its approach was objectified in machine form. Electroacoustic synthesis enhances our understanding of sound because it tests acoustical models and their realization techniques against the reality of human perception. Technology in this role acts as a means to verify human knowledge.

Dynamic Behavior

Whereas the constancy of electrical power permits high speed uniformity, its ability to start and stop the flow of power nearly instantaneously produces the opposite acoustic result—the switching transient. The word "transient" in this context refers to any signal that is non-repetitive, particularly if it involves a sudden change from one state to another. The temporal behavior of sound (which is termed "dynamic" behavior) is extremely important for the identification of sounds and the perception of timbre. Therefore, electrification produces new kinds of dynamic behavior, and hence timbral qualities, that do not occur naturally.

To understand the implications of these phenomena better, we need to refer to psychoacoustic evidence and some acoustic laws (Roederer, 1975). During the initial portion of a sound, called the "attack," the sound pressure pattern is building up to its maximum "steady state." This portion, which may last only a few milliseconds, contains what are called *onset transients*. In the case of a musical instrument, the onset transients occur during the period in which the inertia of the instrument's physical material is being overcome as it is set in vibratory motion. Interestingly enough, it is this fleeting transient stage that contains the most information for the brain to identify the sound. From the point of view of information theory, this fact is not surprising because it is during the attack portion that there is the most change, the greatest amount of unpredictability and the most noise (literally, since we hear a "chiff" at the start of a note). Because this complex amount of information is processed first by the auditory system, it is the most useful for quick identification of the sound. Again we see demonstrated the brain's abilities to detect subtle differences in very complex input.

Once the sound reaches its steady state (which in natural sounds is never *exactly* steady, but rather has small transient fluctuations), recognition has already occurred, pitch has been identified (if there is one), and timbre has been perceived, at least as a gestalt. In other words, the sound has "settled down" into a predictable pattern, and the brain only monitors further changes that deviate from it. The time to build up to this steady state is greatly reduced with electrically powered devices; that is, they can switch on and off quite abruptly. Consider the mechanical siren with a rotating, perforated disk. It has to build up to the speed that produces a pitch in the audible range, and to do that it has to overcome its own inertia. We hear it begin as a long upward glissando. An electrical siren, on the other hand, produces its pitch practically instantly. The modern ambulance and police car make effective use of this suddenness of attack in urban traffic where the abrupt start of the sound will be more prominent than a slower buildup.

A similar example is that of various types of whistles. The steam whistle depends on a pressure buildup of steam to produce a sound. Therefore it is not only characterized by a breathy, somewhat vocal timbre, but also by a gradual and rather slow buildup of the various harmonics. The result, still to be heard in a few remaining factory whistles or a reconstructed steam locomotive, has an attractive timbre and good carrying power. It is also characterized by being influenced by temperature and other atmospheric conditions. Therefore the sound is never exactly the same, even when sounded a few minutes apart, because the temperature of the horn itself will be different, and other conditions may have changed. The modern compressed air horn is electrically powered but the actual sound is made by the sudden release of air pressure through the horn itself. It therefore has a much sharper attack and greater uniformity of timbre, often with many high harmonics.

The electronic horn, on the other hand, produces an electronically generated sound which can be switched on and off very quickly. Its sound, being produced by fixed waveform oscillation, is simpler and not as rich as its earlier counterparts. Whether it carries as far and is as noticeable as the older models is a matter of debate in many coastal areas where these horns have replaced the older type of foghorn known as the diaphone (a compressed air horn of great power). Naturally, the replacing of the familiar horns, combined with the simpler, less unique sound of the electronic replacements, results in a mistrust of the newer models by the locals.

The on/off switching transient also results in the rather modern sound of the *click*. This modest sound that increasingly populates the soundscape is an excellent example of a transient. The sound can only be produced mechanically by the impact of two objects, but in that case it takes on some of the resonant quality of the objects themselves. Human clicks made with the tongue are components of some languages and other types of communication without words. For instance, they are useful in echolocation and general "testing" of a space (as in the tap of a blind person's cane) because their brevity prevents the environmental response being masked.

The frequency content of the click is always broadband. There is an inverse relation of frequency to time that dictates that the shorter the time window during which sound pressure changes, the broader the band of frequencies it produces. Even a short burst of a low frequency sine tone (cut on tape for instance) produces a click. Only when the time window is enlarged to several periods of the sound does the click disappear and the impression of pitch emerge. Therefore, the spectra of all clicks include a wide range of frequencies, and electrical transients, being uncolored by resonances and unconstrained by the physical inertia of objects, can have a very short duration and a broad bandwidth.

Finally, the speed of switching between states is constrained in the physical world by natural laws. It cannot be done instantaneously, but electrical systems shorten the time switching takes in comparison to mechanical systems which have to overcome physical inertia. Therefore, the police siren can switch from "wail" mode (a continuous glissando) to "yelp" mode (a rapid up–down pattern) nearly instantly. The latter mode is usually used when going through intersections in order for the sound to be heard better.

The telephone system depends on the rapidity of switching for making connections, and newer electronic technology has speeded up this process.

However, many phone systems still produce switching transients that can be heard as very loud clicks. Because of the close proximity of the receiver to the ear, the actual pressure levels to which the ear is exposed can be over 100 dB. They pose a threat to hearing with frequent exposure. The auditory system has what is called an "averaging time" of about 35 milliseconds during which it monitors incoming information. Short transients in the microsecond range simply do not register for the brain and therefore are not heard as being loud (they do not occur in nature, and it is more efficient if the brain screens them out). However, such transients can cause damage in the inner ear because they are transferred to it directly via the eardrum and bones of the middle ear (Brüel, 1976). It is a case where what one doesn't hear *can* be harmful.

Response Characteristics

Whenever sound or an audio signal is processed by a device, including the auditory system itself, we may describe the type of processing in terms of the effect it has on certain parameters of the sound. For each parameter, the device is said to have a *response* characteristic. Response is usually shown on a graph which compares the input signal to the output, or which compares the output to a standard (Fig. 15). In order to account for the quality of elec-

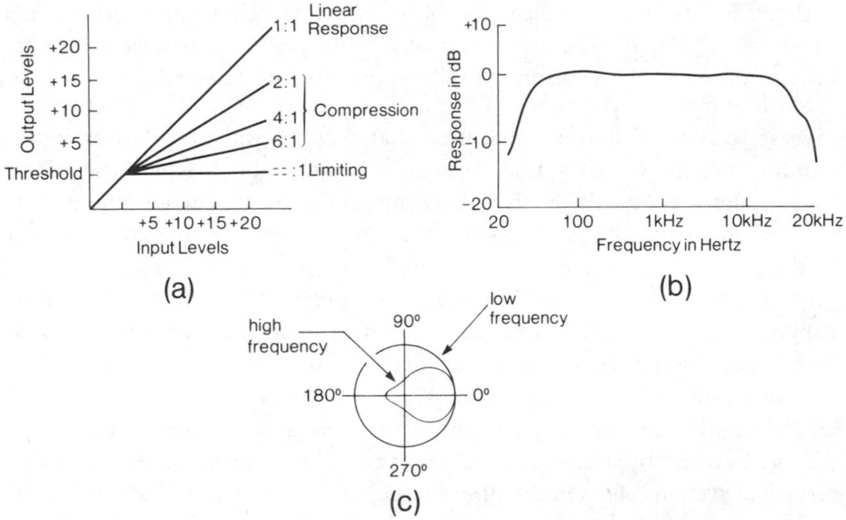

Fig. 15. Three types of audio response patterns: (a) for intensity levels, showing linear response and the non-linear response caused by compression and limiting; (b) for frequency, showing a typical "flat" response across most of the audio spectrum; (c) for direction, in the case of an omni-directional microphone, showing equal response for low frequencies and more limited response at higher frequencies.

troacoustic sound, including communicational problems of distortion and background noise, we need to give a brief survey of these technical terms. For a more detailed account of recording and studio techniques see (Nisbett, 1972; Runstein, 1974; Keane, 1980; Alten, 1981; Thom, 1982).

Linearity and Dynamic Range

The response of a system to various intensity levels is usually described in terms of the ability of the system "to maintain linearity." Linearity means that equal amounts of input result in proportionate amounts of output. Shown graphically as a plot of input versus output, a linear system is represented by a diagonal line at 45 degrees (Fig. 15). Another way to conceptualize the process is that the relative loudness between quiet and loud sounds is preserved through linear amplification. All levels are boosted, but they stay in the same relative proportions. The range of intensity levels (in dB) that a system can handle is called its *dynamic range*. The dynamic range of hearing is about 120 dB, whereas with audio systems, one can expect a good analog tape recorder to have a dynamic range of about 60 dB (i.e., 1 million times smaller!). Disk recordings, optical soundtracks, and television have a considerably smaller dynamic range.

Background noise is found at the low end of the dynamic range of any audio system. It is produced by thermal energy within the channel of transfer itself. High intensity levels, on the other hand, risk driving the system into saturation or overload. With the auditory system, this maximum level is the threshold of pain. Audio systems must be prevented from damage occurring due to such overloads, and therefore a "limiter" is introduced into the system which prevents input levels from exceeding a certain amount. In terms of a response diagram, a limiter is shown as a flattening out of the diagonal line at the top end. No matter how much the input level increases beyond the limiting value, the output remains the same.

Because of the discrepancy between the natural range of sound intensities and that which can be handled by the audio medium, and because of the risk of overload and distortion, audio signals are often "compressed" in order to fit within the dynamic range of the system. Instead of the system maintaining linearity, the relative proportions between loud and soft are reduced during compression. For instance, the range of sound levels within an orchestra may vary by over 70 or 80 dB from loudest to softest. Good recording levels place the given dynamic range within that of the recording device, but in the case of large ranges, a recording level that avoids peak saturation places the quiet sounds close to the background noise. Compression of the signal optimizes the signal-to-noise ratio for *all* sound levels. The effects of compression can be counteracted through the opposite process of expansion, though this is seldom done during reproduction.

The ear seems strangely insensitive to the effects of compression, at least by comparison to other kinds of manipulation. Perhaps it is because the dynamic range of hearing is constantly being adjusted with threshold shifts. We do not experience absolute standards of loudness, only relative ones. For instance, a quiet sound in a quiet environment does not have the same loudness as the same sound in a noisier environment. One only has to compare a clock ticking at night, when it may seem very loud, to its sound during the day when it may not be noticeable at all. The effects of compression only become obvious when the dynamic range is so reduced, such as in television broadcasting, that our sense of *relative* loudness is offended. If we are familiar with the live sound, for instance that of an orchestra, and we do not hear the same relative proportions between full orchestra and solo instruments in an audio version, the difference will be quite noticeable. Compression is also used in popular music recording, as well as in radio broadcasting where it is used to extend the range over which the signal can be heard, and to affect the listener's level of attention. We will return to this type of use in chapter 11.

The ear, however, is very sensitive to distortion, particularly that caused by the overloading of dynamic range by peak signals. The result is some form of "peak clipping" of the signal, i.e., a distortion of the waveform itself where its peaks are flattened. Any change in waveform causes a change in frequency content and therefore a change in timbre. The effect on the sound is always gross and quite noticeable. The peaks in the voice are usually the consonants, particularly the plosives (p,b,g,d), and therefore one often hears a reproduced voice distorting on these sounds.

Frequency Response

The most common type of response measurement, and the one to which the ear appears to be the most sensitive, is that of frequency response. This kind of response is shown graphically as intensity level versus frequency (Fig. 15). For each frequency along the horizontal axis, the corresponding response or output level is shown vertically. A level that indicates no change between input and output level is arbitrarily marked as the 0 dB level. Therefore, negative output levels indicate that the response of the system is to deemphasize those frequencies. For instance, the response of most cheaper loudspeakers falls off at the low and high ends because these frequencies cannot be reproduced accurately. Levels above the 0 dB position indicate an emphasis that is given to certain frequencies. Loudspeakers are usually designed to have a "flat" response, i.e., to reproduce all frequencies within the audible range equally. The ideal response diagram is a flat line, though in practice, variations within plus or minus 1 or 2 dB are regarded as a reasonable equivalent.

The frequency response of the auditory system is not flat, as documented by the Equal Loudness Contours (Fig. 16), the modern version of the earlier Fletcher–Munson curves named for the researchers at Bell Labs who first investigated the phenomenon in the 1930s. In fact, the ear's response at

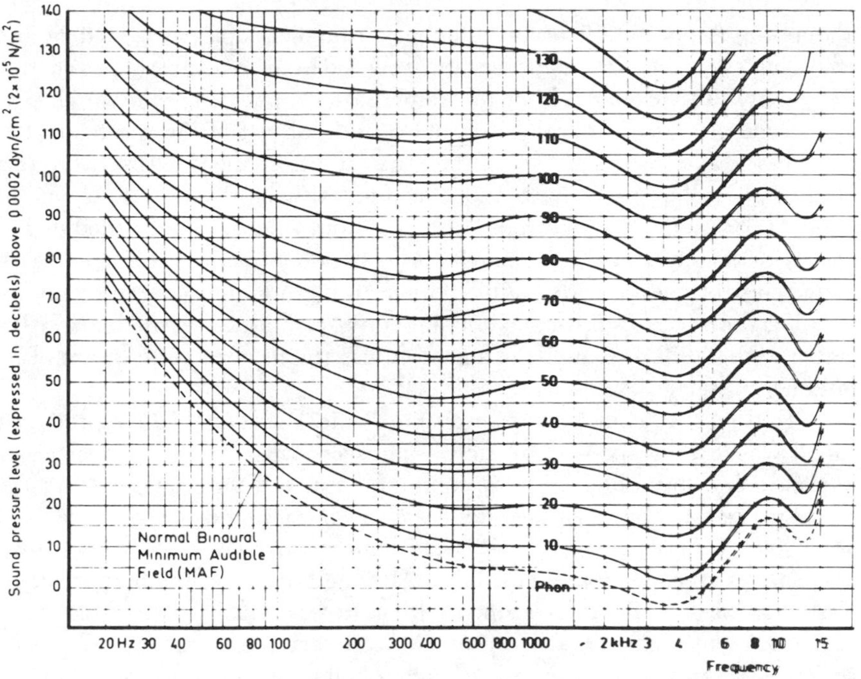

Fig. 16. Frequency response of the auditory system as a set of equal loudness contours for pure tones. The normal threshold of hearing for persons aged 18–25 years is also shown at the bottom (from ISO recommendation R226).

low intensity levels is quite curved at both the low and high ends, indicating that sensitivity drops off at these extremes. (The contours are always presented in the opposite manner to a frequency response diagram; i.e., they show how much the intensity level would have to be *raised* at any given frequency in order to restore equal loudness sensation; hence their U-shape corresponds to an inverted U-shape on a frequency response diagram). The "loudness" control on some amplifiers is intended to compensate for this aspect of the auditory system for *low* listening levels; however, one often observes its use at higher levels for boosting bass response in popular music.

The term "equalization" is used to describe any intentional alteration of frequency response. Standard curves of equalization are part of the recording process, both for disk and tape. The recording curve for disks deemphasizes the low frequencies and emphasizes the highs; during the reproduction process the reverse equalization curve is used, so that the net result prevents any coloration of the sound. The reason for this process is to minimize groove noise on records and hiss in the case of tape (for the latter, curves that work in the opposite manner are used, and therefore tape and phono inputs on amplifiers are different). Equalization is also used by the recording engineer, the composer, and now the home user as well, to change the quality of the sound, either to compensate for poor recording quality or room acoustics, or simply to bring out a desired part of the spectrum. Because of the extreme sensitivity of the ear to subtle changes in spectrum, this kind of control is immediate and effective. Although its alternate names "correction" and "compensation" indicate that it was originally intended to correct deficiencies in the signal, the process now provides the listener with active control over sound quality (either through simple tone controls on amplifiers, or actual third-octave, half-octave, or full-octave equalizers). Inevitably, the ability to alter the signal makes the listener more aware of its internal character.

However, in contrast to the technical ideals, much of the reproduced sound we hear has poor frequency response because of the deficiencies of loudspeakers. Probably the most common cases are the telephone and the transistor radio. The small telephone speaker has a frequency response from about 300 Hz to 3,000 Hz, just wide enough to transmit voice with an adequate degree of comprehensibility. Although one loses the high frequencies, such as the sibilants (s,sh,ch), their loss is usually compensated by redundancy in the words themselves. More interesting is the low frequency region. The fundamental, or lowest pitch, of all adult voices is below 300 Hz. The fundamental of a typical male voice is around 100 to 150 Hz, and occasionally lower; therefore it is transmitted and received with greatly reduced strength, yet we do not hear the voice as suddenly that of a child. The same occurs with transistor radios which cannot properly reproduce the bass sounds in music. The brain, however, comes to the rescue by its ability to "fill in" the missing fundamental on the basis of the higher harmonics whose cumulative periodicity is the same as that of the fundamental (i.e., two cycles of the second harmonic, three of the third, four of the fourth, and so on, repeat their aggregate pattern in the same time as one period of the fundamental). Therefore, although the actual sound of the fundamental is not there, the brain's *pattern recognition* ability reacts as if it were.

Designers of telephone equipment and cheaper loudspeakers have not ignored the value of the brain's ability to compensate. What the brain doesn't need, they don't have to produce if economy, not full fidelity, is the primary criterion. For the telephone company, this means that the quality of the microphone and speaker in a telephone can be the cheapest (i.e., carbon type), and that a smaller bandwidth of frequencies can be transmitted. The load that can be carried by a communication channel depends on the bandwidth of the individual message. Therefore, with a smaller audio bandwidth for each message, more of them can be multiplexed onto the same channel, and the transmission made more cost effective.

A second type of reaction to the telephone's limited frequency response is that in the acoustic world, a voice with a weak bass component indicates that the sound is coming from a distance. Indoors, the low frequencies of the voice are amplified through room resonance, but outdoors, if there are no reflecting surfaces, the low frequencies tend to fall off faster with distance. Therefore, the learned response to an acoustic signal with deemphasized low frequencies is to attribute its quality to the factor of distance. This association neatly corresponds to the psychology of using the telephone to speak over large distances. Voices *sound* distant over the phone both because we know they are distant and because the acoustic cues are telling us so. However, the person at the other end could be in the next room and sound just as distant. On the other hand, full frequency response in a telephone would make the voice seem closer *and* positioned at an intimate distance from the ear. Whereas we can easily keep a caller at a psychological distance on the telephone in its current form, one wonders how interpersonal communication would change if the technical quality of the phone system were suddenly to improve!

Directivity

Lastly, we come to the response of an audio system to direction and spatial position. With microphones and loudspeakers, this type of response is termed "directivity," "directional characteristic," or "field pattern." It is conventionally shown as a polar diagram where each part of the 360 degree range of directions is marked on the circumference of a unit circle (Fig. 15). The 0 dB response (equivalent to the "flat" position for frequency response) is indicated on the circumference, with lesser levels of response inside the circle. Such diagrams are commonly used to describe various types of microphones, such as omnidirectional (equal response in all directions), cardioid (response greatest in front, falling off to none at the back), bidirectional (front and back only), and shotgun (response focused and magnified in a single direction).

Similarly, loudspeaker radiation patterns can be indicated on polar diagrams. Because of the acoustics of sound propagation, low frequencies "bend" (more properly, "diffract") around obstacles whose proportions are smaller than the relatively long wavelengths of low frequency sound. Therefore, frequencies in this range generally spread out evenly around a loudspeaker, unless its dimensions are too small to produce them in the first place. High frequencies, on the other hand, do not diffract easily and consequently are more directional. They also do not bend around the head and as a result sound fainter at the farther ear (an effect called "sound shadow").

What does the concept of "fidelity" mean when applied to spatial position? If we refer to the way in which the auditory system detects spatial directions (on the basis of time and intensity differences between the signals arriving at each ear), or the sense of depth (relative strength between the direct and reverberated signals), then it is clear that conventional microphones, with their various response patterns, do not "hear" the way the ear does. Moreover, when recorded sounds are played back through a loudspeaker (a fixed source), or groups of loudspeakers, they are clearly different from the originals which may or may not come from point sources. Although the quest to reproduce the concert hall, or any other space, in your living room proceeds unabated with current audio technology, the emphasis is not strictly on fidelity but on creating an effective *illusion*. After all, it takes a certain suspension of disbelief to imagine a concert hall in your living room in the first place. The audiophile, and even the casual listener, has become used to—and probably prefers—the artificial electroacoustic image that can be conveyed through stereo and quadraphonic equipment.

An interesting reversion to the pseudonatural came with the introduction of binaural recording during the 1970s, or as it is popularly known, *kunstkopf* or "dummy head" recording (Gerzon, 1975). The idea is simple enough: place the microphones in the ear canals of a carefully modelled artificial head, or else wear small electret microphones in your own ears such that the outer ears (the pinnae) provide the same reflections as they do normally. In fact, the idea had been demonstrated in 1933 at Bell Labs by Dr. Harvey Fletcher, using a suitably wired mannequin named Oscar, but it did not go any further as a recording technique because of the lack of commercial two-channel equipment (Stevens & Warshofsky, 1965, p. 99). The technique was revived in Germany in the late 1960s and used by the West German radio for various documentaries. The carefully modelled head with pinnae sat on a box to simulate chest cavity resonance, and was called the kunstkopf, or artificial head. Commercial versions soon became available, some with less realistic looking heads and ears, others that were designed to be clipped to the recordist's ears. The technique is as effective as it is simple. The microphones pick up the differences in sound between the two ears just as they occur normally. This includes coloration of the sound by the pinnae, as well as time and intensity differences between the signal at each ear.

For binaural recording to be effective in reproducing the spatial aspects of an environment, the results must be listened to on lightweight headphones. Because all of the coloration by the environment and the outer ear is already present, the sound should not come from loudspeakers and pass over the listener's pinnae a second time. The result, therefore, is a very intimate type of listening. Headphone listening, which has become an integral part of most people's audio experience in the last few decades, is normally characterized by the sound appearing to originate *inside* the head (the phenomenon called "in-head localization"). The reason is the same as for the appearance of a "phantom image" between two speakers when the same signal is fed to each. As the intensity of the sound in one speaker is varied, the apparent location of the image moves towards the speaker with the stronger intensity. The effect is a somewhat crude spatial placement, and although the phenomenon does not occur naturally, the brain interprets it readily. With headphones, the two speakers are at the ears, and therefore the image appears to come from within the head. Because binaural recording incorporates the time differences that are involved in binaural hearing, the image appears to originate *outside* the head, as in normal hearing. To a generation accustomed to the "inner space" of conventional headphone listening, this reversion to a "natural" image is novel and even disconcerting. One awaits a marriage of kunstkopf and walkman to overlay one environment with another and give the lie to the old adage that you can't be two places at once!

Fidelity and the Artificial

We have briefly summarized some of the technical issues that are connected with the reproduction of spatial images with audio technology. The field is vast and encompasses endless details about loudspeaker design (such as how many components a speaker should have, what kind of enclosure, and whether phase coherence should be maintained between the parts), as well as multiple loudspeaker placement and the simulation of directional and distance cues with delays, digital processing, and various types of encoding. From the point of view of communicational processes, the technical details are less important than the listening and buying habits, among others, which are encouraged by such developments. What begins as a discussion of fidelity in spatial reproduction eventually becomes an interest in the technically sophisticated creation of the artificial. The significance of technology is not that it re-creates life, but that it creates new *images* of life. Sometimes the images are "larger than life," in that they enhance the natural or extend our perception into entirely new domains. Too often, however, the audio image is "smaller than life," because as we have observed, the quality of electroacoustic sound, both environmentally and in the media, is frequently poorer than the richness of natural sound.

The enhancement of the natural, as made possible through more sophisticated forms of audio technology, brings with it the possible preference for, or even addiction to, the artificial. The audiophile may prefer to listen at home than in a crowded concert hall with more or less adequate acoustics and coughing neighbors. We obviously are touching on listener preferences here, and the point is not to approve or disapprove of anyone's listening habits, only to observe implications. Familiarity with electroacoustic sound, like most acquired tastes, can produce divergent results. One may become more discriminating (there are as many audio clichés as there are uninteresting soundscapes), or more jaded. We may become more in tune with the natural acoustic environment (with its "perfect fidelity"), or more anxious to shut it out and live in an audio cocoon. We may go on an endless search in the universal soundscape, or sit home to be comfortably reassured by the old favorites, the top 40, or the background audio wallpaper.

Analog and Digital

Perhaps no current development more aptly illustrates our theme of the paradoxical nature of electroacoustic technology than the current rise of digital technology and its impact on the soundscape, as well as our listening habits. The paradoxes arise between what is possible and what is actual, between the potential offered by technology and many of the actualities brought about by compromises in its realization. In order to understand the implications of digital technology on the soundscape, we need to review the basis of the digital representation of sound (Mathews, 1969; Moorer, 1978; Bateman, 1980).

In the previous chapter we discussed the essential nature of the audio signal which has been transduced from acoustic to electrical form. The kinds of signals involved can be termed "analog"; in fact, the sound wave itself is an analog phenomenon par excellence because it is created by a *continuous* change in pressure. The audio signal is a continuously changing voltage that is designed to correspond exactly to variations in sound pressure. Therefore, we normally refer to audio signals and their manipulation as "analog" signals and processes.

Digital representation of sound is achieved by *sampling* the analog signal, usually at a fixed rate on the order of 20 to 40 kHz or more, and storing the discrete numerical values (called "samples") obtained through this process. This kind of sampling is done by an analog-to-digital converter (ADC) which converts points along the continuous curve to binary numbers, the conventional representation of digital values. The greater the number of samples per second that describe the audio signal, the more accurately small variations (i.e., high frequencies) can be represented and preserved. The actual relationship of sampling rate to frequency (or bandwidth) is that the sampling rate must be at least twice the highest frequency to be represented. Therefore, audio signals with frequencies up to 15 or 20 kHz must be sampled at 30 or 40 kHz respectively. If lower sampling rates are used, then the signal should be filtered first to prevent the distortion called "foldover" which occurs when frequencies higher than half the sampling rate are converted.

The reverse process is called digital-to-analog conversion, and is performed by a digital-to-analog converter (DAC). This device converts binary numbers to a proportionate voltage level. For instance, binary numbers in the range of ± 2048 are converted to voltage levels in the range of ± 5 or ± 10 volts. Note that the positive and negative portions of the audio signal are interpreted as positive and negative numbers. The output of the DAC is a voltage that resembles a staircase (Fig. 17), i.e. it has discrete voltage steps, even though it is an analog audio signal at this point. In order to smooth the signal (and remove unwanted high frequency components above half the sampling rate), the signal is filtered by a low pass filter.

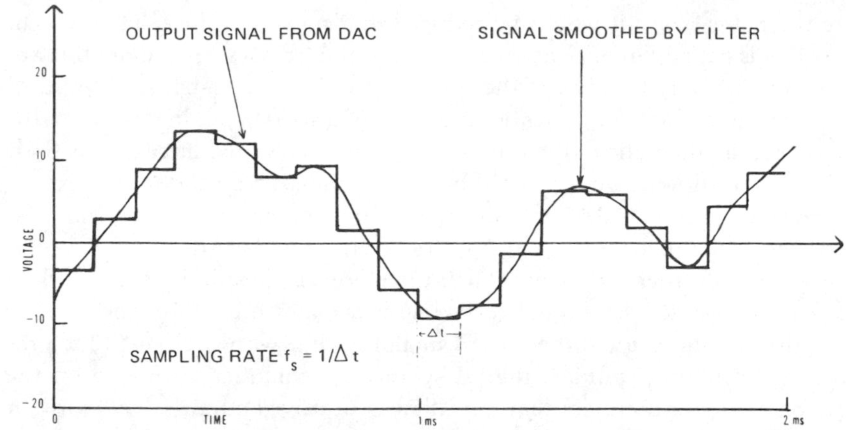

Fig. 17. Production of a sound signal by digital synthesis. Numbers stored in the computer's memory are converted to discrete voltage steps by a digital-to-analog converter (DAC) at fixed time intervals Δt, as shown above along with the resultant signal smoothed by a low-pass filter (from *Handbook for Acoustic Ecology,* B. Truax, ed., Vancouver, British Columbia, A.R.C. Publications, 1978).

Thus, the digital "transduction" process includes the digitization of the analog signal by the ADC, its storage and/or manipulation in binary number format, and its reconstitution as an analog signal by the DAC. The "black box" model from chapter 1 could equally well apply to digital audio if audio signals were substituted for the acoustic parts, and digital representation for the audio part. In other words, digital audio is a "box within a box" in this model. At the moment, no direct conversion from acoustic to digital form is possible without an intervening microphone and analog signal stage. Similarly, digital audio relies on a loudspeaker at the other end for transduction back into sound.

In comparison to the response characteristics by which an analog signal's quality is measured, we can mention two corresponding factors in the digital representation of sound. The first of these is the sampling rate, as already described, which determines the bandwidth of the sound which can be represented. Note that the emphasis is on the highest frequency that can be sampled accurately, whereas it can be assumed that low frequency and DC signals pose no problem in terms of their representation.

The second factor is the maximum size of the individual sample, which is described in terms of the number of binary bits available. Each bit represents two values, 0 or 1, and the binary word, composed of *n* bits can represent 2^n numbers. For instance, three bits can represent 8 numbers, those from 0 to 7. An audio signal could not be stored very accurately with only three bits, since it would be reduced to 8 possible values. This type of distortion is called "quantization error," and it decreases when more bits are used. Another way to think of the quality of the digital signal is in terms of dynamic range. Each doubling of amplitude of a signal is an increase of 6 dB. Therefore, the theoretical dynamic range of a digital signal increases by 6 dB with every additional binary bit. The conventional 12-bit format can represent signals with a 72 dB dynamic range, and the newer 16-bit format extends the range to a theoretical limit of 96 dB. The best dynamic range of analog tape recorders is about 60 dB; therefore, the possibility of around 90 dB dynamic range with digital recording is a major breakthrough.

Just as one can synthesize an analog signal with a circuit that produces an oscillating voltage, digital synthesis techniques are based on the creation of binary numbers that "oscillate" (positive and negative), without necessarily being derived from an analog source. They can be calculated from a formula, for instance. But whereas the production of analog voltages is a matter of circuit design, and the user only has control over the *parameters* of the processes which the circuit performs, the production of binary numbers for digital synthesis places the level of user control at a micro level that is not possible with analog circuitry. Hence, the power of digital synthesis, as well as the digital processing of analog signals, is in the *precision* of control. The designer may typically control individual samples at rates of 30,000 samples/second! Needless to say, the large amounts of data involved require strong control methods (since obviously one cannot specify all of the samples directly), but this problem raises complex issues which we will leave to the final chapter. However, at this point it should be clear that the digital representation of sound is a major change in the way in which sound can be controlled, and therefore thought about.

Another advantage of digital audio that is frequently mentioned is the question of background noise. The digital copying or other manipulation of a sound does not add any additional noise, as it does in analog versions, where for instance, every "generation" of a sound on tape inevitably adds background noise and tape hiss. During the conversion of digital samples into sound, noise will of course be added during the analog stages. Also, errors of various kinds can result in conversion inaccuracies. However, it can be stated that in general digital audio is the cleanest and most accurate technology for treating sound.

The "Digital" Soundscape

Given the technical advances made possible by digital audio technology, what are the corresponding environmental implications? First of all, we can observe that digital technology in general is the first truly *silent* technology ever created. It is therefore ironic that in order to communicate with it (in the sense of getting information in and out of a computer), we inevitably introduce noise. One only has to visit a computer room with its fans to keep everything cool, its humming fluorescent lights, and its whirring disk drives, to hear that the use of this technology is far from silent. Most such rooms are perfect illustrations of a lo-fi/high-tech environment. More subtle are the sounds that are deliberately introduced into machines to replace the aural cues that people supposedly need. Computer terminals often generate audible clicks when a key is hit in order to give the user the response expected from mechanical and electrical typewriters. Even the digital clock radio has its distinctive click as it turns the minutes, as if the aural cues of time cannot be left behind.

However, the digital sounds that are populating the new soundscape to the greatest extent are the ones in video games, toys, appliances, and even telephones. Buzzes, beeps, and chirps are programmed as signals to the users of everything from pocket calculators and watches to automobiles. And the ever increasing use of the simulated sounds of engines, guns, human, and alien voices, as well as musical tones, in nearly every form of game and entertainment is inescapable to the listener. The paradox is that such sounds can be generated cheaply through the microcircuitry of the "chip" by which any specialized circuit can be miniaturized. However, in order for the production of such a chip to be cost effective, it must be mass produced. Therefore, in terms of sound quality, the crudest algorithms for producing sound are used, sampling rates and bit sizes are scaled down, and the cheapest loudspeakers send the sound to the listener. Hence, the quality of mass-produced digital sound is poorer than almost any analog audio signal, and the public, entranced by the novelty and convinced of the inevitable progress of technology, tolerates the new arrivals to the soundscape without really listening to them.

Video games, however, have attracted public concern, not for their sounds, but for the social implications of their being a fad, and perhaps an addiction, for children of all ages. Others point to the mental agility and hand-eye coordination that skill at such games promotes. The crudeness of the digital sound may be aesthetically offensive, but it is an expected part of the reward system inherited from pinball machines and a stimulation for the player. What happens, however, when such machines are grouped together in an arcade is that the combination of all of them, besides producing an unimaginable cacophony of acoustic violence, generates a noise level in excess of 80 dB and a completely lo-fi, non-listening environment. The danger to hearing and socialization is probably no worse than the typical bar or lounge with amplified music, but it is also no better.

Interest in computer music in the form of digital synthesizers has also increased over the last few years. Many personal computers incorporate digital synthesis of one sort or another. Unfortunately, however, the quality of sound that is produced is usually no better than that of an electronic organ (which dates from the 1930s), and the emphasis on keyboard control ignores most of what has happened musically since then as well. The easiest type of digital synthesis to implement in mass-produced circuitry is fixed waveform synthesis, as we described it earlier in connection with electronic music. The uniformity of spectrum and dullness of timbre does not change with a digital realization; if anything, digital technology makes it even more exactly uniform and boring. However, perhaps the experience of actually making music, with small portable instruments such as the Casio, after some decades devoted mainly to its consumption (following the demise of the parlor upright), will change the public's concept of musicmaking and promote a greater interest in its more experimental, electroacoustic forms, as described in chapter 13. New technology by itself—without careful design or an understanding of how it can improve communicational patterns—as often as not degrades the soundscape and alienates the listener.

10

The Listener As Consumer

In the last two chapters we have documented some of the enormous changes in the (re-)production, manipulation, and consumption of sound that electroacoustic technology has brought about. The changes affect the very nature of listening by transforming some of its most basic characteristics. In the discussion we frequently referred to paradoxes, ironies, and the "double-edged sword" of technology because, as with most innovations, there are always conflicting implications to change. New potentialities always have their price. We could easily polarize the issues involved, pro and con, but we would miss many of the subtleties inherent in technological change. In this chapter we will examine, as objectively as possible, some of the dualities with which the listener is faced and the fundamentally new role the listener plays, i.e., that of the consumer.

Sound and listening often seem to be a paradigm for other types of relationships within society and the environment. Therefore, the changes in listening habits brought about by audio technology are not only important to the student of communication, but may also interest the more general observer of society. For instance, the experience of "cutting oneself off" from the environment through portable headphone listening, or the deliberate use of radio and background sound to create one's *own* environment, may be symptomatic of a general trend away from environmental awareness and community involvement. Listening involves personal experience that is more immediate than, for instance, changes in demographic patterns or economic policies (although the effects of the latter are certainly regarded more seriously by most individuals). It is a property of the mediating function of sound that changes in it or the way it functions both reflect other changes in society and, in turn, bring about further change. Trends in listening habits, therefore, may closely correspond to other social and psychological trends or be the precursor of developments yet to come. Consumerism for the listener may only be in its infancy.

Many listeners seem unaware of the relationship they have to technology and how their listening habits have been shaped by it. Some may even feel frightened by equipment and alienated from using it. They may be surprised by the idea that they *already* have a deep-seated relationship to technology that has been conditioned by years of exposure to its products. The power of technology in our lives is disturbing at first, particularly when it affects something as personal as listening. However, it is useful, and perhaps even liberating, to examine one's own listening and consumer habits, not to feel guilty but to understand them and take responsibility for their effects.

Extension and Simplification

The fact that technology is intended to extend human capabilities is well known; that it is accompanied by a parallel trend toward simplification may be surprising. Given the intimate relation in public rhetoric between technology and such words as "progress," "advances," "innovation," or even "development," it is not surprising that most people associate technological change with increased complexity. Such clichés as "our fast paced world" or "this complex society" reveal a deeply felt belief that all change leads to greater complexity. It is tempting to add to this equation the further development of the human brain, which we are told has not evolved to its full potential. Technology is even credited with bringing about a "new consciousness" or an "expanded awareness." That it brings about change is not an issue; what needs further examination is that those changes which seem to promote a greater complexity between the elements of society may be counterbalanced by corresponding simplifications of those relationships.

We have already described many instances of the dual nature of electroacoustic processes vis à vis simplicity and complexity. The ability to "abstract" a sound from its original context allows unlimited possibilities for it to be put into new relationships. New sound and syntax lead the listener to new meanings, and new mediating roles for sound create new forms of communication, at least potentially. On the other hand, the same technology allows exact repetition, precise uniformity, and mass reproduction that provide *less* information to the brain and much less variety than in the acoustic equivalents.

For instance, the same uniformity in electrical power that allows sophisticated machine design results in its acoustic character being highly repetitive and undifferentiated from other machines. The philosophy of machine automation leads to the equivalent in commerce, i.e., product uniformity, modularity, and streamlined processes. A greater number of products may be available, but the differences between them may be less. The phonograph record, for instance, makes it possible to hear the words, music, and soundscape of practically any culture, past or present. Compared with this potential wealth, the range of recordings that are readily available, and actually owned and listened to by most people, is amazingly small. Similarly with radio, the range of choices, even on the FM band, is quite limited and tends to be grouped into five or six main types of format. What technology extends, its organization (in terms of economic factors such as marketing and distribution) simplifies.

Much the same can be said for the depth of listening, as well as its breadth. When we hear too much, we actually listen to very little. When we know that a sound can always be repeated, it is easy not to be very attentive the first time. When sounds from every part of the globe come to us instantly, the world seems to shrink to the size of a "global village," but do we feel any greater sense of neighborly responsibility? And the "faster paced" the world seems to become, as reflected in the tempo of commercial radio, for instance, the more time seems not to move at all. Even in acoustics, the "whitest" and most neutral of all sounds is the one that changes randomly the most (i.e., noise); it may have the most information, but it also has the least meaning.

The attention and concentration that is required to listen carefully and understand sonic relationships deeply is generally not encouraged by the lo-fi environments in which we too often live or work. Although steady sounds are less distracting to one's concentration, they also contribute to an environment with less acoustic definition, less meaningful information, and less reason to promote interaction. Moreover, the information processing nature of the brain dictates that when too much information is presented to it in too disorganized a fashion, there is a tendency to "skim" the content, rather than analyze it carefully. In other words, more may be experienced, but less is absorbed.

A particular case of skimming in listening occurs with the use of sound in radio commercials. A typical commercial lasting 30 seconds may incorporate one or more voices, sometimes acting out a short story or situation, mixed with music and sound effects. One might expect such a sequence to contain a great deal of information, given this density of elements. However, commercials are designed to simplify the message such that it "gets across" even when the listener is not paying attention to it. The sounds used are not to be listened to directly; they are intended only to evoke a response or association. And because the desired response must be the same for the largest audience, these associations are stereotypes, just as the characters and music are.

Most ads are not trying to convey specific information, unless intended for a limited time only as with an upcoming event. For instance, products such as records and films are never advertised with specific prices or locations included; instead, the *name* is emphasized (since it is new and must be memorized). It is surrounded with sounds that suggest the imagery that the advertiser wants associated with the product. Whether the image is excitement, escape, happiness, relief from anxiety, security, or social success, all sounds used, from the type of voice to the style of music, language, and sound effects, are designed to convey it. Because very little actual information is to be recalled, the product need only be surrounded by a "psychological context" so that when the decision to buy is made, one choice will come to mind with the proper "reward" attached to it.

Such ads are good examples of the paradox between the increased complexity of juxtaposition of sounds made possible through technology, and the resulting simplicity of the information that is conveyed. The listener has only to make the correct associations on cue. Moreover, the listener is identified as being a member of a "target group" based on demographics of age, social class, and economic status. Each subgroup is appealed to with different styles of music, voice, and product presentation. In fact, each radio station designs its format for such a specific group. The style is always readily identifiable, even with very short exposure, and therefore the listener immediately recognizes it and responds accordingly. The relationship of listener to station becomes static and predictable.

A more subtle example of our theme comes with listening to phonograph records or tapes. The ability to become extremely familiar with a piece of music through more frequent hearings than normally possible with live performances can potentially lead to a greater understanding of it. Moreover, different performance versions can be compared, and historical changes can be observed. In the case of mainly improvised music, such as jazz and many non-Western musics, the permanence of the recording extends its influence. In fact, it would be hard to account for the spread of familiarity with different styles of jazz performance in this century apart from the recordings that have made them accessible. Likewise, the renewed interest in early music stems largely from recordings made by a few groups who specialize in it.

On the other hand, recordings become so familiar that they resemble pictures on the wall that always seem the same and demand little attention. One may even become so used to a particular recording that a live performance may be irritating because it differs from the "old favorite," or because it cannot acoustically reproduce the technically enhanced studio sound. Even the flaws and imperfections in a recording may become permanently ingrained in the memory; one may be surprised when the live performance doesn't "skip" or "pop" in the same place, or in the case of opera, when it doesn't pause for turning the record over! Perhaps the most typical listening association that is built up with a familiar recording is the anticipated beginning. Even if the different cuts on a record are quite unrelated, their progression becomes so familiar that one "hears" the beginning of the next one, at least mentally, before it starts. I'm not referring to the actual "pre-echo" caused by print-through between layers of tape or grooves of a record, though this phenomenon may assist the mental anticipation.

All of these examples point to an increasing standardization and commoditization of the listening experience. The mass product may be a technological extension, but it sounds the same everywhere in the world, every time it is reproduced. Its consumption *simplifies* the relationship of the listener to sound and contributes to an homogeneity of the soundscape. However, electroacoustic technology also produces different kinds of listening attitudes which are extensions of those found in the acoustic world; we will now examine two of them.

Analytical and Distracted Listening

In chapter 2 we identified three levels of listening that function in the natural acoustic environment, namely listening-in-search, listening-in-readiness, and background listening. Each represents a way in which the brain processes information and determines its significance. Also, each type of listening is valuable for survival, orientation, and all forms of communication. Our discussion of the changes brought about for the listener by technology suggests that each of these forms has adapted itself to the new communicational environment. The active nature of listening-in-search is extended to what may be called "analytical" listening where the sound itself is searched for information. Background listening, on the other hand, can be closely identified with the experience of "distracted" listening, that is, where the listener is actively engaged in other activity. We will begin by examining the former.

In situations where sound is the conveyer of information, it functions in a quasilinguistic sense as a "signifier" of that information. One identifies a particular sound as indicating the presence of an object or person, or as reflecting a specific state of the environment. But once that information has been received, the sound itself is "discarded," in the sense that it is not important *what* sound brought the information. The linguist Ferdinand de Saussure referred to this property of language as "the arbitrary nature of the sign" (Saussure, 1966, p. 67), and to some extent the same concept applies in acoustic communication.

In any example of listening-in-search, one scans the environment for a particular sound of importance, or in the case of echolocation, one listens for the environment's response to the sound one has produced. We listen for the footfall of someone expected, for the clock to strike the hour, or for the rain to slacken off. Whereas in the linguistic case *any* vocal sound can represent an object or idea as long as it is "agreed to" by the community, patterns and associations in the soundscape are built up over the years around *specific* sounds, and therefore their qualities become associated with their meanings. But, as in the linguistic case, once the pattern has been identified and its meaning assessed, the sound is probably dropped from short-term memory.

For instance, we may be able to recognize the footsteps of a friend from among hundreds of others, but to describe the sound with enough accuracy that someone else could do likewise is usually very difficult, not only because of the problem of language, but also because the sound is not *consciously* analyzed and stored in terms of its parameters.

Now, it might be argued that in an echolocation example, where a blind person listens for environmental coloration of the tap of a cane, the sound is in fact being analyzed. The process is analytical in the sense that it is a property of the sound that signifies the information, but the cognitive process is based on pattern recognition in which the timbral coloration and reverberation cues are compared to thousands of previously experienced examples. The process is largely unconscious, as suggested by the fact that until fairly recently it was controversial whether the sense of hearing, and not some other sensory mode, provides the necessary information to a blind person, based on what such people say about how they orient themselves. Only when experiments were performed in which each sensory mode was isolated in turn did it become obvious that when hearing was blocked, the ability to navigate was impaired (Supa et al., 1944; Griffin, 1959, p. 131 ff.).

How does electroacoustic technology make listening more analytical? Most obviously, it takes the sound out of time and allows it to be repeated, as well as subjected to machine analysis that renders it visible. A somewhat similar analysis occurs when we repeat a word over and over until the linguistic meaning is minimized and the sound itself remains. We begin to note the acoustic peculiarities of the sound, much the same as when children play with words, stretching them into fantastical shapes *as sounds*. Repetition allows the sound to enter a kind of "laboratory" of perception where it may be dissected.

A second type of situation in which analysis occurs is when a tape recording of an interview or conversation is played back and the participant becomes an observer. One's attention in any interchange is constantly shifting between oneself and the other, so it is common to miss a lot of what the other person is saying and to be unaware of the effect of one's own behavior. By extricating oneself from the immediacy of the situation and listening to the patterns of communication with the perspective of the intervening time, one can listen far more analytically, and perhaps detect deeper implications than were obvious in the original situation. Needless to say, most of that kind of acoustic subtlety is lost in a transcription of the same material.

A tape recording of any environment, when listened to carefully, makes us more analytically aware of it. Without the interference of visual and other sensory input, and without the kind of focusing we constantly use in listening to shut out what we don't need, the tape recording presents us with as objective an aural representation of a subject as possible (the colorations described in the last chapter notwithstanding). By re-presenting the environment to us, the recording allows us to perceive it afresh.

Analytical Listening in the Sound Studio

Another type of analysis in listening occurs when one has the sound on tape in an editing studio. Once one can actively *manipulate* the sound, even in the simplest manner, such as cutting and re-arranging it, one begins to hear the sound as structure as well as content. One notices, for instance, where there are pauses and breaks because these are good points for splicing, but also one comes to realize how these spaces *function* in spoken language. If such pauses or "extraneous" sounds (such as "mm," "uh," etc.) are removed, the meaning may be altered and the natural flow of the speech damaged. For instance, if the space between sentences or phrases is eliminated, the listener is deprived of the pause that allows what has been said to be absorbed. Violent "jump cuts" between phrases and sentences are frequently heard on radio when material is too closely spliced together to sound natural. From the point of view of semantics, one can say there is no "closure"; the listener is constantly propelled onto the next idea. Verbal pauses have the same importance as punctuation in written language, and their removal has a similar effect to the absence of punctuation in prose. Not only is speech harder to listen to, but there is no time to understand what is being said, either directly or implicitly.

In the media world where "time is money," editing is necessary to force content to fit a given format. In the acoustic world, form arises from the shape of content, but in the media, the time frame, arbitrary as it is, is the shaping factor. Even sports events must have "time-outs" to allow for commercials, and in news reporting, what someone says must fit the time slot allotted. Issues are simplified and "catchwords" predominate. On television news, the voice of the interview subject is blanked out (even when one *sees* the person speaking) and only allowed to surface for a brief sentence or two, selected by the news editor as being the most important. The TV journalist, in control of the mike and in a favorable camera position, interprets the item in a concise summary—something one presumably cannot trust the interview subject to do succinctly enough.

Even when the time constraint is not as rigorous, as with documentaries and interviews, the same principle seems to dominate. Voice material is cut, not to preserve the natural rhythm of speech, but to fit into tight structures for short attention span listeners. As a result, everyone starts sounding the same—concise, articulate, fastpaced. When was the last time you heard a storyteller extemporizing on radio, or even a natural sounding conversation? Those whose voice and manner of speech do not conform to the concise style, or which cannot be edited into a facsimile of it, are never heard on radio or TV. Moreover, those who have a glib verbal facility for speaking that way naturally are favored as "lively" interview subjects, regardless of what they have to say.

One of the many lessons of the editing room is that structure shapes and determines the communicative impact of content. The very fact of being able to design structure in relation to content makes one more analytically aware of it, even in conventional listening situations. If simple editing has this effect, then the extended possibilities of audio manipulation and mixing of signals enlarge the scope to amazing proportions. However, one only has to hear conventional media productions to discover that the potential does not guarantee the actuality. Transformation and mixing techniques become standardized, and like strict time formats, they shape the content, no matter what the content may be. Under the pressure of production deadlines and conformity to mass appeal (essentially "what sells"), audio techniques are applied indiscriminately to all material and all situations. Listen, for instance, to the way in which background music is used in most productions. It is almost always totally unrelated to the subject matter, having been chosen because it can "hook" the audience's attention and satisfy their conventional expectations. It is generally faded in and out at will and juxtaposed with other pieces, regardless of the musical validity of such manipulations. And in the case of visual media, music is used to overlay the content of the visual image with an emotional and cultural layer that *interprets* the image for the audience and manipulates their response.

Finally, let us contrast such media clichés with the possibilities found in the modern electroacoustic sound studio (Appleton & Perera, 1975; Keane, 1980). Even the simplest manipulation of a sound reveals its structure and promotes an analytical understanding of it. To use Piaget's formulation, to know an object is to act on it. A simple drop in speed of a tape, for instance, lengthens each sound and lowers its pitch; one hears the sound "in slow motion" as it were. Details that pass by too quickly in "real time" now become apparent. Interestingly enough, once discovered at slower speeds, these characteristics often stay evident when the sound is heard again normally. In other words, there seems to be a transference in perception from the technical transformation back to the original.

The repetition of a sound via a tape loop allows it to be studied in greater detail as well. Timbral manipulation via filtering or equalization changes the sound, but also makes one more aware of its components (such as the low frequency part, the middle, or the high, and the particular dynamic quality of each). Spatial modification, such as the addition of reverberation or placement in a stereo or quadraphonic space, allows the sound to be heard in different environments. Finally, more aggressive manipulation, such as electronic chopping or modulating of the signal, tape echo, and feedback, allow new sounds or sound patterns to be derived from the original, and all these "offsprings" reflect the character of the parent.

Sound synthesis—the artificial creation of sound—adds a further dimension to this process, one which to an even greater extent promotes analytical listening. Because one has precise control over each acoustic parameter during synthesis, each change one makes must be evaluated by listening analytically to the result in order to effect further changes. Traditional analog synthesis, as in the voltage-controlled electronic synthesizer, involves the designer in an interactive process where each change in a knob or other setting leads to a corresponding change in the sound. In contrast, digital synthesis usually involves a numerical specification of the desired parameter value, though more recent systems allow such values to be determined interactively as well. In all of these cases the composer can be said to compose the sound as well as the structure within which it is placed.

Technological control over the internal structure of sound has naturally led to a renewed interest in timbre, and the desire to give it a more important role in the compositional process. Timbre in traditional Western musical forms has largely had a supportive function to keep various melodic parts separate and to provide "color" or a specific quality to support various musical effects, e.g., an oboe or English horn for a "pastoral" melody, or a flute for bird-like images. The enlargement of orchestral resources to incorporate new colors, such as by the addition of more percussion instruments and new styles of performance, has gradually expanded the range of timbre found in instrumental music from the end of the 19th century to the present (Erickson, 1975; Reynolds, 1975; Battcock, 1981). Electroacoustic technology extends the range of timbre further by making it possible to bring *any sound* into a composition through tape recording, and to create new sounds through the transformation of recorded ones or by electronic synthesis. Although we have only introduced these possibilities here, we will return to them in more detail in the final two chapters.

Distracted Listening

We have already indicated many of the ways in which electroacoustic technology favors what in chapter 2 we termed "background listening." All of the factors in electrification that produce a new soundscape of redundant, low information sounds are contributors, as is the prevalence of background music, whether the commercial product, radio, or stereo units. Exact repetition and predictable formats in broadcasting also reduce the amount of new information reaching the listener. And finally, the general trend away from the aural sense as a source of information in daily life tends to make people focus their attention elsewhere and keep nearly all sound in the background.

How does the electroacoustic situation differ from the kind of background listening found in the traditional soundscape? The distracted listener superficially resembles one for whom a particular sound is in the background of perception. Neither is paying attention, but presumably each can if the need arises. With the distracted listener, however, at least two aspects of the listening process are different. First of all, the sound itself is often one that would normally have been considered a foreground sound, such as voice and music. Except in the case where such sounds are overheard, speech and music have traditionally been intentional forms of communication meant to be listened to as foreground sound. Today they increasingly occur as background sounds which the distracted listener blocks out.

Secondly, the distracted listener usually *chooses* the sound which is kept in the background. The use of radio, records, tapes, and even television as an accompaniment to daily life is a frequent occurrence. Through repetition, a psychological dependence builds up between the listener and the background sound (Mendelsohn, 1964). What begins in the natural soundscape as the brain's ability to focus attention on what is of immediate importance and screen out what is not, changes to a situation where the listener *needs* the background sound in order to function. What are the reasons and uses for this type of listening?

The most general answer is that the sound is used to fill a gap or deficiency in the environment, whether psychological or physical. If the environment is noisy or distracting, background music (or even white noise) will mask it. If an activity is boring or frustrating, pleasant music will make it seem easier to endure. Loneliness and lack of personal contact may be countered by use of radio. And for the young, popular music and commercial radio provide an instant form of peer group image to adopt.

The problem, if there is one, with the role of background sound as a surrogate in these situations is that, at the very least, it does not change the problem or fill the deficiency—it only appears to. The intruding noises are still there, jobs are still unfulfilling, time only seems to pass more meaningfully through the artificial structure of radio, and the "friends" that the radio offers are the same for thousands of others, with no possibility of a real, personal relationship. However, more serious perhaps, is the fact that the surrogate relationship often becomes a dependency that prevents, or at least discourages, the person from taking any action that will lead to a lasting solution. The media in particular feed on these needs and seek to perpetuate them in order to keep their audience's allegiance. One station offers to "get you through the day" or help you "survive the rush hour," presumably by stimulating enough nervous energy so that you can cope with it. Another reminds you with every station promotion that it comes "from your friends" at the station; never have the actions of friends been as self-serving as this!

The challenge for radio is to design its format so that the commercial messages get through to the distracted listener. The solution is through careful control of the audio signal and the sequencing of program content; we will document typical examples in the next chapter. The intention of such techniques is to maintain the listener's attention as long as possible and promote station loyalty. Frequent use is made of the station call letters, logo and "headers" (i.e., phrases that are frequently used to describe the station), combined with positive associations of "what they do for you." Promotions where listeners are given rewards for advertising the station (by displaying posters or stickers with the station's logo on it, or even by answering the phone by saying "I listen to . . . ") increase ratings and allow the station to command a higher price for its advertising. In essence, the station buys the audience and sells it to the advertisers (Smythe, 1981).

The use of frequent repetition, whether of a radio station logo or a commercial product theme, makes such sounds function like a keynote for the distracted listener. Whereas the keynote sound, through its prevalence, reflects a basic fact about the environment, the frequent repetition of station logos and product jingles is intended to entrench the product in the memory and surround it with a particular image. The association can be built up even in the distracted listener, because the sound is still processed by the brain and the incoming pattern compared to previously experienced ones. In fact, storage of the pattern with the associations of its surrounding context is probably *better* done at an unconscious level, because the point of desired action is not in the present but at a future date when choices are to be made. Too conscious a level of perception might promote rejection; the seed takes better root without such screening. Distracted listening, therefore, is a profitable phenomenon for the advertiser, and so it is not surprising that many aspects of the media encourage it as a habit, even outside the commercial situation.

Consumerism

From the examples already given in this chapter, one can see that the listener can be a consumer not only in the sense of buying recorded sound. Specific listening habits assist the consumer process and are encouraged by it. The point where persuasion becomes manipulation is difficult to determine; however, it is clear that new technology is quickly seconded to the arsenal of advertising techniques and that through the results, public awareness and attitudes (including listening habits) are being shaped. The sheer prevalence and economic power involved means that we cannot avoid or ignore what is happening. It is unlikely that any of the traditional creative disciplines have access to either the technical sophistication of the commercial world or the audience it attracts. Yet, the arts must deal with the public sensibilities that have been significantly shaped by commercial forces. And so must the educators, legislators, and other professions.

In case there remains any doubt in the reader's mind as to the amount of time the average North American spends listening to electroacoustic sound, one may refer to reports such as the 1979 Nielson study which shows that television viewing alone ranges from about 23 to 38 hours per week for various age groups.[1] In my own survey of 156 university students entering

---

[1]A. C. Nielson Co., *1979 Nielson Report of Television,* Illinois: A. C. Nielson Co., 1979, pp. 8–9.

TABLE 1

Survey of Electroacoustic Listening Experience among Students:
Time Spent Listening to Electroacoustic Media by 156 University Students on a Weekday and Weekend Day

	Weekday Totals				Weekend Totals				Estimated Weekly Totals (Hours)
	Self Minutes	Other Minutes	Total Minutes	Total %	Self Minutes	Other Minutes	Total Minutes	Total %	
T.V.	63.5	44.7	108.2	27.0	89.3	61.0	150.3	27.6	14.0
Radio	78.2	50.5	128.7	32.2	92.6	47.4	140.0	25.7	15.4
Stereo/tapes	58.0	25.3	83.3	20.8	88.7	56.3	145.0	26.6	11.8
Film	18.0	0.4	18.4	4.6	35.0	3.9	38.9	7.1	2.8
Telephone	19.4	16.7	36.1	9.0	21.5	19.1	40.6	7.4	4.4
P.A./intercom, etc.	4.0	6.4	10.4	2.6	8.6	8.6	17.7	3.2	1.4
Other	6.3	8.8	15.1	3.8	6.7	6.8	13.5	2.5	1.7
TOTAL	247.4	152.8	400.2 (6 hr. 40 min.)		342.4	203.1	545.5 (9 hr. 5 min.)		51.5

% in Background or "Other" Category

	Weekday	Weekend
T.V.	41.3	40.6
Radio	39.2	33.9
Stereo	30.4	38.8
Film	2.2	10.0
Telephone	46.3	47.0

	% Audio Only	*Audio + Visual Media*
Weekday	64.6	31.6
Weekend	62.9	34.7

an introductory course in electroacoustic communication between 1979 and 1982, in which they were asked to monitor their electroacoustic media listening habits during one weekday and one weekend day, the total estimated consumption per week for all forms was in excess of 50 hours, as shown in Table 1. Interestingly enough, radio listening accounted for the highest percentage of the total, particularly during the week, and the total of all audio-only media (radio, stereo, telephone, P.A.) exceeded that of audio+visual media (television, film) by a two-to-one ratio. The students were further asked to distinguish between active or foreground listening ("self" initiated) and that which is background or overheard ("other" activated). Although this distinction is not entirely identical to the distracted listening versus foreground listening concepts already discussed, it is somewhat similar (one cannot be a truly distracted listener and monitor the activity at the same time). The results show that television, radio, and records or tapes are frequently (up to 30% or 40% of the time) classified as background listening, with the latter increasing dramatically on weekends. If nothing else, the study shows that the amount of exposure people have to technologically reproduced sound is sufficiently high (6 to 9 hours per day) to have a significant influence on listening and other habits.

In conclusion, let us attempt to summarize the implications of consumerism for listeners and the listening process. First, there is the obvious commoditization of goods and services (i.e., audio equipment and products, recordings, functional prerecorded music, etc.), as well as the less obvious commoditization of the listening *experience* itself. Car radio or home stereo listening, disco environments, the acoustic "wallpaper" of background music, heavily amplified concerts, portable headphone listening, and brand names such as "Dolby stereo" film presentations, are all examples of listening experiences which one buys as a consumer. Moreover, such consumption can be as conspicuous as any other form of prestige-oriented consumerism. What one buys (aurally) is as much an economic status indicator as any other class factor.

Commoditization brings with it a standardization and simplification of both form and content that is consistent with mass production philosophy. The nature of the simplification has already been discussed at length in this chapter and the previous one. The general implication is that the product becomes a static object, not a unique and dynamic entity. It also takes on an "exchange value" that usually exceeds its "use value." In the natural acoustic environment, sounds only have use value, or else they are ignored. The economics of Western culture gradually evolved to the point where musical experience entered the marketplace in a similar manner to the buying and selling of art objects. However, it remained for 20th-century technology to provide the technical basis for storage, mass reproduction, and global transmission that allows the aural experience of audio products to have primarily exchange value.

Secondly, consumerism changes the basic nature of the flow of aural communication. Whereas traditionally, the sound source is closely linked with the "communicator," today's audio advertising and audio products are the outer voice of powerful, but hidden, commercial interests. Exactly who is one listening to? Superficially, the sources may still be voices, musicians, environmental noises, or synthesized sound effects, but we know that these sources are not really speaking for themselves; they are the aural equivalent of the graphic advertisement and the billboard. They are sent by someone else, and that someone is no longer another individual. And like mute objects that can be seen but do not see, such voices are heard but do not hear. The listener listens, but is not listened to.

A great deal of literature concerning media has debated whether they involve a one-way or two-way flow of communication. The technocratic argument sees the one-way *signal* flow as the source of the problem and proposes technical solutions (e.g., two-way television such as the Telidon system). Those favoring a critical communicational approach point out that even if the media signal is one-way, the consumer responds through the economic force of purchasing habits that support the commercial media (i.e., radio isn't free). For the listener, this means that the chain of communication enters via the ear but continues on via the pocketbook, and not via the mouth. The listening consumer is rendered mute, and perhaps this fact alone accounts for the lack of emphasis on speech skills, voice quality, and rhetoric in public life. The soundscape may be too noisy for conversation, but the marketplace is completely deaf!

Finally, the consumer's use of audio as a surrogate, filling in the physical and emotional gaps in life, and the resultant dependency it creates, makes the listener vulnerable to the explicit and implicit values which are inevitably communicated by those using the media, whether commercial, governmental, religious, or private interests. Television has been particularly singled out for the way in which its content communicates middle class values and portrays social stereotypes. The export of such products from the U.S. throughout the world, often flooding local markets, is justified by the American concept of the "free flow" of information (Schiller, 1969, 1973). We will return to the larger impact of audio media on the community in chapter 12. Here we will consider how consumerism in listening assists the propagation of sexist values.

The audio industry itself is completely male dominated; therefore it is not surprising that its products and services often show a sexist bias. Audio technology, as a part of technology in general, is clearly understood as a seat of power, whether economic, social, cultural, or communicational, and men have never been far from any source of power. The situation seems even more irrational than in traditional industries, because there is clearly no biological or social basis for the discrimination. Yet, sexism flourishes in audio-related matters, as one can quickly see from a typical audio engineering convention or the clientele at your local stereo component store. Judging from the populations of the young found in video game arcades and home computer outlets, the male dominance in technology is not likely to change with the next generation either. In its worst forms such sexism takes on an ethos of "techno-macho" where the technical possibilities of audio power and control are reflected in individual behavior.

Thus, the ads for stereo equipment emphasize power and control, not for the sake of "audio quality" which is the ostensible justification, but for the image they create for the (usually male) buyer. In radio advertising, where voice is everything, the bass-boosted male voice is the norm when success, confidence, and power are being sold, particularly in ads aimed at the young. For the older audience, a more sedate version of the same voice serves to emphasize paternal protectiveness, stability, or authority. Similarly, female voices are often portrayed stereotypically and in a manner intended to be heard from a male perspective.

With radio and television functioning as a frequent accompaniment to daily life, the communication of such values seems impossible to escape. Moreover, the distracted listener does not consciously screen and evaluate what is being heard, and therefore is a prime target for what might be termed the subliminal inculcation of values. In fact, one might even argue that since the aural faculty cannot be "turned off" like the visual, and because it has developed to handle input at several simultaneous levels, it is a more effective modality to assist advertising. Comparison, though, is not the point, and in television the two are designed to act in a complementary fashion, although it is often observed that the aural part can stand alone, because advertisers know that people often are not watching commercials, but are within earshot.

The path to a solution may simply be a matter of exposure to alternatives. Just as North American children may grow up thinking that society is like what they see on television (with its high proportion of doctors, policemen, entertainers, sports figures, and middle class families), so too the listener is exposed to a limited range of music, advertising images, time flows, and even types of listening experiences through the commercial audio media. Critical listening and a careful evaluation of existing and developing technologies are necessary for the individual to understand how to create alternatives and regain control.

11

The Electroacoustic Media: Audio Mediation

In chapter 4 we introduced a simple model for acoustic communication in its various forms (speech, music, soundscape) that shows structure as the mediating force between sound and meaning. That is, the way in which a sequence of sound is structured determines the type of meaning, or levels of meaning, it communicates, provided the listener has the appropriate tacit knowledge (i.e., competence) to decode it. Although the types of structure and operational rules vary considerably among acoustic communication systems, concepts about structure and syntax are needed for any communicational analysis. Therefore, in describing audio media, we will emphasize a structural type of analysis as distinct from a purely content-oriented one. Moreover, because audio forms of communication are artificial languages, not natural forms, their structural features represent explicit (though not necessarily conscious) design choices that are made for specific functional purposes.

What distinguishes a model as communicational, in contrast to those arising within the study of a particular system (e.g., linguistic, musical), is the inclusion of the pragmatic level, that is, the notion of *context*. For instance, music is traditionally analyzed for how it is structured, not how it functions socially. Communicational meaning can only be assessed when a message is understood within its context. The meaning of a message can differ when it occurs within a different context, and conversely, two different messages may have the same meaning within a single context. (What does a piece by Debussy mean when heard in a supermarket?) Therefore, the context in which the communication occurs must be included within any media analysis. Unfortunately, from the perspective of simplicity, media contexts are multilevelled and include the contexts of both the sender and receiver, and in the case of mass media, the hidden context of the social, economic, and political role of the medium within "the system."

Our analysis in this chapter will focus on radio, mainly because it is a clear example of a purely audio medium with well-defined structural properties and functions. Of course, radio has been overshadowed by television in terms of public awareness, advertising revenues, and critical analysis. The survey results quoted in the previous chapter indicate, however, that radio listening occupies at least as significant a portion of the daily listening experience (of the people quoted) as other media. Except for Tony Schwartz (1973), who has a long history of involvement with sound recording, media analysts have concentrated on television and tended to reflect a visual bias, despite warnings from McLuhan (1964) and others that modern electronic media behave according to auditory models, in contrast to the visually-dominant print media. It is assumed that the concepts introduced here in terms of radio will find direct applicability to other media where audio–visual relationships must be considered.

Our approach emphasizes the *mediating* role of a medium between its consumers and their environments. In chapter 1 we suggested that sound always mediates the relationship of the individual to the environment, creating, influencing, and shaping habitual patterns. Throughout part I we showed how those relationships may be interactive or alienating, binding or isolating, therapeutic or oppressive. Electroacoustic technology, by breaking the constraints of the acoustic world, reshapes those relationships by extending traditional ones and by creating entirely new forms.

In our discussion of the listener as consumer, we argued that commoditization of the listening experience changes the fundamental role of listening from the traditional interface between the person and the environment to a one-way, passive consumption of audio products. The person's response is voiced in economic terms through purchasing habits. We also pointed out that media consumption may create a psychological dependency for the individual through its surrogate function in contexts that are incomplete in themselves. However, as with all technology, the mediating role it plays also offers the promise that new and better communicative relationships may be formed, whether extensions of the natural or those that are artificially designed. It is these alternatives which we will explore in the last two chapters. However, for alternatives to be successful they need to be informed by a clear understanding of existing practice, and no better example can be found than the present-day radio medium.

Form and Content in Radio

Most descriptions of radio programming are based either on content analysis of the program material, including advertising (Simpkins et al., 1974), or on the estimation of radio "reach" related to the listening habits of the audience (Young, 1972). Although these approaches have merit for their intended purposes, they do not deal with the structural aspects of radio programming which affect its impact, specifically its "holding power." In most cases, these studies assume an idealized listener who is reasonably attentive and presumably *remembers* specific pieces of information. Such an assumption could be made in the earlier days of radio when many commentators saw the educational force of radio for "serious listening" (Lazarsfeld, 1940), but today one cannot assume this level of listening. Actual listeners are more likely to be distracted, that is, engaged in other activity with the radio on as a background accompaniment or masking agent of unwanted sounds in the environment (Mendelsohn, 1964). Content analysis alone cannot show how advertising succeeds in communicating to this kind of listener.

The content analysis approach treats advertising from the literary point of view, counting and classifying words and images, to the ironic extent that radio resembles a printed text to be analyzed, rather than an aural experience. For instance, in one study, award-winning commercials were found to use:

> more action words, . . . shorter words and shorter sentences, fewer uncommon words, fewer abstract words, more personal or human interest words, and were *written in a more readable manner.* [emphasis mine] (Felsenthal et al., 1971, p. 312)

They also were found to employ a "suspense factor" and a "non-repetition factor" to maintain listeners' interest. Although such findings are consistent with the model of the distracted listener to whom only the simplest and most accessible features of the ad "get through," it is questionable whether these *textual* attributes alone reflect the true cause of the commercials' success with consumers, or simply the judges' opinions as to what constitutes a good commercial.

Radio is a highly stylized, artificial medium where program format has evolved into distinct styles that are usually recognizable to experienced listeners after a few seconds of exposure. Content analysis ignores what is most familiar to the listener—the types of voices heard, the manner of delivery, the use of background music and sound effects, and the location of the ad within the overall program structure, including intro's or extro's from a live announcer. How things are said (structure), and within what context they are said, are argued here as having a greater influence on the distracted listener than content. Another way to clarify the relation of content and structure is to relate them to the parallel functions of *station selection* and *audience holding power*.

The purpose of radio is to attract the largest audience and hold its attention. In the case of commercial radio, the audience thus delivered can be sold to advertisers (Smythe, 1981). The better the station's ratings with listeners, the more valuable its time on the advertising market. Since the audience is a commodity, the larger it is and the more buying power it represents, the more valuable the station's time becomes on the market. Program content, or more accurately its *style* of content, is what initially attracts the audience. The radio listener usually justifies the choice of station on the basis of a preferred style of music, announcer, program material, and information. In fact, all such content is specifically designed to appeal to a particular social class and age group as its "target audience." We argue, however, that such content-oriented choices are simply the *minimal* criteria for the listener; program content must minimally satisfy the greatest percentage of prospective station listeners, but beyond this basic criterion of acceptability it has little importance. Once the listener has accepted the station's content and style, the question remains as to what *holds* the listener's attention such that a habitual choice of the station is made.

We argue here that it is the structural features of the program organization that actually hold the listener's attention and, moreover, condition the listener's acceptance of the commercial message. The type of structure used by the station is decided upon either consciously through consulting agencies which design radio formats, or operationally through the evolution of "what works." It is designed not only with a specific socioeconomic class as target, but also with a specific listening context in mind. Whereas content strongly correlates with socioeconomic variables, structural features reflect the listening environment, which in contemporary society is most commonly the distracted listening situation where radio accompanies other (usually boring or uninteresting) activity.

For radio to remain successful as a surrogate so that it is the listener's habitual choice, it cannot in fact "complete" the situation. It only makes the situation tolerable so that the listener comes to rely on its presence. It must appear to make time pass more meaningfully, but in order to thrive on the *inadequacy* of the situation, it must perpetuate it. For a noisy environment, it provides a constant level of masking, for loneliness it provides the company of a reassuring (but unreal) friend, for boredom it provides "entertainment," for meaninglessness it provides "information," but only what is amusing, non-disruptive and, most of all, what is non-conducive to thought. Real solutions require profound social change or assertive individual action; commercial radio, like advertisers, must perpetuate dissatisfaction. Therefore they help maintain the status quo.

Once we understand the social and economic reasons why radio must hold listeners' attention, then we realize the importance of radio's structuring of sound in time. If the content were inherently interesting (as in literature, film, music, and so on), the evolution of the material itself would be sufficient to maintain interest. But with radio, the unrelatedness of the various bits of material prevents the content from being "self-organizing" in the same way. The content of radio must be poured into a predetermined mold whose structure is a predictable, repetitive pattern that is effective in holding the listener's attention. The structure itself must provide the variety, the continuity, and the apparent "logic" to hold the attention, since the content cannot. No coherent form of communication could ever be made to fit within a predictable string of 30-second, 1- and 3-minute packages, which in fact characterize the music–commercial–music sequences of radio. In natural forms of communication, content generates form; in radio, content simply "fills up" standard forms. To understand radio form is to understand the logic that guarantees the holding power that radio has on listeners.

Radio Structure

In our discussion, radio structure is assumed to mean the way in which separate "units" of program material are put together into a continuous chain, where the unit is loosely defined as a separable, coherent piece of program material with a definable beginning and end. Such units include news, weather, sports, reportage, announcer talk, ads, music, and silence. Each unit can be easily discerned by listeners as such, and the transitions between them often signal shifts in listener attention, such as "tuning in" to a favorite song or a tantalyzing bit of announcer patter, or "tuning out" to the news or an ad.

There are two ways in which we will put such units into context. First, we consider the total stream of program material and the placement of all units within it. Therefore, the unit is not analyzed apart from its relation to the whole. It can be assumed, for instance, that when an announcer introduces an ad, the listener's level of attention (drawn by a familiar voice) will be different than if the ad were immediately preceded by music with a sharp transition between them. Secondly, we also consider the total listening context within which the program is heard, including time of day, station type, and all factors surrounding the listening experience itself (where it occurs, simultaneous with what other activities, at what loudness level, whether habitually of infrequently, and so on). Unfortunately, empirical data on listening habits is difficult to find. In short, we want to be able to analyze aspects of radio structure which correlate with the perceptual strategies of listeners in a realistic way.

Rhythm

Rhythm may be thought of most generally as the pattern of successive durations of events, whether they are individual sounds or, in this case, program units. Occasionally the units overlap, as with announcers talking over music, but these occurrences may be treated as separate units or, if sufficiently short, the overlaps can be ignored. The rhythmic structure of radio can be viewed at a macro level where different patterns and densities of elements occur at different times of day. For instance, commercial radio typically increases the number of items per hour and the total ad time during the rush-hour periods when listenership is at a peak. The strong circadian rhythm is also characterized by events that occur at regular and expected time intervals, such as news reports, and these repetitions punctuate the overall flow into identifiable segments. When identical rhythmic patterns of elements occur repeatedly, we may speak of an "isorhythmic" pattern which increases redundancy at the structural level.

Our use of the term "rhythmic structure" in referring to the durational pattern of sequences of program units is in contrast with the more conventional notion of rhythm as the property of sound sequences which have a beat or regular accent. The speed of speech and music in radio is significant and becomes identified with the station format or "image." An "up tempo" station is one which is generally devoted to fast music and speech, a fact which may attract the listener's attention and loyalty. The physiological and psychological response to rhythm is largely involuntary (as exploited by the Muzak corporation and other designers of background music for work and consumer stimulation), and therefore the speed internal to programming units is important. It makes radio a dependable form of stimulus which can be used by listeners.

Rhythmic energy at the structural level, however, is judged according to the variety found in successive durations of program units. For instance, a low rhythmic evaluation would be scored when programming consists of units of equal duration, such as an endless succession of 30-second spots. Even if the tempo within each unit were high, the uniformity at the structural level would provide no variety, only boredom. Such boredom is typically found in jobs where the amount of time spent on each unit of work is identical. A high degree of rhythmic energy would be found in programming with a great deal of variety in unit durations, short, medium, and long, interspersed in such a way that no successive units belonged to the same durational class.

What is meant by "durational class" is a range of durations that are arbitrarily regarded as being equivalent. Although arbitrary, such classes tend to be observed by standard radio formats in which commercials are typically 30 or 60 seconds, music comes in 3- to 4-minute cuts in popular music, announcer intro's are about 10 seconds, and most station logos are less than 3 seconds. Items less than 10 seconds fall within the short-term memory span, and larger durations may be ordered according to a logarithmically increasing scale such as 11–33 seconds, 34–67 seconds, 67 seconds to 4 minutes, greater than 4 minutes. Such a scale, or one that mirrors typical program lengths, may be used to evaluate rhythmic structure.

Two specific measures that can be used are, first, the population distribution in each of the 5 durational classes (called A to E), and secondly, the number of "suspensions" in each class, where a suspension is the side-by-side occurrence of two units in the same durational class. To evaluate the former, one may take the highest scores in two *non-adjacent* classes. The classes must be non-adjacent in order to comply with the notion of structural rhythmic energy being created by alternations of dissimilar durations. The distribution of units gives a simple representation of how a typical pattern of programming consists of units of certain durations. Such patterns may be observed to shift throughout the day, particularly when a station squeezes more items per hour into peak broadcast times. Populations that fall into dissimilar classes indicate the amount of variety in rhythmic energy. For instance, an "up tempo" station whose units cluster around the shortest two classes shows less variety or energy than one where there is a mix of short, medium, and long durations. Similarly, the notion of suspension distinguishes between different orderings of the same population. For example, the sequence of units:

A A A B B B C C C D D D C C C B B B A A A

has the same population as the sequence:

A C B D A C B A D B C A C B A C B D A C B

But the first has far less rhythmic energy because of its large number of suspensions; there are none in the latter (though it should be noted that neither case is necessarily desirable). Note that the percentage of suspensions is inversely proportional to the degree of rhythmic energy; the greater their number, the less energy they produce.

Further, the number of items per hour (i.e., density of units) may be seen as both an indicator of the expected attention span and a determinant of the perceived sense of time flow. Robert Ornstein (1969), in his book *On the Experience of Time,* has proposed a model which uses what he calls a "storage size metaphor" to explain the relation between the subjective experience of time and the structuring of the material within it. His hypothesis is that:

> In the storage of a given interval, either increasing the number of stored events or the complexity of those events will increase the size of the storage, and as storage size increases, the experience of duration lengthens. (Ornstein, 1969, p. 41)

According to this model, the subdivision of a given period of time into a greater number of small units, such as the individual program units of an "up tempo" station, will *lengthen* the subjective sense of time flow. The listener has the impression that "more has happened" within the time span, i.e., that time has passed meaningfully. Working counter to this trend is that the pattern of events is highly predictable for the habitual listener (therefore easier to encode, in Ornstein's terms). The individual units, many of which have been heard frequently before, are not complex. Therefore, a balance is achieved between the structural complexity of a high density sequence and the ease of its absorption.

However, one cannot apply Ornstein's model to radio too literally because it implies that there is some form of "storage" of the input data. In most of his experiments, the listeners are presumed to be attentive but passive. He assumes that they are hearing, encoding, and storing *all* of what they hear. A problem solving approach, on the other hand, would postulate a more dynamic situation in which the incoming sounds provoke hypothesis formation about their structure and their potential "sense." For instance, in one experiment, 10 prerecorded sounds are played in two configurations, one where each sound is repeated 20 times before going on to the next, and the other where the order of the sounds is randomized. Ornstein postulates that the second sequence is more complex, and therefore the experiences of equal durations of each one are judged unequal in subjective terms (the more complex one seeming longer). If "understanding" the experience were equivalent to remembering it, then fewer rules would be required to store and recall the repetitive sequence. However, in the model of listening used here, a "repetition hypothesis" could be made quickly for that sequence, but verified only after the sequence changed. New information would occur only when new sounds were introduced. With the random sequence, a "random hypothesis" could also be made quickly, and thereafter only some perceived regularity would be significant. Therefore, the first example might provoke a slightly higher ratio of problem solving activity to passive monitoring, and the second one (by remaining uniformly random) might seem longer, i.e., more boring, not more complex.

What this model and our critique of it has to say about radio structure is that the listener's subjective sense of time flow can be altered by factors such as the number of subdivided programming units, the complexity of their organization, and their redundancy (at both the level of form and content). The holding power of the station is increased by promoting structural continuity and redundancy (i.e., making it easier for the listener to absorb by requiring less mental effort). The purpose of structure in commercial radio is to combat both fatigue and boredom. To achieve the former, the tempo of the content must be stimulating and high energy; to achieve the latter, the durations and complexity of individual items must be reduced, and smooth, predictable transitions between elements must be maintained.

Intensity and Dynamic Range

The intensity level of the radio signal and its dynamic range (from lowest to highest intensity level) is generally regarded as only a technical concern, and not as a factor that influences the listener or a significant component of the structural design of radio. As remarked in chapter 9, the ear seems remarkably insensitive, at the conscious level, to distortions in dynamic range, at least by comparison to other forms. However, we will argue here that this objective variable has great importance in controlling the *attention level* of the distracted listener. Signal strength is also a key factor in determining the reach of the radio signal, and therefore it has economic consequences in terms of potential market size.

The median intensity level of each program unit correlates with its perceived loudness, and just as a uniform sequence of durations becomes predictable and boring, so too do similar loudness levels. In fact, constant intensity levels fatigue the auditory system, and apparent loudness falls off (the phenomenon called adaptation). In terms of radio, the effect of constant levels is a kind of "fading away" into the background. On the other hand, sudden shifts in loudness may raise the level of attention of the distracted listener, but too great or sudden a shift produces the annoying "startle reaction" which may cause the listener to change stations. Therefore, dramatic shifts in intensity level are generally avoided, and changes in *dynamic range* are more effectively used.

Compression in Foreground and Background Format

To understand the role of signal level in holding the listener's attention, we must introduce the notion of "foreground" and "background format" to describe program structure. Although many specific types of format are used and given names in the industry (because program structure commonly follows such standard formulae), these general types of format represent two extremes which function in opposite ways. "Foreground format" refers to a program structure that constantly attempts to keep its signal at a foreground level of listening attention, even when the listener is engaged in other activities. It competes for as much attention as possible, even though, paradoxically, it is not meant to be attentively listened to. By contrast, background format is designed to be heard only as background sound, and therefore remains at a background level of listening attention. Foreground format keeps its signal riding at a high level of modulation with a relatively small dynamic range in order to stay "high" in the listener's awareness. A background format station, knowing that its signal will be listened to at a lower volume level, keeps its signal at a fairly consistent level to *avoid* attracting attention. It also uses smooth transitions between elements (usually slow fade-ins and fade-outs with silence in between) for the same reason.

In foreground format, the signal is compressed both in time (through abrupt transitions that allow no instant of silence when attention, and revenue, might be lost), and in dynamic range. The former is achieved by precise cueing and overlap of elements, and the latter is the result of audio "compression" techniques. Compression is used in disk recording and radio transmission to reduce the dynamic range of the signal to fit within the restricted range of these media. A related technique called "limiting" prevents the signal from exceeding a level that is safe for the recorder or transmitter. Compression constantly adjusts the instantaneous signal level such that low levels are raised to keep them significantly above the background noise, and peak levels are reduced. Therefore, the entire signal can "ride" higher in the dynamic range available without risking distortion.

The first economic implication of compression in broadcasting is that it allows a higher level signal to be heard over a wider area that therefore encompasses a potentially larger target audience. Moreover, compression ensures that the signal-to-noise ratio will be improved, particularly on cheaper receivers such as transistor radios. Thus, a compressed signal which has few quiet parts, and rides as close to full modulation of the carrier as possible, has the best chance of sounding distinct at the greatest distance from the transmitter. Foreground format stations, particularly when aimed at the young who presumably cannot afford expensive sets, typically utilize high degrees of compression.

In addition, we offer the hypothesis that changes in dynamic range correlate with the "listening level" of the audience; that is, a program unit with a greater dynamic range is more interesting or attractive to the ear than a highly compressed signal of nearly constant loudness. The principle on which this hypothesis is based is that the greater the variety in a stimulus, the more potential interest it has for the brain. A further hypothesis is that control of dynamic range is a subtle and extremely effective method used in foreground format radio to manipulate audience attention. A clear example of how this technique works is shown in the graphic level recording in Fig. 18 which documents a segment of a typical AM foreground station.

The entire signal rides near maximum modulation. The music in particular has a very narrow dynamic range of less than 5 dB, because it uses no silences or "diminuendo" passages, and also because it has been compressed during the original recording session, the record mastering and possibly further during broadcast. The crucial transition comes when the announcer appears *over* the end of the song, allowing the listener no chance to withdraw attention or switch stations. The presence of a live human voice of familiar identity presumably raises the listener's attention level slightly. The announcer carries the listener smoothly into the commercial by offering brief bits of information (time, song title, etc.). He also reinforces station identity with a station ID (a frequent occurrence in this type of format, designed to promote station loyalty and make a clear distinction from similar sounding competitors).

The transition to the commercial is amazingly tight—not even the graphic level recorder can detect a momentary pause. The dynamic range of the commercial is 10 to 25 dB, several times wider than that of the music. Contrary to popular belief, ads are *not* louder than other program content (if they were, the listener might be annoyed by the sudden increase and turn down the volume); instead, the dynamic range is wider and the commercial seems more *aurally interesting*. Attention is shifted to the ad without the listener realizing it. It is not unrealistic to see foreground format as using music as "filler" to attract station loyalty and pass the time (with passive listening) in between commercials as foreground, high-interest points.

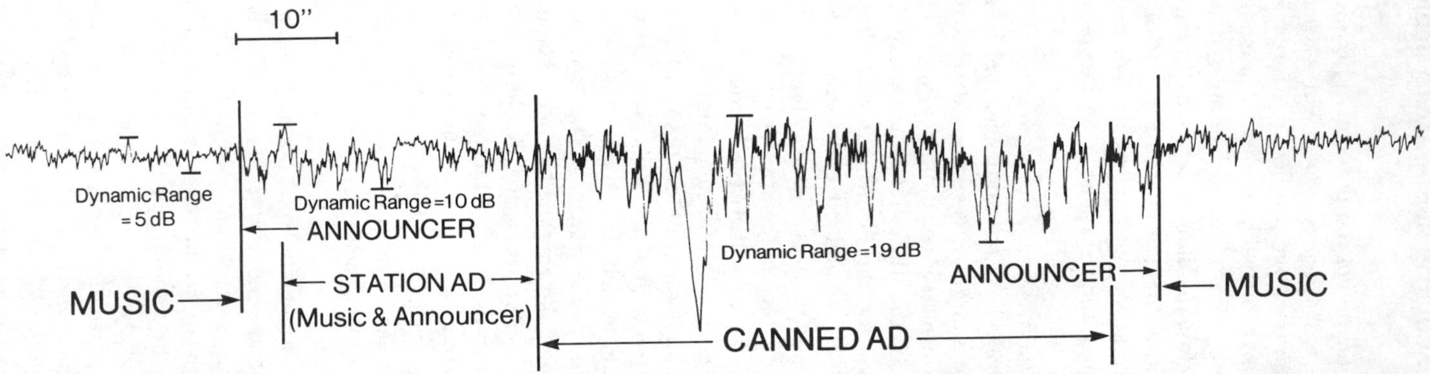

Fig. 18. Graphic level recording of an AM radio signal, showing the larger dynamic ranges of the ads in comparison to the highly compressed music signal. The drop in signal level during the canned ad is a dramatic pause in the commercial, a feature not found in the transitions from music to ads because of the announcer's presence as a bridge. The signal is from a foreground format rock music station in Vancouver, British Columbia.

However, the implication of shifting dynamic range is not always the same. In foreground format with high compression, the shift in dynamic range, found most often with ads and news, is attention getting simply because the range of everything else is even smaller. The dynamic range of the ad may, in fact, be numerically smaller than that found frequently in background and "middle of the road" stations. But simply because such changes are numerous in those formats, any specific one does not stand out, particularly if the listening volume level is low. Again, it is the context of the signal that reveals its significance. In foreground format, commercials "get through" to the distracted listener because of the various "hooks" in the content and because of the shift in listening attention produced by an increased dynamic range. In background format, the ads often have the same dynamic range as the music, but they attract more attention (even in a background situation) because they are faster and more varied than the music. Moreover, their frequent repetition means that they act almost at a level of hypnotic suggestion.

Continuity

Compared to the objectively measured variables of rhythm and intensity level (essentially the "horizontal" and "vertical" aspects of the radio signal respectively), continuity or coherence in the flow of program elements is a much more subjective variable and depends on how the listener interprets what is heard. It involves how adjacent elements are related, and includes both the manner of the transition between them (abrupt or "segue," fade-out/fade-in, and cross-fade or simultaneous fade-out and fade-in), as well as the relation of the two elements in terms of content, style, and form. The temporal juxtaposition of material first became technologically feasible in film, and Eisenstein (1942) was among the first to be sensitive to the power of the "montage" of juxtaposed images. For him, the connection between images, as well as their individual characteristics, creates a *new* level of meaning that does not exist in either separately.

Conventional radio, however, is not creative in its use of juxtaposition between program elements, and generally only uses the technique effectively in commercials. The purpose of radio is to attract and hold an audience, and therefore continuity must be designed to serve that purpose. The problem is to balance the need for change (not letting any one element become tedious) with the need for a smoothness of flow between often unrelated elements. Further, the moment of transition between elements in foreground format is a vulnerable point because at the completion of any meaningful piece of communication (e.g., music, speech) there is a "cadence" or point of repose where all ideas are culminated, and the mind is free to turn to something else. If that "something else" is another station, then the listener must be given no opportunity to have that freedom of choice.

The announcer's role (at the structural level) is to make the bridges between program units and to carry the listener's attention along to the next item. In foreground format, the announcer usually comes in over the end of a song (the musical point of repose where attention could be shifted) to draw attention away from the cadence and on to a commercial or other material. In the densest foreground formats, the announcer's actual time allocation may be less than 3%—simply enough to bridge items, even if it means raising the voice (both in pitch and loudness) to be heard over them. Apart from required content such as station ID or announcer ads, what is said is usually trivial, because it is the structural role of the voice that is important and not the content itself. The distracted listener does not *want* to be disturbed by anything requiring thought, and the bored listener merely wants to be entertained.

Because typical car radio listeners can quickly "punch in" a new station, the competition for attention is fierce—stations cannot risk boring their audience. Therefore, during rush hours in particular, items are switched rapidly, commercials are inserted more frequently, and the announcer's job is to make it all seem coherent. On commercial stations, news breaks are also regarded as vulnerable points where listeners can be lost. Some stations have moved to irregular times for news to minimize their predictability, but the general trend is to "soft" news—essentially an extension of the announcer patter that includes a high percentage of "human interest" or "novelty" stories and little in-depth reportage. Another technique is to "advertise" the news, that is, to preview the most interesting story and leave the listener "hanging" for more information.

In order to measure degrees of continuity in a manner that is analogous to the methods proposed for rhythm and intensity, a scale of program unit types such as the following can be constructed:

1. News
2. Sports
3. Weather
4. Reportage
5. Announcer

6. Logo 12. Silence

7. Ad (voice only)
8. Musical Logo
9. Musical Ad
10. Music & Announcer
11. Music

The specific order of these categories has been chosen to establish a scale going from the most formal, linguistic program type (news) through to the least formal, non-linguistic program material (music). As we move through 1–5, the style of language becomes looser and more informal, perhaps even spontaneous, and through categories 7–11, linguistic content progressively disappears in favor of musical content. The station logo (prerecorded) stands in a neutral, central position, equidistant from both ends, as does silence which is regarded as having a special, if neglected, role that allows it to be equidistant from *all* categories.

We hypothesize that when program categories are ordered appropriately, the size of the "step" from one category to another indicates the smoothness of transition between units perceived by listeners. Thus, a program sequence will appear to be smooth when the steps between adjacent or next-but-one units are relatively small. Conversely, a large jump (from news to music is the largest and most discontinuous step in the above example) will contribute to a sense of disjointedness for the listener, as program material switches levels or degrees of seriousness with no transitional step.

Most typically, high density foreground stations with a large number of units per hour show a high degree of continuity, whereas low density stations (background music or government funded ones) show a low degree of continuity. (The data on which these conclusions are based will be discussed later.) The explanation seems to lie in the degree of standardization that a foreground station typically uses to fit short bits of material together and keep the listener's attention. The ordering is predictable and avoids sudden jumps between unrelated material (usually through frequent use of announcer talk and station logos). Attention is never attracted unnecessarily, only at commercial breaks.

With a background music station, transitions do not need to be smooth in the sense described, as the overall tempo is slow, and the program units are often separated by silence which evens out any transition. A government-funded station, such as the CBC, often shows a high degree of discontinuity when music is used as "filler" in waiting for the next item to occur at its proper time. Music is often crudely faded in and abruptly squelched in this process. In Canada, the situation is exacerbated by the transition between local and network programming which cannot be easily coordinated. It is a clear case where national broadcast policy (the balancing of regional and national interests) makes a tangible appearance in program structure.

Commercials

We have suggested above that the communication of advertising messages to the listener is inherent in the purpose of commercial radio. It is of considerable interest, if only from the point of view of acoustic design, how such messages can be communicated to someone who is not really listening! However, we know that the auditory system is *always* monitoring input (even during sleep or when conscious attention is not involved), and therefore, messages get through if structured properly. Commercial stations are not the only ones whose structure must accommodate ads; publically supported or "community" stations must solicit both listeners and subscribers. Therefore they often resort to ads that in both form and content often resemble those of the commercial stations to whom they claim to be an alternative.

Ads can be classified as "announcer ads," that is, those read live by the announcer; "canned ads," which are prerecorded and may be either of local origin or part of a nation-wide promotion; and "station ads" which are promotions for the station itself, either live or prerecorded. Announcer ads have an obvious basis of continuity in that the voice is familiar and the words can be blended into the overall announcer output. They capitalize on the fact that the listener will presumably have no defences against hearing the voice and therefore will not attempt to screen it out. Music that resembles the style usually played on the station is used similarly at the beginning of many canned ads, both to attract attention and to obscure the commercial being identified as such. Even when a canned ad is locally produced with another announcer's voice, its familiarity to the regular station listener may achieve the same effect. Announcer ads typically follow "public service announcements" for which the listener presumably also has a low defensive threshold.

Canned ads are the high-cost and high-paying sources of revenue, and are frequently the best designed items heard on the station. Their appeal is as calculated as that of a well-designed "hit" song, and often just as effective in producing sales. Although the advertiser buys time during a certain priority period (e.g., prime time) and not a specific position within the stream of program events, most stations seem to follow certain patterns in the strategic placement of such ads. We will describe only a few of the more common sequences, one of the simplest types of which is the classic "arch form":

M–A–B–C–B–A–M

where M refers to music, A to announcer talk, B to an announcer or station ad, and C to the canned commercial which is placed in the middle (the "keystone" position of the arch) with the other units spread symmetrically around it. The advantage of such a sequence is that it draws the listener smoothly out of the music with the announcer's voice, leading to the announcer ad, then to the main ad itself (with usually a sharp transition effected by the announcer having the "cart" on which it is recorded precisely cued). The sequence ends by going smoothly back into the music, perhaps a little more quickly on the "downward" side of the arch. A closely related sequence is the "back-to-back" form:

M–A–C–C–A–M

where two canned ads are placed side by side. However, common sense dictates that the second ad is usually the better of the two, so that it remains the "high point" and isn't upstaged by the other one. A canned logo will frequently be inserted after the last canned ad or just before the music, in order to act as a reminder of station loyalty (which is based on the choice of music that is then offered as a "reward" for having listened to the commercials).

The Commercial Image

Unfortunately, both space and the nature of the print medium do not allow an in-depth analysis of the techniques found in the commercials themselves. To do so would mean falling into the trap of literary content analysis by ignoring the sounding nature of the material. Structural diagrams of the commercial, showing music, voices, and sound effects, are useful in analyzing the design of the various components. However, careful consideration has to be given to the *images* created by these sounds, as it is these images, more than the literal linguistic meaning, that is designed to be associated with the product or service in the mind of even the distracted listener.

Commercials are not intended to motivate listeners to action "on the spot" (although the older style of heavy-handed ad did at one time assume a more attentive listener who could "phone right now" or "rush to the store"). Instead, the intended time-frame of the action is later, and it is then that the learned images must function to motivate the listener in the desired way (Schwartz, 1973). In chapter 8, we referred to the literal quality of commercials in the early days (particularly the 1930s) when product names had to be spelled, memorized, and made iconically recognizable. The "jingle" was devised to assist this process musically. In the post-war period, commercials increasingly moved to more abstract images. The soft drink that emphasized its low cost and type of bottle before the war soon became identified after it with "those who think young." Soon advertisers were marketing "the . . . experience" or an "escape to the world of . . . ," and promoting other kinds of "lifestyles." They associated these abstract images with their products which corresponded less to actual needs and more to inculcated desires.

Radio advertising is clearly designed for those who are not listening, just as magazine advertising appeals to those who are only glancing. It capitalizes on the fact that in background listening, auditory *patterns* are absorbed with little conscious screening, even when specific pieces of information are not being remembered. When one actually takes a detailed and attentive look at the text of such commercials, they often seem silly or absurd. Although intentional, comical absurdity may be used as a "hook" for the jaded listener, the absurdity found in the conventional ad suggests that it is not, in fact, meant to be consciously listened to (just as with background music). When it is heard as an *aural image,* on the other hand, it may suddenly seem coherent and meaningful—the absurd "soap opera" story suddenly becomes an image of tension resolved through the "heroic" intervention of the advertiser, or the image of personal fulfilment achieved through the consumer's act of purchase. The more educated listener rebels, at least intellectually, to such overt forms of manipulation. Yet, as in the case of noise or background music, intellectual defenses are powerless (in the opinion of this author) in the face of the involuntary physical and mental responses such phenomena produce. Critical awareness may help, but snobbery or out-of-hand dismissal ("it doesn't affect me!") certainly will not.

Characteristics of Radio Formats

In conclusion, we will very briefly survey and summarize some of the structural characteristics of AM radio formats and some of the alternatives. Much of the qualitative discussion of the last section reflects a quantitative study done by the author on four AM stations in Vancouver (Truax, 1979). The numerical results are too bulky to quote here at length. The measures which produced the data, however, are based on the three parameters discussed in the last section, namely rhythmic energy (based on percentage populations in dissimilar durational classes and percentage of suspensions), intensity and dynamic range (the RMS values of the median intensity levels and dynamic ranges in dB), and continuity (percentage of transitions between adjacent "two-field" or next-but-one "three-field" program unit types, as ordered along an arbitrary scale such as the one quoted). The data for each station was collected for three 1-hour broadcast segments distributed at key times during the broadcast day. However, a much more extensive study would be necessary for the specific numerical results to acquire general significance. The qualitative patterns suggested by the data, though, are distinctive features of typical radio formats. We may summarize the structural features as follows (see above for more detailed discussion of terms):

A. Foreground format, "top forty" station:

- largest number of items/hour (less than 1 minute per item on average);
- durations cluster around short and medium short range (polarized short-long);
- high percentage of "diminutions" (i.e., items followed by those of even shorter duration) giving a sense of forward momentum;
- high degree of signal compression;
- intensity level rides near maximum modulation;

- dynamic range small (less than 4 dB on average);
- high degree of continuity between items;
- little change at different times of day;
- least amount of announcer time;
- high percentages of music and ads;
- low percentage of news.

B. Middle-of-the-Road, "talk show" station:

- large number of items/hour (about 1 minute/item);
- durations cluster around short and medium short range (polarized short-long);
- lowest percentage of suspensions giving a sense of forward momentum;
- moderate variations in intensity level and dynamic range;
- high degree of continuity;
- music used sparingly;
- high percentage of ads (nearly every second item is an ad).

C. Background format, "easy listening" station:

- low number of items/hour;
- durations in medium short and long classes;
- largest number of suspensions (momentum is toward stasis);
- moderate to large variations in intensity and dynamic range;
- low continuity scores;
- high percentage of music and news;
- most music at midday;
- lowest percentage of ads.

D. Government-funded, "national" station:

- lowest number of items/hour (over 1.5 minute/item);
- uniform distribution of durations over all ranges;
- longest individual items;
- low percentage of suspensions (momentum is steadily forward);
- highest level of intensity variation, particularly for music;
- low levels of continuity with highest discontinuity when programming is polarized between music and news;
- high percentage of reportage and other information-oriented items;
- format shifts during day.

FM Stations

Many listeners regard FM band stations as having a higher standard of broadcasting quality, both because of the wider bandwidth stereo signal and what is thought to be a more intelligent programming style. Announcers are usually less frenetic and more mature sounding, in keeping with the older age of the target audience. The "album-oriented rock" format also includes longer selections of music and more background information. However, the argument presented here that content is designed to be minimally acceptable to the target audience and structure holds their attention, seems to apply to FM formats as well. The content is distinctively more "mature," but the structural features that have been described here (in particular the ad sequences) are not different. One can hear the same types of transitions, and sometimes even the same ads, on FM as on AM.

It is generally true for all types of commercial radio that the percentage of ads in terms of the number of broadcast items is about twice that of their percentage in terms of broadcast time. That is, the frequency of occurrence of ads as *program items* in the rhythmic pattern gives them more weight than would be inferred from simple broadcast time allocation (which is the basis of federal regulation). For instance, ads may occupy less than 20% of the broadcast time but be every third item on average. Even if the percentage of broadcast time for ads drops on FM, their *relative* frequency as part of the structural rhythmic pattern stays significant.

In the distracted listening situation, it is the transition from one item to the next that provides the potential shift in listening level. Music provides the usual background during which attention is not generally focused; with a transition comes the potential to reengage a more active form of listening. Commercials and station logos, being shorter and more compact, can easily attract more attention, even if they do not occupy very much time. FM listeners are not inclined to switch stations rapidly; ads therefore do not have to have a high broadcast time allocation to be effective.

A recent addition to the FM band in the U.S. is a type of background music station that is completely automated. The "station" itself is nothing more than a rack of equipment on which prepared tapes are played with precisely controlled transitions provided by a "canned" announcer. A small variety of formula patterns are used to sequence a certain number of songs with a recap or preview of their titles and artists, along with station logos and transitions to ads. The only exception to the all-canned format is news, which is delivered by a live announcer, but in a style compatible with the depersonalized format. There are no "time checks" because essentially time does not exist on this type of station. It is the same 24 hours a day, and there is literally no one on air to provide the necessary link to the "real" world.

Not surprisingly, according to the distracted listener model we are using, this type of station is very popular with listeners. It is also clearly cost effective. It exploits the use of radio by people as an "audio environment," not as a source of information or even entertainment (at least in the conventional sense of the word). It presents a uniform and dependable audio world with as few intrusions from the real one as possible. A completely machine-controlled broadcast station is probably not too far in the future.

Advocates of *non-commercial* broadcasting, supported through either government or community funding, generally point to the lack of ads as a main source of attraction for these stations. However, as described above, station promotion in the case of community radio generally takes the same *structural* place and form as ads on commercial stations, even if the content or style is more palatable. The word of caution that structural analysis has to offer would-be designers of "alternatives" is that changing content without changing form is only a superficial level of change. Moreover, the lack of purchased advertisement may attract the same kind of distracted listener that prefers the automated, background music station just discussed because it presents fewer distractions. Listening habits may remain the same even when content changes.

Fortunately, many of the people who are producing community radio are sensitive to the "sound" it projects. They are exploring more fundamental differences in programming, for instance, by involving live music on air, instead of only recordings and by presenting a wider range of opinion, music, and, literally, "voices" than is heard on commercial radio. Programming by and for special interest groups ("minorities" if you will) who are ignored by the homogenization of conventional media often brings with it new sounds and new forms.

Such pioneering work may seem to take radio back to its early days, when broadcasting was more experimental, the contact with the community more direct, and the energy more spontaneous. However, we cannot ignore the fact that not only has society and the media changed profoundly in the interim, but so has the very nature of listening habits. Can alternatives work when public sensibilities and appetites have been schooled for years to prefer the "slick," the artificial, and the technologically impressive? Regular radio listeners are sophisticated in terms of what they think constitutes "quality" sound and professional programming practice. Well-intentioned amateurs cannot compete for long, even when motivated by worthy ideals. It is with these problems in mind that we will turn our discussion in the last two chapters of the book to the question of what constitutes actual alternatives and good electroacoustic design.

12

The Acoustic Community As Market

In chapter 5 we introduced the concept of the "acoustic community" as a system within which acoustic information is exchanged. The nature of electroacoustic technology changes both the type of acoustic information involved and the dynamics of the system's behavior, in the sense that traditional space/time constraints no longer apply. The system of communication may extend worldwide both as a direct communication link and in the sense of the international marketing of audio products and services by multinational corporations. Or the system may be as simple as the use of amplified sound in an otherwise conventional soundscape to give speech an acoustic advantage or to introduce music that originates from a completely different context. The effects on the soundscape as a "community" may range from a simple extension through to complete transformation in definition and behavior. From a communicational perspective, the collectivity of listeners functioning as consumers changes from a community to a market.

Redefinition of the Acoustic Community

Most of the rules by which the acoustic community functions are fundamentally altered by the introduction of technology. In chapter 8 we illustrated the extension of the profile of an acoustic sound (a churchbell) to the striking proportions of the area covered by a broadcast signal. Whereas all of the people within an acoustic profile share the experience of being able to hear the same sound (with subtle environmental variations), only those with access to the appropriate receiving equipment within the *electroacoustic profile* can hear the sound, and usually the amount of variation is slight, given the degree of standardization in equipment. Almost by definition, the members of the electroacoustic community are fragmented into subgroups in which they do not necessarily share the simultaneous experience of a specific sound; what they have most in common is the experience of being a product consumer.

Radio operated on the principle of simultaneity even in its early days by choosing (and later allocating) specific broadcast frequencies for individual transmissions. All broadcast signals are simultaneously available in the radio spectrum, and the listener's receiver "tunes in" to one of them. The degree of specificity of the signal was augmented after the Second World War as radio stations targeted specific populations which their product was to attract, and to which programming and advertising could be slanted (Sterling & Kittross, 1978). Modern cable and satellite communication systems provide an even greater range of program choices, and in addition, they actually *identify* the consumer as a subscriber who pays for the service. However, by requiring payment, such systems threaten to stratify audiences along economic lines. And finally, two-way videotext systems such as Telidon change the dynamics of communication such that the subscriber has "free" access to a data bank, although at the moment the access is mainly to alphanumeric information and visuals, not sound.

The community model for two-way communication systems has been established for many years through the publicly accessed radio frequencies allocated for various purposes, e.g., ham, short-wave, citizen's band (cb), etc. The sense of community that has developed around each of these technologies is remarkable. Amateurs, hobbyists, and enthusiasts of every kind devote hours to developing their systems and using them to talk locally and internationally. Codes, jargon, slang, and broadcast nicknames proliferate with the initiated. The content of the messages exchanged usually revolves around the technology itself, as operators discuss signals, rigs, and their experiences in contacting others in the "system." It is clear that the *fact* of communication in this manner is equally as important to them as the content—the message really is the medium.

The application of computer technology and its concepts to these kinds of systems offers new possibilities for many more such "subcultures" to exist, even if the audio component is abandoned in the process. In videotext systems (Woolfe, 1980; Chorafas, 1981), users can select the information they wish, they can send and receive "mail," and even carry on "dialogues" on topics of their choice. In other words, the final stage of the electroacoustic community, as it becomes more and more specialized, simultaneous, global, and multi-levelled, transcends the need for sound (Martin, 1978). Information is exchanged without its acoustic or audio transport vehicle, and the auditory dimension remains only at the level of an organizing metaphor. Tony Schwartz, for instance, describes the similarity at the micro level between auditory perception and that involved in a television image created by a scanning process, i.e., a time-based signal flow. He states that:

> in watching television, our eyes function like our ears. They never see a picture, just as our ears never hear a word. The eye receives a few dots of light during each successive millisecond, and sends these impulses to the brain. The brain

records this impulse, recalls previous impulses, and expects future ones. In this way we 'see' an image on television. (Schwartz, 1973, pp. 14, 16)

What will be the implications of the loss of sound as a physical, sensory and corporeal vehicle for communication in the communities of the future? If urban environments are increasingly isolated and sealed off from the natural environment, if speech and face-to-face communication is progressively replaced by electronically mediated forms that do not depend on acoustic communication, will sound function at all positively in defining human society? Most of the past predictions made about the impact of technology and media on society have proved wrong—television did not replace film or radio, and the automobile is still with us. Home entertainment and information systems may supplant other forms, but can they satisfy the human need for social gatherings, the sense of belonging and control over one's environment? Will the increasing prevalence of technological sound put a premium on purely acoustic experiences in compensation, if only nostalgically? Will the decline of importance of verbal communication and the soundscape as a source of information result in a greater emphasis on music as a replacement for both? If such conjectures about the future appear too risky, what we can analyze with greater certainty is the present, and so we will proceed to examine the impact of technology on two levels of "community" that are part of our common experience, namely changes in small-scale environments and changes at the level of the mass market.

Electroacoustic Sound in the Community

In chapter 9 we described many of the changes that electrification brings to the soundscape through the new sounds that are introduced. All of these changes affect community definition and patterns of communication, frequently in a negative manner unless particular care is taken. For instance, many community sound signals are electrified, and some involve the production of electroacoustic sound. One may ask whether such sounds function as well as or better than their acoustic counterparts, whether they have the same aesthetic appeal, and whether they reflect the uniqueness and character of the community.

In terms of purely functional criteria, one might ask whether the signal can be heard as far and as clearly—an issue in the debate surrounding the electronic replacements of the older type of foghorn. A less obvious functional problem may be whether the electronic signal has the same ease of identification based on its acoustic character, i.e., whether it can be readily recognized and remembered. Unless carefully designed, electronically produced signals may seem "thin" when compared to acoustic ones, and if overly amplified, they become shrill or distorted. Carrying power depends on the nature of the environment, as low frequencies carry better in some and high frequencies in others; the former require large amounts of amplification to be reproduced electronically.

Many churches, lacking bells and/or bellringers, have installed electronic chimes that broadcast from their towers. Even if they are functionally equivalent and seemingly appropriate (by playing religious music), the question remains as to whether they are as aesthetically satisfying as traditional bells. The sound of electronic chimes is not as rich as that of bells because the sharp attack transient (or "strike note") of the latter is muffled. Moreover, all versions tend to sound alike, and if two churches install similar ones, they may be indistinguishable, whereas every bell has its own character. It is unlikely that such chimes could ever be regarded as a unique community soundmark, given their predictable timbre. One church in a small Saskatchewan town plays a record of Gordon MacRae singing hymns from its belltower, and although this electroacoustic signal may be unique and not found elsewhere, its larger-than-life image is marred by accompanying static and a jarring "clunk" as the machine turns off!

Audio transmission systems, such as intercoms and public address (P.A.) systems, are generally problematic because of the distortions they introduce and the difficulty of integrating them into the acoustic environment in which they are to function. Systems operating in noisy environments are notorious for sounding garbled, and those in reverberant spaces suffer the same fate as any speech sound by being masked. On the other hand, people seem amazingly oblivious to communication problems caused by faulty P.A. systems. They seldom realize why they are missing what's being said, and are usually hesitant to suggest that something be done.

The problem of what we might call the "size" of the auditory image is typically found in electroacoustic communication systems. Sometimes the image is "smaller than life" in the sense of providing a distorted, low bandwidth signal because of the poor quality of the microphone and loudspeaker being used. For instance, when a clerk or teller is speaking through some such device behind a glass partition, the voice may be hard to understand and seem ironically distant (given the visual proximity). The listener is forced to used a raised voice in responding, and often ends up feeling alienated by this depersonalized contact. People who are dependent on such forms of communication, such as airline pilots and train engineers, develop a remarkable facility for decoding speech from what seems to the uninitiated as a hopeless noise. In chapter 8 we described the "larger than life" image of the voice amplified through a loudspeaker, with its typically enhanced bass response. The connotation of the magnified loudness of the voice and its increased bass resonances is that of power. Even the average person lacking in rhetorical skills can fill a space with vocal sound that appears to emanate from many directions simultaneously. I am sure that most people would imagine that if God were to be heard, His voice would come through a P.A. system!

R. M. Schafer (1977) refers to Plato's ideal community having a size of 5,040 because that is the number that could be conveniently addressed by a single orator, presumably without amplification. Today we seem to need a mike for groups of even 25, and most speakers using a mike make no compensation in their style of speech for the problems created by amplification in poor acoustic situations. Moreover, unless a delay system is correctly used in a P.A. system in a large space, the direct sound of the voice, arriving a bit later than the amplified sound, may cause confusion. In the worst case, such systems amplify only the communicational *problems,* and in other cases, the amplification unduly enhances the authority and influence of the speaker over the minds of the audience. Amplified messages, whether political, commercial or public service, when broadcast from vehicles moving through the streets, have the ability to command more attention than most other forms—with little scope for response. Some ice cream vendors even advertise their wares by repeatedly broadcasting an amplified, electronic version of the traditional bell from their trucks, thereby driving the neighborhood to distraction for many blocks! Amplification automatically confers an aura of authority on any message, and puts the recipient at an immediate disadvantage to respond.

Few electroacoustic sounds have existed long enough to acquire symbolic importance in the human mind, but some electroacoustic phenomena, such as the loudspeaker and perhaps radio, have achieved the status of a powerful metaphor. The omnipresent power of the loudspeaker suggests a political metaphor of the centrally controlled state that is everywhere but never seen. Although one might think first of Hitler's famous remark about the importance of radio and the loudspeaker in his takeover of Germany (Hale, 1975), politicians and religious leaders in North America (who were sometimes one and the same, particularly in the late 1920s and 1930s) used the same media in reaching mass audiences and achieving a "grass roots" appeal unimaginable in any other way. Because radio listening had a more social role in those days, with the members of one or more families gathering around it in rapt attention, the message found its way into literally the center of countless households. The disembodied voice, originating from afar, carried with it a sense of power that extended the scale of the community from the immediate region to national and international proportions. The individual's ties to an image of community or country now had an immediate, perceptual manifestation as well as a metaphorical significance.

Background Music

Closely related to the ways in which electroacoustic signals and amplified sound alter particular soundscapes, is the impact of all forms of "background music" and other types of sound designed not to be listened to attentively. In the previous chapter we discussed the use of radio by the distracted listener and identified some of the implications it has for the listening process. It also has larger implications for the sense of community. By creating its own ambience and imposing a predefined character onto it, background music essentially *isolates* an environment from any connection it may have to a larger sense of community. Whether the sound level is low or high, it creates a "wall" that isolates the individual or group. The wall may have a social function to define (and protect?) the group, as when young people use "their" music to shut out the adult world which, ironically, is responsible for production of the music in the first place. Or, the function may be acoustic, when background music is used to mask the sound of intrusive noise. Perhaps the most common use of background music by people who consciously choose it, is as a physiological and psychological stimulant to counteract the fatigue, boredom, or loneliness of modern life—"audioanalgesia" Schafer (1977, p. 96) calls it.

The problem from the perspective of the community is that: first, background music blocks other sounds from being heard and thereby reduces acoustic definition; second, it imposes its own mood and character onto the environment, instead of reflecting and enhancing the character of the environment itself; and finally, it is perceived as originating from the "outside" commercial world, the invisible seat of power. This commercial world operates on the principle of the mass market and the homogenized, standardized product. Therefore, the proliferation of background music internationally means that every soundscape starts to resemble every other; local cultural influences are subsumed or emasculated into a bland, universal style. Uniqueness, which is central to the community, is obliterated. In Innis's terms, the international audio industry is spatially dominant, wielding its influence across the globe, and challenging the time-based systems of the oral tradition and the print medium (Innis, 1972). The soundscape is no longer a channel of communication and a contributor to community definition. Instead, it is simply a painkilling background to profit.

The Impact on Community Design

The effects of electroacoustic technology on the acoustic community may be judged in terms of the three characteristics of a well-functioning acoustic system described in chapter 5, namely variety, complexity, and balance. For the first two, there are conflicting influences. Variety may be lessened by the standardization of audio products, but on the other hand, technology can introduce a wider range of sounds into the environment, albeit with the risk of their having less internal variation. Standardization, and hence predictability, may lessen the complexity of information conveyed by electroacoustic sound, but at the same time, the ability of such phenomena to break normal space/time constraints means that information from a wide variety of other contexts impinges on the environment. The patterns of communication flow within a community may be much more varied (for instance, think of the simultaneous telephone links occurring at any one time), but it is open to question whether such links add to or merely *replace* traditional ones. Do telephone links replace neighborly chats or extend the scope of what constitutes the neighborhood? Likewise, it is debatable whether the complexity of technological forms of communication assists community definition, fragments it into countless "subcultures," or redefines it completely on larger scales that are less related to human, auditory dimensions.

Finally, the impact of electroacoustic sound is most noticeable in its adverse effects on the *balance* of a soundscape. Once sounds can be taken out of any context, manipulated and introduced into any other, at any loudness level, there is no guarantee that an acoustic balance will be maintained. Already in 1930 in New York, according to the noise study reported in chapter 8, radios and loudspeakers were a major source of complaint and the subject of municipal ordinances. In the intervening years, the same sources have proliferated throughout the world and given the power to unbalance a soundscape to nearly everyone. The domination of space, which is inherent in audio media, whether on a local or global level, attacks a fundamental balancing force within the soundscape (unlike time-based media which demand only repetition). Digital technology has added ubiquity to the control of space by miniaturizing the hardware to the point where high-pitched beeps, buzzes, and pseudo-human voices can emanate from even the smallest places. Everything "speaks" even if no one communicates.

The balancing forces created by the natural laws of acoustic behavior, or by social and cultural patterns, do not and probably cannot control the impact of technology on the soundscape. The reason is simple; as a force, technology does not originate from *within* the environment, but rather is imposed on it from without. Its artifacts are not constrained by the same forces as the natural soundscape, and so there is no guarantee they will be compatible with it. Therefore, electroacoustic design must involve not only the composition of the artifact itself, but also its *integration* with the environments into which it is introduced, within the constraints of the medium itself.

The highly critical tone of this discussion, intended partly to counterbalance the more usual unbridled optimism of technical utopianism, suggests that to a very large extent, the impact of electroacoustic technology is a "zero sum" operation. For every advance or new possibility, there is a corresponding price. When one gains from one perspective, one inevitably loses from another. The "gains," being good selling points, are the most obvious, and it seems to be a part of human nature to ignore the "losses." Our implicit belief in the *inevitability* of technological change requires that the losses be minimized. We *must* believe that things are getting better, or else we might not participate in the game. Throughout all of the chapters in this section of the book we have attempted to formulate a more accurate picture of the assets and liabilities inherent in the current situation than that offered by proponents of the audio industry. Supported by such knowledge, we can begin to assess the directions in which a "net gain" may be achieved, if any. Without the influence of good electroacoustic design strategies, technology can only make things worse, or at best, strike an even balance of zero gain. In the final two chapters we shall explore the principles on which alternative design strategies may be based. However, before proceeding, we need to touch on the final, and in some ways, the most important aspect of electroacoustic technology—its political and economic force at the international level.

The International Audio Industry

Unlike all of the other forces that affect acoustic communication, electroacoustic technology is controlled internationally by a multibillion dollar industry that is so vast that it has never been documented in its entirety with any detail. At best, with a great deal of digging, one can form a composite image of one section of it, such as the recording industry, audio equipment manufacturing, or the background music business. Most political economic studies of the mass media concentrate on particular media, such as newspapers, telephone or cable companies, and the television or film industry (Smythe, 1981). The complete picture is beyond the scope of this book as well, but in order to appreciate the dimensions and controlling force of the industry, we will attempt to summarize some of the available facts about the recording and background music parts of it.

A good profile of the international music industry has recently been published by the Planning and Research Department of the Finnish Broadcasting Company in which they estimate that "retail sales of records and cassettes in the West for 1977 were . . . 8–9 billion dollars, the United States accounting for over 3 billion, or about 40%" (Soramaki & Haarma, 1981, p.7). The U.S. market grew to $4.1 billion in 1978. Following the U.S. in sales of over $200 million in 1977 were Japan, Germany, the U.K., France, Canada, the Netherlands, and Australia. Estimates for sales in the Soviet Union are in the $600 million range for 1976. The report comments on the "cultural influence of Anglo-American music" in popular music, and its dominance in large markets such as Japan and Germany which export little national music of their own.

Following a pattern of increasing concentration of the market in the hands of a few large companies, a pattern common to many areas of economic life, the international music industry is dominated by five large multinational companies who control over 60% of the market, identified as follows:

> The three largest are obviously CBS (USA), Polygram (The Netherlands/Federal Republic of Germany) and EMI (U.K.), each of which has an estimated 15% of the entire music industry market in the West (1980). The next two are Warner Communications (USA) and RCA (USA), with respective market shares of 9–10% (Warner) and 7–8% (RCA). (Soramaki & Haarma, 1981, p. 8)

Medium-sized companies in the field include A&M (USA), Bertelsmann/Ariola-Eurodisc (Federal Republic of Germany), K-tel (USA), MCA (USA), and Motown (USA). Most of the major companies are involved in other aspects of the entertainment industry and/or the manufacture of hardware. For instance, the Polygram group, which controls labels such as Philips, Vertigo, Mercury, DGG, Polydor, MGM, and British Decca, is jointly owned by Philips of the Netherlands and Siemens in Germany, both major manufacturers of electronic equipment. In 1979, EMI was taken over by Thorn Electrical Industries Ltd. On the other hand, Warner Communications was formed from a merger of several labels when Warner Bros. Records took over Reprise in 1964, Atlantic in 1967, and Elektra and Asylum in 1970 and 1972, respectively. All of these companies are branching out internationally, particularly into third-world countries in recent years. Recorded music is a powerful and subtle vehicle for cultural domination. Herbert Schiller quotes Dr. Joseph Klapper of CBS as stating that:

> the broadcasting of popular music is not likely to have any immediate political effect on the audience's political attitude, but this kind of communication nevertheless provides a sort of entryway of Western ideas and Western concepts, even though these concepts may not be explicitly and completely stated. (Schiller, 1969, p. 106)

Recorded music is also a good example of the unidirectional flow of cultural products, as imports from the countries that are the markets for American and European music form a small percentage of sales. Given the enormous number of records produced every year and the highly competitive market situation, no record sells without a strong backing from advertising and exposure on radio, through concerts, magazines, etc. Therefore it is not surprising that the system favors the few recording artists who can deliver a commercial success; the backing they receive dictates the styles and trends that survive and flourish.

The general result is that most consumers are exposed to a quite limited range of musical styles—limited by contrast to the potential variety that exists. Essentially they are kept musically ignorant. Local successes and trends are quickly picked up and integrated into an acceptable, international commercial style, whether it is black music, disco, or new wave. Genuine musical talent obviously exists throughout the industry, but the focus of this discussion is to show that the commercial basis of the industry creates a largely homogenized sense of community that lacks variety and depth, and that spans most of the world with identical products.

Although the use of background music extends back as far as Edison's experiments in 1915, the major research and experimentation with the functional use of music was done just prior to the Second World War (Cardinell, 1948). It proliferated initially for the patriotic cause of increasing wartime factory production and easing worker fatigue and boredom. Cardinell estimates that by 1943, 8,000 factories in England (90% of British industry), and 6,000 in the U.S. were furnishing music for their employees (Cardinell, 1948, p. 356). After the war, it appears that employee preference, and presumably that of management, dictated its retention. By this point, the Muzak Corporation was the largest supplier of functional, background music. Clients included not only factories, but various kinds of offices, stores, restaurants, and public buildings, for each of whom specific types of programs were produced. Today, Muzak claims to service "43 of the 50 largest industrial firms," as well as most major restaurant chains, and over 60,000 clients in 21 countries.[1]

Proponents of the background music industry claim that it stimulates production, efficiency, and sales, that it ameliorates employee psychology, and that it creates pleasant moods. Critics charge that it manipulates people (both workers and consumers), that it pushes workers to produce more and to ignore their own physical needs, and that it induces a passive acceptance of boring and alienating work situations and environments (Yale, 1970). Whatever the interpretation, there is no doubt that it has resulted in a large industry that is controlled by multinational corporations.[2] Besides those marketing background music, such as Muzak and Q-Music, there are numerous smaller companies and individual entrepreneurs offering other types of programmed musical services, tailored for specific markets and environments. In fact, the larger companies appear to be losing ground to the smaller competitors on the basis of individualized product design. Many such services are providing what they term "foreground" music, by using original artist recordings and playing the music at a higher listening level. Background music, on the other hand, is typically highly compressed in dynamic range, limited in bandwidth, and designed to be played at low volume. Most companies produce their product on tapes that are distributed to their clients, but in some cases, the signal is transmitted on the FM band,

---

[1]Muzak Corporation, promotional literature.

[2]Muzak Inc. was a subsidiary of the Wrather Corp. from 1963 to 1971 when it was merged into the Teleprompter Corp., whose major activity is in the cable television market. In August 1981, Teleprompter merged into a unit of Westinghouse Broadcasting Co., a subsidiary of Westinghouse Electric Corp., who changed its name to Group W Cable (NY) in 1982.

and most recently, satellite telecommunications technology is being used for transmission.

From this brief overview, it can be seen that the music industry is controlled by powerful commercial interests for whom any notion of musical quality is subservient to their market interests. Even the competitors of the large firms are more likely to be imitators rather than innovators, and hence the range of choice provided in the industry is surprisingly small. The net result is not only that the listener becomes a consumer and the acoustic community is replaced by the audio marketplace, but also that the norms established by the industry become the prevailing models for design, of both the product itself and the environments into which it is introduced. Alternatives are not readily available, and promising innovations, like new technology, are quickly "bought up" by the industry and recast into commercially viable forms. This process raises two vital questions which we will deal with in the last two chapters. The first concerns what alternatives exist for the individual. Can the same technology be used creatively within environments and with listener attitudes that are largely shaped by the commercial industry? Is all technological experimentation compromised from the start, or can true alternatives still flourish? Secondly, what are the principles on which an alternative sense of electroacoustic design can be founded? In part I we have proposed principles for acoustic design, but the question remains in what way they can be adapted to, or extended by, the new technological possibilities.

13

Regaining Control: Electroacoustic Alternatives

Our presentation of the impact of technology on acoustic communication has thus far argued that its effects are largely a "zero sum" operation, i.e., that every new possibility is balanced by a corresponding loss. Extension in one area is accompanied by simplification in another. Moreover, the vested interests in the audio industry and the commercialism of the media suggest that much of the new potential offered by technology is under their control, and that individuals, as well as the soundscape, are victims of their power. With technology controlled by others shaping channels of communication, listening habits, and a fair amount of the sound environment itself, one can be left wondering whether there is anything which the individual can do to regain control.

At a certain level, the industry that propels technology forward is indeed beyond the control of the individual, and the mass media today are such powerful institutions that an individual can exert little influence on them and seldom gain access. But those are not sufficient reasons, in my opinion, to justify ignoring, avoiding, or hating technology. Countless opportunities exist for alternative uses of the same tools, and numerous individual examples can be cited of imaginative ideas that could only be technologically realized. My own involvement is as a composer for whom electroacoustic technology is the primary means for exploring new ideas in sound, and so I have no doubts as to its usefulness. Therefore, these last two chapters will be devoted to a description and analysis of what might be called the "creative alternatives" of electroacoustic technology. Whether the reader is interested in the use of technology as a personal creative outlet, or is simply willing to become a more appreciative listener to the efforts of others, I trust this account will be enlightening and perhaps inspiring.

Most people probably do not realize the extent to which conventional uses of technology in the media influence common perceptions, standards, and expectations. Only the experience of alternatives throws such norms into perspective, and if for no other reason, alternatives serve a valuable purpose. The problem, however, is to distinguish the merely new (and with technology, everything seems new) from what is truly original. My own criterion is that what is most valuable is what changes the way we think about things, the way we perceive the world—in short, our patterns of communication. From a communicational perspective, we might say that it is what changes the *process* of communication that is important, and not simply what replaces conventional content with something different.

In this chapter we shall present examples of such alternative uses of technology, particularly those which have general applicability and those which, to some extent at least, have changed the process of communication through sound. A discography of work by those referred to in this chapter is included on pp. 225–226. In the final chapter we will analyze the principles involved in electroacoustic design and establish some criteria by which its effects may be judged. Further, we will look at the new possibilities offered by technology to design systems by which sound may be created and organized, that is, the potential it offers to design the process as well as the artifact.

Recording and the Document in Sound

The ability to record sound, in essence to transfer it permanently to a physical medium, has always had a certain fascination attached to it, from the earliest days of Edison's phonograph (1877) and Berliner's gramophone (1887), which were originally designed both to record and reproduce sound, to the magnetic wire recorder invented by V. Poulsen (1899). The ability to store and reproduce sound is the most fundamental fact of electroacoustic communication and the one that has done the most to change the listener's relationship to sound. Even today, the modern tape recorder provides a relatively inexpensive and accessible medium for the exploration of sound on a personal basis (Dwyer, 1971; Keane, 1980). However, its effectiveness as a tool depends not only on the technical expertise with which it is used, but also on the attitude of the recordist. If the machine is used as a substitute for listening (as is sometimes implied in the phrase "I've got it on tape"), then one gains little from its use, but if it is used as an *extension* of listening (in the spirit in which the telescope and microscope function for the eye), then one is constantly learning something about sound and soundscapes.

Following its commercial introduction in North America in the latter half of the 1940s, the modern tape recorder was often referred to as a "sound mirror," suggesting that it reflects an image of sound to the listener—a concept that in some ways is more accurate than the implied objectivity and neutrality of a machine that simply records sound by transferring it to tape. The mirror may "color" reality through its representation, but it also frames reality, and hence makes us more intensely aware of it. Therefore, it is not surprising that many people have used the tape recorder to enhance aural awareness, in both themselves and others, and to explore the communicative potential of the document in sound.

One of the first people to capitalize on the reflecting power of the tape recorder was Tony Schwartz, a New Yorker, who in 1946 devised a portable version of his tape machine and went about recording the rich soundscape of New York. Through his earlier experience of recording folk singers, he had acquired an interest in folklore, and when he started recording, he realized that he was surrounded by a living folklore in his own auditory environment. In that year he started a year-and-a-half-long study of the soundscape of his postal zone, New York 19, a study which resulted in a Folkways recording of the same name. He also started an exchange of wire and tape recordings by mail, and reports that he "exchanged recordings with over eight hundred people in fifty-two countries, and accumulated some twenty thousand songs and stories" (Schwartz, 1973, p. xii). Schwartz's work also focused strongly on children's songs and the sounds of play, and he published several recordings based on this material. What makes his work stand out is that he used a new technology to change our notion of sound by suggesting that there is value in the "common" sounds of the environment and the soundmaking of the common people. Technology is not just for recording speech and professional musicians, but can be used to change our awareness of all forms of sound and music. Moreover, through radio, recordings and mail exchanges, he communicated with a wide audience, enabling listeners "to experience actual sounds—sounds that served vital communicative functions in people's lives" (Schwartz, 1973, p. xiii).

An extension of the same approach occurred during the 1957–1964 period at the BBC with the creation of eight musical radio documentaries that are collectively known as the "Radio Ballads." They were researched and produced by folklorists Ewan MacColl and Peggy Seeger, and BBC producer Charles Parker. Each program told the story of a different group of people and was based on hundreds of hours of interviews. They also included the creation of songs in the folk tradition that were derived from, and skillfully interwoven with, the language of the people. The authors were aware, not only of the unusual methodology they were devising, but also of the new role that music and sound was playing in these broadcast documentaries:

> They were not conceived as background music, punctuation or as 'spot numbers' whose function was to relieve tension or to provide a little colour in an otherwise somber statement. They were designed to form part of a continuous text which would move freely between speech and song or, when combined with visual images in a film, they would form part of the total language of the medium. (MacColl, 1968, p. 5)

During the recording process, the producers discovered the richness of the natural language of the so-called uneducated workers—the age-old rhetorical techniques of the storyteller in modern form. By contrast, they found that their " 'educated' informants used words to convey information and, simultaneously, to conceal their feelings, while the labourers used language in order to reveal themselves to us in the course of conveying information," (MacColl, 1968, p. 8). Radio documentaries, up to this point, had primarily been concerned with conveying information, and had relied on professional announcers to deliver that information in an articulate manner, even if the result was hard to listen to for any length of time. The producers of the Radio Ballads used technology to change those basic assumptions by deriving both the form and content of their programs from the language patterns of the common people who embodied the program subject. The songs, though newly composed, were derived from the experiences of the people and the speech patterns which they used to portray them. In fact, the songs were so effective that old-timers sometimes claimed to have known them all their lives!

In the production of "Singing the Fishing" (around 1960), a new studio technique was developed to bring the prerecorded speech and the live performance of the songs together with amazing synchronicity. Instead of all the elements being prerecorded and then cut or mixed together, the playback of the tapes became part of the live musical performance in the studio. The integration of the various elements that was achieved had no precedent. In the resulting program, the story is communicated both through a unique mixture of song and music, and by the form of the program which is derived from that material, not imposed on it. The producers also transferred their techniques to more contemporary subjects (e.g., the physically disabled, teenagers, and professional boxing), showing that not just folk traditions could be treated in this way. But in 1964, with critical acclaim for this work at its peak, it was curtailed by the BBC as being too expensive; radio production budgets were shrinking, and listener surveys showed that disc-jockey programs of popular music could attract a larger audience at less cost.

Interestingly enough, most of the innovative work in the sound documentary during the 1950s and 1960s was sparked by radio production, despite the influence of television (although the quality of TV drama during that period might have been an influence in keeping standards high in competition). In Europe, state-owned broadcasting systems have continued this tradition into the 1970s and have encouraged such production with the Prix d'Italia awards for excellence. In Canada, a CBC producer named Imbert Orchard continued the tradition we have been describing with his work in "aural history" and his innovations in the design of what he calls the "document in sound."[1] His work was aided by the relative youth of the country and the fact that many of those who pioneered its development were still

[1]Imbert Orchard, "The Documentary in Sound," unpublished manuscript, no date; "Tape Recordings into Radio Documentaries," *Sound Heritage*, 1974, *3* (1), pp. 28–40.

alive, particularly in the West. Beginning in the early 1960s, he set about recording such people, as well as native Indians, throughout the various regions of the province of British Columbia, each with its own character, history, and soundscape. His work includes two major series of programs, "From the Mountains to the Sea" and "People in Landscape." Orchard's interests were production-oriented for radio, but he also saw the value of such documents as living history, worthy of archival protection. As a result, he contributed to the founding of the Aural History division of the Provincial Archives in Victoria, British Columbia.

In his sound documentaries, he brought a fresh approach to the design component by incorporating sounds which operate, in his term, at different "levels of remove." These levels include (in order): actuality, running commentary, recall and reenactment. Each level of remove represents an increasing distance between the listener and historical reality, but each can be effectively used to make that history come alive. The juxtaposition and interweaving of several such levels in Orchard's works create a unique sense of flow that is evocative and multi-levelled. He uses the fact that the listener can easily recognize the level of remove involved, as well as whether the material is extempore or prepared, and plays on the counterpoint that results from their interaction. His training in the theater accounts perhaps for the sensitivity and vividness of his use of the voice in running commentary sections, a technique which he uses with great effectiveness to draw the listener into a scene.

At the macro compositional level, Orchard creates forms that reflect his subject. In "Skeena, River of the Clouds," for instance, he creates a flowing "stream of consciousness" in sound by skillfully linking different speakers, sometimes with such smoothness that each seems to continue the thought of the previous one without a break. The river of voices flows as relentlessly as his geographical subject. In "Fortunate Islands," on the other hand, he creates islands of voices, each group having its own character and linked by the ambience of the boat ride by which the various Gulf Islands are visited. Through their blend of language, literature, history, and the soundscape, Orchard's work uses technology to make the listener more vividly aware of landscape and the people of its past.

Another more controversial innovator of radio documentaries is Glenn Gould, the Canadian pianist who left the concert stage in 1964 to devote his energies to studio recording (Payzant, 1978). Although less well known than his recordings of the classical repertoire, the radio documentaries are a fascinating use of the medium from a completely different perspective. The main works are a set known as *The Solitude Trilogy* which are studies of people in isolation, including "The Idea of North" (1967–1968), "The Latecomers" (1968–1969), and "The Quiet in the Land" (1975–1976). Their style derives from a very dramatic use of voices, one that constantly places them in various relationships—conversation, debate, argument—against a "keynote" background. The relationships, needless to say, are contrived by editing and mixing, as each of the subjects was interviewed separately. In "The Idea of North" the background is the sound of the train journeying north, on which the various characters are supposedly travelling and reminiscing. In "The Latecomers" the sound of waves forms a constant accompaniment to the islanders who debate the virtues of their isolation.

The techniques used by Gould are described by him as creating a kind of "contrapuntal radio," which in many cases means a simultaneity of voices (Jessop, 1971). He justifies the resulting complexity, and even texture, from the listening experience of following more than one conversation at a time, particularly when the language used is redundant or closely related in subject matter. On this point, Gould seems to be reflecting the contemporary soundscape which increasingly contains simultaneous elements or "crosstalk." The listener's attention is divided, not focused, and there is a tendency to "skim" the content; on the other hand, can the documentary listener be enticed into a more attentive involvement with an increased rate of information processing? Gould suggests that the listener has greater freedom to evaluate different sides of an argument when they are presented such that one can focus on individual voices at will. He feels that it is important "to encourage a type of listener who will not think in terms of precedence, in terms of priority, and collage is one way in which to do it" (Jessop, 1971, p. 21).

His layering, though, is not random as suggested by his frequent references to musical structures and contrapuntal techniques that are designed to allow several voices to fit together in an intelligible manner. He contends that "every line stacks up against the line opposite, and either contradicts it or supplements it, but uses, in any case, the same basic terminology."[2] In "The Idea of North," the layering is only used in the prologue, a technique which Gould suggests was only an afterthought designed to shorten the length of the program to the required duration (Jessop, 1971). The voices weave in and out, and because each has a distinctive style and psychological feeling, one simply gets a general impression of the characters who are later to take prominent roles. Although there are formal relationships between the voices in terms of specific words or concepts that are similar between them, the listener probably hears the sequence for the first time as a way of establishing the character of each person, rather than as conveying specific information. The tape medium, by its very nature, implies the possibility of many hearings, and therefore the designer of the tape documentary can profitably utilize different layers of meaning, some of which are apparent the first time and others which reveal themselves only with great familiarity.

---

[2] *Radio as Music* (film), CBC, 1975.

Conversational overlaps seem to occur frequently these days, and perhaps Gould was only slightly ahead of his time in using them, but the tradition of theater where the "one voice at a time" rule is extremely strictly observed has a lasting influence on the documentary designer. I have observed the difficulty of getting actors and actresses with traditional training to speak in a musically inspired counterpoint, even when the content of their lines is clearly redundant, i.e., utterances the audience would find predictable on the basis of their established characters. It is not surprising that Gould's innovations received much criticism on this point. In "The Latecomers" where such layering abounds, the stereo medium is much more felicitous in providing spatial separation between the voices, a difference that the auditory system constantly uses to distinguish between simultaneous input. In fact, the stereophonic mode has provided composers of documentaries and other types of works with an invaluable framework for incorporating lateral space (not just depth perception as in the monophonic mode) as a dramatic and structural variable. Spatial placement and movement can provide an aural metaphor for the relationship between characters. In "The Quiet in the Land," the use of spatial variation, combined with a wider range of elements (e.g., various styles of music and voice), intensifies the counterpoint but at the same time preserves a clarity in the debate between the sacred and the worldly. The result is that this program seems to be the most satisfying of the three.

Disk Recording

The locus of Gould's other contribution to our understanding of electroacoustic design is his treatment of the disk recording (Gould, 1966). Throughout his long career as a recording artist he regarded the medium he was dealing with as an independent entity, something that should be dealt with on its own terms and within its own potentialities. In essence he regarded the disk as a "document in sound" whose production artifices are as inherent to it as those of any other electroacoustic process. He criticized attempts to make the recording a copy of reality; for him it was not a passive recorder of events but an independent medium through which one could create a *new* reality, one that was often impossible to achieve in live performance. He used technology to change his relationship to the music. This meant, first of all, getting out of the showmanship business of the concert stage which, he felt, encouraged styles of performance that were not appropriate to the music. In the recording studio and the editing room, different versions of the same piece, each with its own musical validity, could be tried out and evaluated. The ability to splice is not just a way of eliminating extraneous sounds, but, in his approach, a powerful technique to create a new realization of the music by combining "takes" that may have been widely separated in time or intention. That is, "by taking advantage of the post-taping afterthought, . . . one can very often transcend the limitations that performance imposes upon the imagination" (Gould, 1966, p. 53).

Gould's process is typical of the way in which technology, creatively used, turns its effects back into a new awareness for the listener. The splice that represents the technical possibility of joining two elements that *might have* existed originally in that juxtaposition, but didn't (and couldn't have because it was beyond anyone's imagination), once performed and its effectiveness absorbed, changes the way we understand the work. Possibilities suggested through the use of a machine become incorporated into human awareness.

However, Gould also imagined that this highly interactive interplay with technology which is inherent to the electroacoustic compositional process could be transferred to the home listener as an antidote to the passive relationship which mass media consumption encourages. Even the relatively simple modification possibilities provided by home entertainment equipment could be used by the "new listener" to make choices and musical experiments. Critics were sceptical that such an idea would take hold, other than in the technical fiddlings of audiophiles, for whom musical content is generally secondary to a fascination with the technical means. However, listeners to home audio systems do seem generally more discriminating today as high quality reproduction becomes more accessible. But can one expect that the consumer process on which the industry is based can be changed from within, by use of its own products? Will not such possibilities simply be absorbed within marketing strategies as yet another illusion of freedom given to the buyer?

Gould's emphasis on the artistic possibilities within the recording medium itself extended the work of many other innovators, one of the most notable of whom was John Culshaw, a producer with British Decca until 1967, who produced the first complete version of the Wagner *Ring* cycle of four operas on stereo recordings, beginning with "Das Rheingold" in 1958. In his entertaining book, *The Ring Resounding,* Culshaw (1972) gives the story of how it all came about. It is difficult today to imagine the barriers he experienced in transferring a work from stage to disk. His success stemmed largely from his treatment of the stereo LP as an independent medium, different from a live performance with its own potential.

Both the stereophonic format and the long-play record made it possible for Culshaw to achieve greater continuity in the recording of a long work (compared with 78s), and to give the dramatic action an appropriate spatial character. The magical elements of Wagner's operas, which strain the resources of theatrical effects technology, are well suited for the stereo medium where effective illusions may be painstakingly created without the constraints of a real-time performance. The use of a reverberation chamber for the sinister figure of Alberich and the climactic peak of Donner's thunderbolt in Culshaw's 1958 "Rheingold" are still without rival. And when the stereo illusion reached its limit, as it did in portraying vertical distance when Wagner's gods on the Rainbow Bridge call down to the Rhinemaidens in the water below, psychological suggestion came to the rescue. Culshaw wrote an article before the release of the record and drew attention "to the way in which the voices appeared to come from below. In fact, they do nothing of the sort, but the suggestion worked. One critic after another commented on the remarkable illusion" (Culshaw, 1972, p. 102).

Although a great deal of technical change still surrounds the long-play record, particularly with the advent of digital technology, surprisingly few changes have occurred in the communicational process since these earlier examples. If anything, the process of putting performances onto disk and selling them to the home market has become even more standardized, and few people seem to be suggesting other uses of the medium or different approaches to it. The major variable now may be the difference between the large record-producing companies and the myriad independents who operate on small budgets and produce types of music which are not viable on the mass market. The idea of "composing for disk" does not seem to have flourished, after the initial effort by the Nonesuch label to commission works specifically for record from electronic music composer Morton Subotnick in the late 1960s. A few composers take the medium into account when composing by consideration of what fits onto one side of a record, but by and large, composers tend to regard recordings as the most valuable form of distribution for their work, but not as a medium for which one designs the work in the first place—the record itself being the composition. The reason is presumably the lack of control which the creator of the music generally has over the recording process and other stages of manufacture and distribution. The increasing technical specialization of the recording process threatens to exclude the composer from active involvement in it even more.

The gap between composer and record producer seems the most ironic in the case of the electroacoustic composer, the one who works in the tape medium in the first place. What kind of work could be more appropriate for the record medium which itself is derived from a master tape! My bias here is obvious, as I have personally produced two records of this type of music and have found it most satisfying to be able to design the entire "package," as well as its recorded contents. The irony may yet heighten, as we watch what success composers of computer music (particularly that which is synthesized entirely in digital form) have in gaining access to the new digital forms of recording that are now emerging. It would indeed be ironic if, either the digital composition had to go to an analog medium and back to a digital one in order to be recorded, or else if those who are being creative in the medium are denied access to its use as a mode of distribution!

Text-Sound, Electroacoustic Music, and the Soundscape Composition

Never have the dividing lines between language, music, and soundscape been as blurred as when these sounds are used as source material in the sound studio. And never have we been able to experience as intensely the continuum that links these systems of acoustic communication as when electroacoustic technology brings their sounds into the realm of compositional design. The common basis is sound, but in their original contexts, the sounds of language, music, and the soundscape are structured in order to be meaningful. When isolated, fragmented or even distorted in the sound studio, they first seem to lose whatever meaning they acquired through both structure and context. The initial impact of technology seems to degrade their integrity. Although one may become more intensely aware of out-of-context sounds simply because they are isolated and framed by technological intervention, the composer is left with the problem of how to *reconstruct* a meaningful utterance with them.

All sound in the experimental studio, whether of natural or synthetic origin, becomes abstract material awaiting rebirth within a new communicational framework. The temptation is to let the sound remain abstract, justified as art for its own sake. To invent new meaning by creating a structure that allows the sound to speak with a new voice is more difficult—but ultimately it is the only path that can be defended as being original. Let us briefly introduce some representative work that suggests possible paths which have produced a new electroacoustic art. Although the examples we cite concern professional work, and only that which has been recorded, keep in mind that experimentation along these lines can be carried out with the simplest home equipment and a bit of imagination (Dwyer, 1971; Keane, 1980).

The field of what is called "text-sound" composition represents a particular meeting of the sensibilities of the poet and the composer around the premise that language is fundamentally an aural phenomenon (Chopin, 1981). It has grown out of related work referred to as "sound poetry" and "concrete poetry" that extends back to such Dadaist artists as Tristan Tzara, Raoul Hausmann, and Kurt Schwitters who performed their work with all manner of vocal utterances and other noises. Others, like William Burroughs, invented literary techniques that depart from conventional syntax and use of punctuation. A strong emphasis of the contemporary sound poetry movement is in live performance, with a return to the primacy of voice and its ability to turn the printed page into sound. Various performance groups have emerged, some from the literary side, such as the Canadian group, The Four Horsemen, and others with musical background, such as the West German group, Trio ex Voco, the British ensemble, Electric Phoenix, and the Extended Vocal Techniques ensemble from the U.S. Many such individuals and groups use electroacoustic technology, either as an aspect of performance (e.g., amplification, modification circuits, tape delay, or prerecorded tape), or as the compositional medium itself.

A typical example of a text-sound composition on tape is Charles Amirkhanian's piece *Just* (1972). It is based on four words "rainbow, chug, bandit, bomb" which are repeated in a variety of rhythms and juxtapositions, like some complex mantra. It is typical of these pieces that the basic techniques of the sound studio, such as splicing, rearrangement, and mixing, are the methods by which the sound material is explored, and that these methods subsequently influence the style of live performance of the poet and even attitudes toward text organization. Therefore, in *Just* it is not clear how much of the repetition and rhythmic variation was in the original reading, and how much was done through studio manipulation, the techniques of each being similar (as in Burroughs' "cut-up" technique). However, layering of the *same* voice to produce choral effect, echo, or rhythmic counterpoint is only possible in the sound studio, and therefore its use changes the listener's perceptual mode to the level of the *imaginary*. One may seem to be hearing, for instance, an "inner" voice accompanying an "outer" one, or multiple mirrored images of the self speaking independently.

Working in parallel to the dialectic between the real and the imaginary in a text-sound composition, is that between referential and abstract meaning as in the continuum between language and music. In Amirkhanian's *Just*, the words are familiar but their juxtapositions create abstract musical rhythms of the words as *sounds*, rather than referential language patterns. The possibility is left open, however, that the listener may construct a personal interpretation from some conjunction of words such as "rainbow bandit." The musical basis is not accidental, as the words were clearly chosen with rhythmic criteria in mind, namely the 2–1–2–1 pattern of syllables that naturally produce a triple rhythm and can easily be placed in other metric patterns. In his companion piece, *Heavy Aspirations* (1973), based on a lecture by Nicolas Slonimsky which refers to the earlier piece, Amirkhanian uses similar techniques with this "found" material, though more sparingly, to illustrate ideas referred to in the text. Referential meaning (mainly about text-sound and music) is preserved and simply enhanced by repetitions suggested by the text or derived fom musical features of Slonimsky's unique rhetorical style.

Many sound poets and composers have explored the border country between words, sounds, and music, with varying degrees of traditional linguistic and musical meanings present. Audio technology has often provided the means for the exploration. The "audiopoems" of Henri Chopin, for instance, though based on vocal material, have little conventional linguistic content and in a sense, use studio techniques to transcend language. The Swedish composers Lars-Gunnar Bodin and Sten Hanson frequently use language elements as an integral part of their electronic musical compositions. One of the most famous pieces of early European electronic music, *Thema*

(Omaggio a Joyce) (1958), by Luciano Berio, is in fact a text-sound composition, being based entirely on the voice of Cathy Berberian reading the first 40 lines of chapter 11 of James Joyce's *Ulysses*. The highly onomatopoeic text is divided into sound families: phonemes, vowels, consonants (in particular the plosive "b" and sibilant "ss"), as well as words and phrases. Multiple tape loops, speed changes, filtering, and other classical studio techniques are used to create a panoply of vocal sound that borders on the electronic. Berio states that he:

> attempted to establish a new relationship between speech and music, in which a continuous metamorphosis of one into the other can be developed . . . where it is no longer possible to distinguish between word and sound, between sound and noise, between poetry and music, but where we once more become aware of the relative nature of these distinctions and of the expressive character inherent in their changing functions.[3]

The celebratory nature of Joyce's text (which consists of aurally enticing fragments from the rest of a chapter dedicated to music) is mirrored by Berio's virtuosic handling of all the elements of language, from the whirlwind of phonemes on the word "bloom" to the caressing solo voice of the cadential sibilants "pearls: when she. Liszt's rhapsodies. Hissss."

The present author's work *The Blind Man* (1979) is based on a text and reading by Vancouver writer Norbert Ruebsaat and constitutes what might be called a text-soundscape composition. The source material includes the writer's reading and improvisation with the text, as well as environmental recordings of bells, and heavy doors and locks in a library vault. However, a continuum between these materials is established by extracting words and phonemic elements from the voice (e.g., sibilants, plosive consonants, etc.) and extending them into sounds with environmental connotations that reflect and dramatize the poem. The original reading of the poem is interspersed throughout the piece in five segments, but the creation of a longer (16 minute) dramatic environment around the words allows the interplay between the various levels of poetic image as word, word as sound, and sound as image to be experienced by the listener.

Digital voice synthesis and processing have extended the range of possibilities of the text-sound composition. The American composer Charles Dodge has created several works based on synthesized speech (which is, in fact, resynthesized on the basis of linear predictive analysis of recorded speech). The synthesized voice, as used in *Speech Songs* (1973), *The Story of Our Lives* (1974), and *In Celebration* (1975), based on texts by Mark Strand, em-

---

[3]Luciano Berio, liner notes, Turnabout TV 34177.

bodies within itself both the real and the imaginary, as it weaves between literal resemblance of the original and unusual distortions, elongations, and perturbations that reveal its electronic basis. The frequent humor suggested by such manipulations stems from the listener's constant perception of the voice in human terms, and the impossibility of even the most gifted vocal contortionist of producing such gymnastics. Dodge has also exploited the theatrical possibilities of speech processing in *Any Resemblance is Purely Coincidental* (1980), in which a pianist on stage "accompanies" a recorded and digitally manipulated voice of Enrico Caruso to great humorous effect. Musically, the works are extensions of Schoenberg's *sprechgesang* technique of blending speech patterns with melody, but with a vastly extended range of (in)human expression. Linear predictive synthesis techniques have also been used by Paul Lansky in his *Six Fantasies on a Poem by Thomas Campion* (1978–1979) with expressive effectiveness on a more intimate and human scale.

One of the first combinations of voice with purely synthesized sound material is found in Karlheinz Stockhausen's 1956 work *Gesang der Jünglinge*. The text, which is the "song of the holy children" from the Apocrypha to the Book of Daniel, is sung, intoned, and spoken by a young boy, the purity of whose voice is well suited to be surrounded by sine tones and clusters of sine tones. Because the text (in German) consists of repetitive acclamations with no evolution of thought and is presumably familiar to a German-speaking audience, it is amenable to fragmentation and musical variation without its essential meaning being lost. Since the meaning is essentially preabsorbed, "the concentration is directed upon the sacredness; speech becomes ritual."[4] The voice includes both pitched and non-pitched sounds (i.e., voiced and unvoiced phonemes) and a variety of timbres, from the harmonic, through those based on formant regions, to noise-like spectra. This fact suggested to Stockhausen that the vocal sounds he was using could be arranged along a continuum of timbre, as well as pitch, duration, and loudness, and then permuted according to serial principles, which formed the basic structural model in use at that time in Europe. The electronic sounds that were available from the "building blocks" of waveform generators and filtered noise were also treated similarly.

The resulting work is a dynamic series of textures that present a wide variety of constellations of the singularly coherent materials. This structure creates a non-linear sense of form which can be compared to "an individual self-contained world like a crystal, which, when one turns it, is always different, but always the same" (Meyer, 1967, p. 80). In fact, in all of these works one can see the acoustic design principle of balance between variety and coherence being invoked within the extended practice of electroacoustic tech-

[4]Karlheinz Stockhausen, "Music and Speech," *Die Reihe, 6* p. 58.

nology. Careful choice of text and voice preserves unity within the vastly expanded variational possibilities provided by that technology.

Electroacoustic Music

In a very general sense, all instrumental music is constructed from abstract sound material whose qualities arise from the design of the physical instrument itself and the particular techniques for performance on it. With the exception of composers who become instrument builders, like Harry Partch (1974), composers of instrumental music generally use the sounds available to them, rather than design the sound directly. Again, with exceptions such as Steve Reich, Terry Riley, and others, today's composers are also not generally the performers of their own music. In the practice of electroacoustic music, the roles of instrument builder, performer, and composer become much more closely linked.

With analog electronic equipment, the composer is seldom its actual builder (with the exception of composers David Behrman and Donald Buchla who have constructed and used both analog and hybrid digital-analog systems). However, electronic music composers work directly with macro level parameters of the sound; in essence, they compose the sound as well as the music. With digital technology, the composer may have participated in software or hardware development, but even if not, is still more likely to be closely concerned with the details of sound synthesis at both the micro and macro level that were previously inaccessible. Although many electroacoustic composers prefer to dissociate their techniques from traditional instrumental models, both in terms of acoustic and structural models, there are several senses in which electroacoustic music may be seen to build on and *extend* the instrumental music tradition of composition with abstract sound material. Without doubt, electroacoustic technology has changed the communicational system of composer, performer, instrument builder, and audience.

Part of the electroacoustic tradition in music derives from using prerecorded source material (the isolated "sound object" or the environmental "sound event"), following the early work by Pierre Schaeffer dating from 1948 at the French radio (O.R.T.F.), and that of John Cage in New York using found materials of various kinds (Cross, 1968). Schaeffer's work (frequently termed *musique concrète)* led to the formation of the research and production group known as the G.R.M. (Groupe de Recherches Musicales), the most notable of whose composers are François Bayle and Bernard Parmegiani, and also to the founding of independent studios at Marseilles and Bourges (the G.M.E.M. and G.M.E.B., respectively). The latter, directed by composers Françoise Barrière and Christian Clozier, is also notable for its hosting of the annual International Festival of Electroacoustic Music, the only event so singularly devoted to this type of music.

The use of purely electronically synthesized material stems from the work in the early 1950s at the studios of the North West German Radio (NWDR) in Cologne, founded by Herbert Eimert, Werner Meyer-Eppler, and Robert Beyer, and later directed by Karlheinz Stockhausen. Many of the early works of significance were realized in that studio by composers such as Eimert, Stockhausen, Karel Goeyvaerts, Gottfried Koenig, and Bruno Maderna. After 1953, studios quickly sprang up around state radio facilities in Europe and Japan, and around university facilities in England, North America, Australia, and New Zealand. Among the latter is the Columbia–Princeton studio founded by Otto Luening and Vladimir Ussachevsky, whose early experiments and compositions made extensive use of simple tape manipulations of prerecorded sounds. Koenig went on to direct the Institute of Sonology at Utrecht in the Netherlands, a leading studio involved in research, teaching, and both electronic and computer music production.

With the advent of transistor technology in the early 1960s, many modular synthesis and modification circuits could be included in a single device, known as the electronic music synthesizer, such as those designed by Robert Moog, Donald Buchla, and Peter Zinovieff. As a result, electroacoustic music composition became more widely accessible, as well as commercially viable (Strange, 1972, 1983; Appleton & Perera, 1975; Howe, 1975). In many cases, the design of the synthesizer began to take on more traditional characteristics of instrumental music with keyboards, 12-tone equal-tempered pitch scales, and constant timbre per voice. By the time such units became equipped with polyphonic keyboards, some sceptics argued that the designers had merely reinvented the electric organ, which dates from the 1930s. In many ways, the same split between new technology modelling older musical practice and extending that practice is occurring today with the advent of digital synthesizers, as used by composers such as Jon Appleton and Joel Chadabe. Just as the electronic music synthesizer incorporated the new ideas of modularity and a semi-automated control principle called "voltage control," so too, the contemporary digital synthesizer offers the digital potential of memory storage, algorithmic processes, and digital signal generation. All of these features change the communicational environment in which the music is created, but frequently these new concepts are used to mimic traditional models of music organization, thereby minimizing their creative potential and maximizing their commercial viability. The composer whose work has best shown the creative use of the synthesizer while remaining commercially attractive enough to be recorded on a major label is Morton Subotnick, but his work is the exception that proves the rule.

The composer who foresaw the potential of technology for the "liberation of sound" from traditional musical models was Edgard Varèse, a French composer who became an American citizen in 1916 (Russcol, 1972). His most controversial works during the 1920s and '30s attempted to stretch the boundaries of music within the instrumental tradition, even if that meant using only percussion instruments as in the classic 1931 composition *Ionisation,* which was the first to do so. As early as 1917, Varèse had called for instruments which would contribute "a whole new world of unsuspected sounds" (Varèse, 1966, p. 11), but it was not until 1953 that he acquired a tape recorder and interpolated sections of sound on tape between the instrumental sections of *Déserts.* In 1958 he produced his best known work, and his only tape solo, *Poème Electronique* in the Philips studios at Eindhoven in the Netherlands, a work intended for the Philips pavilion designed by Le Corbusier at the Brussels World Fair. The work mixes purely electronic sounds with transformations of prerecorded sounds such as bells, carillon, organ, bits of traditional music, and the female voice. The sounds are clearly demarcated and placed in a multidimensional space, and those derived from prerecorded sources remain identifiable, though fragmented. Each sound element seems to have been chosen for the vividness of the aural image which it contributes to the "poem." The juxtaposition of images is not entirely arbitrary as in a collage, but rather plays on certain rhythmic and timbral relationships that link dissimilar elements. The listener's imagination is invited to connect the images further, or if you prefer, to supply the missing "film" for which this is the soundtrack. The poetic sound images are as vivid as they are evanescent, and the work concludes with a magnificent Varèse glissando which arcs high overhead to carve out a voluminous space that is as open as his imagery and musical vision.

Similar studio techniques have traditionally been used to put the prerecorded sound object under a microscope and find the sonic universe within the single sound. Examples of compositions built up from the single abstracted sound are Hugh Le Caine's charmingly whimsical study of a single drop of water, called *Dripsody* (1955), Toru Takemitsu's *Water Music* (1960), and Iannis Xenakis' 1958 work *Concret P-H II.* David Keane, in turn, has used the Le Caine work as a starting point for an electronic extension of the water drop music in his *In Memoriam: Hugh Le Caine* (1978). In the Xenakis work, the scintillating texture derives from the crackling discharges of smoldering charcoal and illustrates the composer's fascination with stochastic processes, as described in chapter 7. Micro level variations make many stochastic sounds quite interesting, and Xenakis has extrapolated this concept to the macro level in the density and texture of events of his instrumental works. His recent work in digital sound synthesis has returned to a concern for the control of statistical fluctuations in sound pressure as a source of musical material.

The field of electroacoustic music, despite the public's relative unfamiliarity with it, is too extensive for an adequate survey in the present context; however, see (Appleton & Perera, 1975; Deutsch, 1976; Schrader, 1982; Pellegrino, 1983). However, our intent is not to deal with it on a musical level but from a communicational perspective to examine how the new technology changes the design process, and more generally, how it affects our concepts about sound. To do that, we have chosen some representative works that illustrate a characteristic handling of materials along the speech–music–soundscape continuum. We are considering "music" in that continuum to be the organization of abstract sound, that is, sound without referential meaning, except to its source. Because electroacoustic sounds are much more varied in timbre than traditional instrumental sounds and are often non-pitched, traditional harmonic models of organization are not appropriate. The compositional problem is how to find a method of organizing *timbre* that is as structurally powerful as that of tonal harmony. Needless to say, solutions are not easy, and moreover, the resulting pieces require a different type of listening, in the sense that one cannot understand them on the basis of melody and harmony alone; instead, they require greater sensitivity to sound quality and spatial, textural relationships. One of the classic pieces from the 1950s that established a convincing sense of timbral organization is Stockhausen's *Kontakte* (1958), which explored the "contact" between percussion and electronic sounds. However, let us briefly examine two more recent pieces of less well-known electroacoustic music that are based on particularly well-conceived systems of timbral organization, namely *Composition 1972* by the Dutch composer Jan Boerman, and *Pentes* (1974) by New Zealand composer Denis Smalley, who now lives in Britain.

Although the Boerman work follows and extends the tradition of Stockhausen and Goeyvaerts, and Smalley's work grows out of the Schaeffer/G.R.M. tradition (in whose studios it was realized), both organize timbre at a form-determining level and create an appealing sonic environment. Boerman organizes his timbral material along a scale from pitched to noise-like sound, but instead of serial permutations, he uses a complex structural scheme based on harmonic proportions, or what is called the "golden section," where an interval is divided into unequal parts such that the proportion of the smaller to the larger is the same as that of the larger to the whole. The result is a type of "self-similarity" in the structure where proportions on a smaller scale are mirrored at larger levels. Boerman's work plays on a dynamic balance between stasis and movement, just as it finds a balance between pitch and noise, loud and soft dynamics, percussive and sustained sounds, in classical proportions.

Smalley's work, on the other hand, is based on a repertoire of sounds that, although widely ranging between tone and noise, are designed from certain qualitative acoustic properties of the instrumental sounds that form the basic source material. The French title (meaning slopes, inclines or ascents) describes the contours of specific sound layers, as in the explosive attack sounds with long textured decays, and the larger-scale accumulations, as in the attractive middle section where the drone harmonies of the Northumbrian pipes, one of the source materials, gradually unfold and lead to a brief and haunting traditional melody on that instrument. This point where the piece "touches down" into the real acoustic world gives the work a different perspective from that of Boerman's completely imaginary landscape. Smalley reveals the fundamental acoustic basis of his electroacoustic art, both as the source of its aural richness and as the model from which the abstract sound shapes are derived.

Although examples of computer music by younger composers such as James Dashow, Paul Lansky, Stanley Haynes, John Celona, Bruce Pennycook, Jean Piché, and Barry Truax have recently appeared on record, some of the best known examples of digitally synthesized and composed works that have extended the domain of electroacoustic composition are not yet available, such as John Chowning's *Turenas* (1972), *Stria* (1977), and *Phoné* (1980–1981), all composed at Stanford University, or Jean-Claude Risset's *Inharmonique* (1977) and *Songes* (1978). They extend the compositional use of timbre through precise specification of particular combinations of frequencies and their temporal evolution. *Phoné* is based on vocal timbres, and *Stria* and *Songes* explore the domain of inharmonic timbre, i.e., those whose component frequencies are not related by integer proportions and therefore are not subject to the auditory system's handling of the "privileged" intervals in the harmonic series. *Songes* also plays on a smooth transition between digitally-recorded live instruments and their synthesized extensions. Besides its appealing timbral repertoire (produced by Chowning's frequency modulation synthesis technique), *Turenas* is also notable for the precise control of the spatial characteristics of the sound used, both in its quadraphonic placement and the control of local and global reverberation. Sounds are placed in spaces of varying sizes and move through them, as in the opening and closing high-frequency drone in the piece which describes a complex trajectory around the audience. Another recent work, *Dreamsong* (1978) by Stanford composer Michael McNabb, uses digital techniques for the entire continuum of sound we have been referring to, from the vocal and environmental through to the artificially synthesized (McNabb, 1981). Therefore we see that current electroacoustic technology is extending the composer's control over the entire domain of sound.

The Soundscape Composition

Electroacoustic music has moved towards environmental sound in many ways, for instance by incorporating prerecorded environmental sound as source material, by simulating environmental cues such as reverberation, directionality, spatial movement, and even Doppler shift, by the structural use of such variables as density, texture, foreground, and background, and finally, through its performance in a multi-channel speaker environment. Given the environmental orientation of a great deal of electroacoustic music, can one speak of yet another category, which we will call the "soundscape composition," which is distinctively different? Just as the text-sound composition draws upon the unique properties of the word as sound and signifier, can the composer use environmental sound in such a way that it necessitates a unique type of understanding based on the listener's soundscape experience?

The essential difference between an electroacoustic composition that uses prerecorded environmental sound as its source material, and a work that can be called a soundscape composition, is that in the former, the sound loses all or most of its environmental context. In fact, even its original identity is frequently lost through the extensive manipulation it has undergone, and the listener may not recognize the source unless so informed by the composer. In the soundscape composition, on the other hand, it is precisely the *environmental context* that is preserved, enhanced and exploited by the composer. The listener's past experience, associations, and patterns of soundscape perception are called upon by the composer and thereby integrated within the compositional strategy. Part of the composer's intent may also be to enhance the listener's awareness of environmental sound. Whereas the use of *concrète* sources leaves the environment the same and merely extracts its elements, the successful soundscape composition has the effect of changing the listener's awareness and attitudes towards the soundscape, and thereby changing the listener's relationship to it. The aim of the composition is therefore social and political, as well as artistic.

Soundscape compositions occur along a continuum between the natural "found" composition (i.e., a soundscape whose organization is so compelling, varied, and interesting that a simple recording of it may be listened to with the same appreciation that one has for conventional music), through those that are painstakingly constructed from elements such that they *appear* to have plausibly occurred that way, to those which have been substantially manipulated for musical or other purposes, but are still recognizably related to the original environment. Therefore, as with the text-sound composition, a dialectic exists between the real and the imaginary, as well as between the referential and the abstract. The artificial soundscape can never be completely referential because it is always being reproduced outside of its original context which it can never entirely restore. Likewise, it can never become wholly abstract without losing its essential environmental quality. It is the interplay between the two extremes that gives vitality to works of this genre.

Although the term "soundscape composition" has been coined by the composers working with the World Soundscape Project (W.S.P.) at Simon Fraser University to denote the pieces which they composed with source material recorded by project members, the term can equally well apply to works by other composers who may or not have been influenced by, or even aware of, that work. For instance, the 1974 work by New Zealand composer

Jack Body, titled *Musik Dari Jalan* (Street Music), is based on the cries of street vendors in Indonesia. Body uses the classical studio technique of isolating the individual sound object (in this case either the vocal cry or the soundmaker used by the vendor) and manipulating some particular facet of it. In essence, he makes the listener more aware of the sound in isolation and then places the sound back into a simulation of its original environment. The transitions between the sound as studio object and environmental event are the most fascinating parts of the piece, and like most soundscape compositions, the integrity of the original sound and soundscape is preserved, in spirit if not in fact. His later works, based on similar Indonesian material, namely the 1978 piece *Musik anak anak* (Children's Music) and *Fanfares* (1981), preserve the same balance and also make the listener more aware of particular environmental sounds and the soundscape of which they are a part.

Other composers use collage techniques with their environmental source material, as with Makoto Shinohara's *City Visit* based on sounds he collected during a visit to New York City. Luc Ferrari uses environmental sound with minimal manipulation in his *Presque Rien* series; for instance, *Presque Rien No. 1* (1970) is based on sounds recorded at a beach at daybreak which are cross-faded with insect sounds towards the end of the piece. A variant on the soundscape composition technique is the electronic work inspired by a particular environment, such as Henri Pousseur's *Trois Visages de Liege* (1961), or an artificial construction such as Bengt Hambraeus' electronic work *Tides* (1974) which effectively evokes much of the environmental imagery of the seascape.

At the other extreme, a work such as *Wood on Wood on Water* (1978), realized by Anne Holmes at S.F.U., is a superlative example of how recorded material from the natural environment, namely waves, seagulls and the sound of a stick hitting a beached log, can be subtly manipulated into an imaginary "real" environment, that is, one that seems realistic enough to have been plausibly recorded as heard. The composer introduces the seashore environment, with the waves as ambience, and gradually brings the percussive sound of the wood into the foreground, elaborating on its simple rhythms until they are a complex percussion orchestra. After the peak of the rhythmic part has been reached, one suddenly realizes that the waves have come into the foreground and are on the verge of "submerging" the sounds of the log. Thus, the structure of the piece, as well as its material, is based on the environmental experience of the shifting relationships between background and foreground in environmental sound (such as hearing the tide come in over some extended period of time). As the piece ends, the sounds of the wood are muffled and dull, those of the waves dominant, and as a final touch, seagulls are heard again. They were omitted from the mix of the middle section, but their absence and rediscovery play on the listener's experience of blocking out background sounds when attention is focused on foreground ones. The subtlety of the effect is typical of the artifice the soundscape composer uses to evoke and intensify the real through the listener's environmental perceptions.

The educational as well as artistic orientation of the W.S.P. led its members to construct a variety of environmental documents that range along the continuum we have mentioned, from the "found" composition through to the highly manipulated artifact. The clearest example of the former is the 24-hour recording technique whereby some number of minutes of each of 24 hours of the same environment are recorded. From each section of this raw material, a 2-minute representative segment is chosen and carefully spliced or cross-faded with the next segment, keeping the same chronological order of the original. The first such effort, called "Summer Solstice," was recorded in 1974 at midsummer by a pond on the grounds of Westminster Abbey, Mission, British Columbia. It was that experience and the resulting document that clearly revealed the amazing variety and balance within the natural soundscape (see Fig. 9), precisely because the experience was framed and compressed into a time period more conducive to the extended human attention span, namely 50 minutes. A similar document was made of Easter Sunday in the Italian mountain village of Cembra, referred to in chapter 5, as well as shorter sequences of the "dawn chorus" of bird song (from predawn to mid-morning) in various locations.

Another type of simulated soundscape is found in the "Entry to the Harbour" sequence on the *Vancouver Soundscape* document. It comprises the various foghorns and other sounds one would encounter on a ship passing from the outer to the inner harbor in Vancouver, then docking. The motor sound that obscures an actual recording of the journey necessitated each sound being recorded separately and mixed with the appropriate spatial illusion of the sound approaching and receding. Other time compression techniques were also used that have become familiar in the syntax of films where intermediate parts of an action can be omitted without disrupting the overall continuity. At a certain, rather undefinable point, the document in sound transforms itself into the soundscape composition, where the various functions of documentation, pedagogy, and aesthetic gratification start leaning towards a predominance of the latter. Of the many works done at S.F.U., one can mention Bruce Davis' *Games,* based on sounds of play, and the poetic documentary *Bells of Percé*; Peter Huse's *Directions,* based on "found" language of people being asked for directions en route; Howard Broomfield's *A Radio Program about Radio,* a complex collage of historical and contemporary radio sound; Barry Truax's *Soundscape Study;* and the larger collective work *Okeanos* by composers R. M. Schafer and Bruce Davis, and writer Brian Fawcett, which brings together the poetic literature of sea imagery with its myriad sounds.

The composer who has pursued the soundscape composition in its various manifestations the most is S.F.U. composer Hildegard Westerkamp (Zapf, 1981b). Her work includes *Whisper Study* (1975), based on the sounds and words of quietude, *Fantasie for Horns* (1978), which places a rich array of sound signals into various environmental and musical relationships based on their pitch and rhythmic patterns, *A Walk Through the City* (1981), which combines the environmental images of Norbert Ruebsaat's poetry and reading with the urban soundscape, and *Cordillera* (1980) which utilizes analogous components to the previous piece, except around the theme of wilderness. In addition, she has composed documentary-style soundscape compositions *Under the Flightpath* (1981), about people's reactions to aircraft noise, and *Street Music* (1982), which celebrates a different kind of environmental music. She has also been involved in several experimental radio series such as the "Soundwalking" series, first heard on Vancouver Co-operative Radio, which blends soundscape documentary, running commentary, debate on social issues concerning noise, and poetic/musical imagery based on soundscape material.

Conclusion

This brief survey has not been able to do justice either to the range or depth of the work done over the last 35 years, but at least it has indicated the incredible variety of experimentation and composition, as well as some of the themes that have been developed. It is neither prejudicial, nor an exaggeration, to suggest that there is a vast gulf between stereotypical, commercial media products and the highly original work that individuals and groups have accomplished with electroacoustic technology. By definition, the former is all too well known, the latter all too inaccessible and unfamiliar, and through its unfamiliarity, perhaps also strange and exotic to many people. Original work either has no access to the media that could bring it to people's attention, or access only on the fringes—the alternative radio stations who seldom can afford to commission professional work, the small independent record labels, mail exchanges of cassettes, or private publication. Works with artistic merit gain some public access via the poorly funded fringes of the contemporary music community, but this avenue, though it has its ardent supporters and (small) appreciative audiences, also serves to "ghettoize" the work and make it subservient to government patronage. It also encourages only that portion of electroacoustic composition which has "artistic" merit, however the definition may be stretched. As a result, particularly in Europe, composers almost automatically confine their efforts to the production of art music and turn a deaf ear to the entire continuum of social, environmental, pedagogical, and artistic implications of the technology they use—a technology which by no stretch of the imagination is conceived entirely or specifically for musical purposes.

It is not surprising if both the individual member of the public and the professional electroacoustic designer/composer feel constrained by the prevailing communicational patterns of our society. Both need to regain control of technology and its organized avenues of communication. But neither appears to be on the verge of any breakthrough. The consumer's illusion of freedom through the pseudo-democratization of mass-produced home computers and home audio equipment merely contributes to even greater conformity and industry control. New ideas may lead to new products, but new products do not necessarily lead to new ideas. Yet the path forward is clear once we see what constitutes a true net gain from technology, what makes it an actual extension of the human mind. The alternatives and the explorational potential have been demonstrated by countless pioneers. Through them we suddenly realize that the limitations are not in the technology, or even necessarily in its organization. They are in ourselves, in our imagination and initiative to use what is available for our own benefit. It is in fact up to us whether technology will be the massage or the catalyst in our lives.

14

Electroacoustic Design

The examples cited in the previous chapter suggest the range of alternative uses of electroacoustic technology that extend or transform our relationship to sound. If anything justifies the technological embrace on society, it is these creative uses of the new resources, the ones that fulfill the basic definition of what a human "tool" should be—an extension, not a replacement or surrogate. Other uses often impose unwanted artifacts on the soundscape and condition desensitized listening habits. We accept even useful technological aids without realizing that we have to adapt our behavior to their demands and that something is lost in the process, a loss that may not be compensated by the gains we expect. In the worst cases, outright exploitation turns listeners into passive consumers in an attempt to create, control, and manipulate their needs and desires.

Let us examine the claim I am making that a net gain is indeed possible through the creative use of technology by analyzing the general principles that are common to all of the cases that have been cited. In the first half of the book it was argued that acoustic design is both an analysis of how systems of acoustic communication function successfully, and the application of the criteria obtained from such analyses to situations in need of improvement. The analysis of electroacoustic systems of communication, therefore, should lead to an insight as to how technology may be successfully integrated within the acoustic communicational process. It should also suggest how such innovations may be regarded, how they may best be used, and what criteria for electroacoustic design may be formulated. The net result should be an understanding of how technology need not be an inhuman force we cannot control, but rather, how it can be used to extend our awareness, express our creativity and improve human communication.

Principles of Electroacoustic Design

Perhaps the most basic difference between acoustic design and electroacoustic design is that in the latter case, there are no "natural" well-designed models as there are in all acoustic systems. Just as languages are classified as natural and artificial, so too, there are natural acoustic systems of communication and those involving technology that are always artificial. Even the inherently human artifacts of spoken language and music seem, through their traditions in all civilizations, to be "natural" systems. We should remember that in music, it is a relatively recent concept, found only in European music from the Middle Ages and in its descendants, that a composer exists as an individual charged with the personal creation of sound structures. Therefore, the completely artificial nature of electroacoustic design demands both technical expertise (which is an extension of earlier mechanical sound technology), and an implicit awareness of every stage of the design process. Connections with tradition exist, of course, but our purpose here is to show in what respects electroacoustic technology changes the design process. Also, I do not want to imply that creative sound design cannot be done with traditional acoustic means. It is only the *means* that are either traditional or experimental; conventional or innovative forms of expression can result with any choice of medium.

What is common to all forms of innovative electroacoustic design are the possibilities of control over the sound material, the organizational structure, and the communicational environment. The latter is the most frequently ignored at the peril of the success of the communication. Within acoustic systems, the possibilities of control are bounded by the laws of acoustic behavior. The spoken word, for instance, can be designed through the skills of oratory and rhetoric to remain intelligible in large or small spaces that are open or enclosed. Such strategies, however, have to work within the constraints of reverberation and sound diffusion, and those variables can only be altered by the design of the space, not by the design of the artifact. Traditional performance techniques in music have always adapted the musical message to the given acoustic environment. If one treats a musical work as a static object that is always performed in exactly the same way and always with the same participant forces, one will immediately run counter to the laws of acoustics that dictate whether such an ideal performance will work in a given space or not. Therefore, the design of the musical work is not independent of the space for which it was intended (implicitly or explicitly), and the design of a specific performance *must* adapt the original scoring to suit the acoustics of the performing space to whatever extent is feasible within the given style.

Design of the Electroacoustic Environment

Therefore, we see that what is being controlled in electroacoustic design is not fundamentally different from the concerns of acoustic design, but that the methods and possibilities of control have considerably more flexibility. Keep in mind that the "environment" in the electroacoustic case may be nearly independent of the laws of acoustic propagation, as in the case of the telephone or headphone listening. Although the final sound that is heard is still acoustic, in these cases at least, the main determinant of the coloration of the sound by the environment is that of the response characteristics of the medium of transfer. For telephone, this means a restricted frequency range, whereas in high quality headphone listening the bandwidth can be quite large. The binaural format in headphones also allows subtle spatial information in the sound to be transferred directly to the ear without further coloration, either by the environment of the listener or by the listener's own pinnae (i.e., outer ears).

Another fundamental difference in the environmental design component of the electroacoustic process is that the environment in which the sound is ultimately heard is indeterminate or even completely unforeseeable. Sound on tape may be played anywhere at any time, and under quite variable technical and acoustic conditions of reproduction. One can only guess where a radio transmission might be heard and what the listening environment of the person hearing it might be. Moreover, the sound studio in which the design is being tested may bear little acoustic resemblance to the space in which it is ultimately heard. One frequently has to imagine the effects of transferring the sound from a small studio to a large hall, or from the studio to a private living room. At the 1978 World Music Days in Stockholm, tape pieces were commissioned for a concert that took place in the harbor, with a stereo channel on either side—one of the larger stereo separations I have encountered. Certain kinds of sounds and structures worked better than others in that acoustic environment (voice being the least successful), but it was certainly a case where the composer had little chance to test the piece in the space beforehand.

The variability of the destination environment suggests that not only might one have to design the sound so that it works under various conditions, but also that one might want to create several versions of the piece designed for different media and formats (e.g., quadraphonic speakers, FM stereo, stereo LP, headphones, etc.). Each version can be adapted to the restrictions of the medium (e.g., bandwidth, dynamic range, number of channels, etc.), but also each can exploit the possibilities of that medium. For instance, a version with binaural time delays could create sounds whose spatial movement is only audible on headphones. In terms of concert performance, the electroacoustic work *must* be adapted to the acoustic of the hall or space and literally be performed for it, both in the design of speaker placement and in the real-time control of levels, equalization, and channelling. Skilled interpreters of electroacoustic music are needed as critically as those for acoustic music.

A very subtle form of design consideration is the *listening environment* for which the artifact is intended, by which I mean the level and type of awareness of the prospective listeners. Besides the social context, one must consider the psychological expectations of the audience in order to predict how they will react as listeners. One cannot, and should not, assume that people will devote their full attention in any given situation, or that the acoustic environment will be favorable to sound propagation or sensitive listening. If the problem is to communicate a verbal message via loudspeakers, a careful choice of voice quality and style of delivery is necessary, and many such systems also employ an attention-getting signal or fanfare at the beginning of each message. With perambulating listeners, as in a gallery, the sound must make sense at whatever point one starts listening to it, even if it is in the background of one's attention. Therefore, a "linear" form that depends on the listener having heard something earlier cannot be used. Perhaps the most interesting and challenging outlet for such design considerations is the medium of radio. We have described how commercial radio is structurally designed to be effective with distracted listeners, but there are many possibilities with alternative radio formats to design different types of interaction.

For instance, one might keep the same assumption that listeners will generally be involved with other activity and design a sound structure that suggests background listening on their part, but instead of the listener remaining totally passive, changes might occasionally occur that would deliberately attract attention and change the listener's relationship to the sound. The use of slowly moving environmental sound as an unusual form of radio content would establish, first of all, a different time scale for the listening experience. Second, it would give the listener more freedom to change the level of listening attention at will according to what seems interesting at the time. Bruce Davis (1975) has suggested an even more radical step in terms of a real-time "wilderness radio" monitoring channel, which would reverse the flow of radio by broadcasting sound from a carefully chosen wilderness environment direct to the city, thereby providing a different type of long-term listener involvement. Therefore, even a background listening environment can be made more interactive, and less manipulative, than current formats. If such a use of environmental sound seems extreme, one can explore alternative formats with more conventional content. Anything that departs from conventional expectations of radio structure will change the listening relationship of the audience (e.g., live music as opposed to prerecorded, different speech rhythms and timbres, non-linear progressions as opposed to "that was A, now this is B," and most daring of all, the creative use of silence.).

Design of the Sound and its Structure

To return to our summary of the basic principles of electroacoustic design that make it different from traditional means, we should recall that, in addition to the design of the environment, one is designing both the sound and the sound structure. Even when the sound source is prerecorded, one has quite powerful tools for its modification in the contemporary sound studio. When you record the sound yourself, then an even greater range of control is possible, according to choice of mike, its placement or movement and the choice of ambient environment. One may use a mike to capture extreme close-up detail, like a microscope, or multiple mikes for stereophonic images, including binaural recording techniques that provide the perspective of being inside someone's head. Even some smaller mixers include basic equalization controls for adjusting the timbral quality of the sound, as well as allowing sounds to be combined and directed to one or more output channels. In chapter 10 we described the full range of studio possibilities for sound manipulation as providing a "laboratory for perception" because each modification both creates a new sound and makes one more analytically aware of the original sound's structure. The inclusion of some of the basic possibilities in home audio equipment has brought some of this potential within reach of the general public, but the current trend away from reel-to-reel tape, in preference to the enclosed, modular cassette format which is difficult to splice and usually has no possibility for speed changes, suggests that such experimentation is not likely to continue to be encouraged.

Electronic sound synthesis, of both the analog and digital varieties, is reputed to provide the greatest control over the design of sound material. It is also more problematic than that which starts with prerecorded natural (or *concrète*) sounds simply because one is forced to generate the basic material synthetically. All of the intricacies of the physical behavior of the sound source that combine to produce the richness of even the simplest natural sound are unavailable in electronic synthesis. One has to invoke some model of sound production right from the start, and therefore the quality of synthesized sound depends on our knowledge of acoustic behavior as modelled in the equipment used. Most synthesizers are based on the waveform generator or oscillator which has a predictable harmonic content but no time variance (something found in all natural sounds), or else on noise generators whose output can be filtered. These two basic types of sounds can be extended through dynamic filtering and techniques of modulation, both of which can add some time variance to the internal structure of the sound.

Creative or Exploitative?

Without going into the technical problems any more deeply, we can see that the synthesis of sound raises the question of whether one can (or should) model the complexity of natural sounds, or whether one should explore the possibilities that are unique to the medium itself, even if that means creating unfamiliar sounds. For the latter, which naturally attracts the more adventuresome, the acoustic territory is a domain with few guideposts or familiar landmarks. But is the equipment designing the sound or is the composer still in control? And if the sound output is entirely new, on what basis will its organization allow it to become meaningful? The potential is great, but so are the risks. On the other hand, the electronic music that has had the greatest impact on the public is undoubtedly that of the so-called "switched on" variety and its popular music descendants, where familiar pieces or styles of music are realized with electronic sound sources that are designed to resemble instrumental models, more or less. It is a case where one can feel daringly modern and safely traditional at the same time.

In fact, this formula of repackaging familiar forms in electronic guises is practically the only one which finds success in the commercial world, simply because it satisfies the public "demand" for what is new (which is in fact a need of the industry), and at the same time protects them from having to deal with the problem of assimilating anything *really* new. It provides the illusion of change with none of its inconvenience. The soundtracks for the biggest science fiction/fantasy films at the box office use the most traditional styles of music—computer graphics and the romantic orchestra. Even those with electronic soundtracks are imitations of the instrumental equivalent, and cynics might add, a less expensive version to produce. The other standard use of electronic sound in the mass media is to depict the eerie, the strange, and the other-worldly, that is, to reinforce the musical ignorance of the public which regards anything unfamiliar as alien and inhuman. All of these standard uses of technology reinforce the status quo and confirm existing relationships to sound and music. Therefore, by our definition, they are neither new nor creative, and in the worst cases, simply exploitative and manipulative.

How then does one break through this impasse of using technology creatively without losing communicative effectiveness? The answer, of course, is good electroacoustic design, but that answer is also circular since that is what we are attempting to define. Whether the work is artistic or functional, the composer or designer is most successful when the following two levels are considered:

1. the sound material and its structure;
2. the use to which the work is put; its context and environment.

The distinction with the former is quite subtle, because superficially it would appear that the skill involved in producing a conventional commercial product is equally concerned with sound material. One way of expressing the difference in attitude toward the materials is that in the one case, one composes "with" sound, and in the other, "through" sound. In the former, one *uses* sound structures because they are known to have a predictable effect, whereas in the latter, one is in a sense "used" by the sound by being open to whatever meaning it may suggest. It is the difference between sounds "expressing'' something else (e.g., happiness, danger, or a storyline), and the expression arising from their own behavior and structure. One process reinforces an existing communicational relationship, the other extends and transforms it.

For the designer, the difference is both subtle and sometimes very simple. If one is editing an interview, for instance, the difference may be between cutting the material to force the relevant content into a given time frame, and editing it in such a way as to let the person speak ''naturally''—in effect, making the technology invisible. The difference may be between ''using'' existing music as an overlay to hook the audience's attention (ignoring the distancing effect to the subject it also has), and finding other sound material from *within* the subject matter that functions as a more appropriate and revealing counterpoint to draw the audience into a deeper involvement. Likewise, it may mean avoiding conventional ''sound effects'' and creating a sound environment with its own level of meaning that simultaneously ''comments'' on the action. It can mean treating speech for its musical values, orchestrating voices or framing environmental sound to enhance the listener's awareness of the soundscape. In the exploitative approach, there is some justice in that the designer is the first to be manipulated during the studio design process. In the creative approach, even though a great deal of manipulation of the sound may be involved (i.e., the process is still artificial), the designer is the first to learn or experience something new and unique in the process.

Design of the Compositional System

One of the most exciting aspects of electroacoustic technology is that it allows new possibilities for the design not only of sound material, structures, and modes of distribution, but also of the *compositional process* itself. The computing science term for it is ''man-machine communication,'' but let us remove the sexist connotation from that phrase, and refer to ''composer-machine communication.'' We will look at several features of such processes which can change the composer's creative involvement with sound.

Real-Time and Non–Real-time Composition

Current practice separates electroacoustic design systems into studio composition and ''live electronic'' performance. Let us first compare and contrast these new possibilities with the conventional process for the composer who is involved, either in writing notes on paper or in improvising directly on instruments. For the former, the process involves a fair amount of memory and imagination of what the final sound result will be. Structures can be tried out on a piano, but essentially the sound material is a given entity that can only be modified by instructing the performer to use certain playing techniques. Moreover, conventional music notation implicitly determines the kinds of control which can be specified and their degree of precision, with the result that things that appear precise and fixed on paper may be less so in the composer's mind, and that other things which are more important may be left to the interpretive discretion of the performer. Contemporary notational practice has attempted to break through some of these constraints in allowing other types of control, for both precision and deliberate indeterminacy to be expressed (Karkoschka, 1972). However, the general process and relationship between composer, conductor, performer, and even audience has not changed very much within the traditional medium.

For the composer-improviser, the process is bound up in a much more intimate interaction between thought, performance technique and the sound of the instrument. Both the greatest advantage and the greatest limitation of improvising are found in the intuitiveness of the process. Many intermediary stages of notation and composer/performer separation are avoided, but other constraints operate in their place, such as what can be performed and thought out in real-time musical behavior. Some electroacoustic instruments, such as the electronic organ, may change the sound material or the playing technique, but they do not change the musical process very much. On the other hand, synthesizers that implement some form of automation and data memory definitely change the process of live performance by allowing independent activities to be initiated and controlled. The performer may not be directly responsible for the production of all the sound, but rather may also have some role as a "controller" of automated or semi-automated processes, if only to initiate and terminate them. The inclusion of any kind of data memory (such as a sequencer, tape playback unit, or digital memory) lessens the real-time constraint by allowing sound, or control data for sound, to be pre-organized and introduced into the performance at the appropriate time.

In addition, the use of new control devices allows other means of performer involvement in the process, even though the present level of sophistication of such is often criticized as being too primitive. What we are referring to are transducers, that is, devices which convert environmental data (including that provided by the performer) into electrical form for use as an audio signal or control signal. Most such transducers convert a single parameter, such as pressure, velocity, distance, heat, or any biological variable; others pick up brain waves or other signals from any source. The generality of such devices favors multi-media performance since anyone, including the audience, can participate in sending signals and controlling circuits. The problem for the designer is how to map such control signals onto meaningful patterns of sound or other variables. Many devices transmit signals that prove too uniform or erratic to be of much interest. One-to-one control patterns quickly become predictable and boring. Often the problem is how to introduce hierarchic levels of control, because no system of communication with any complexity operates at a single level. The challenge in live performance is how to design a real-time system of communication that shows variety, complexity, and balance in the interaction of all of its elements.

Let us characterize the other kind of design process referred to above as non–real-time composition. In it, the compositional process is separated from the performance process, and electroacoustic technology has a profound effect on both. We have already discussed some of the possibilities for performance, in terms of the format, medium, and environment. The design of the *compositional system* itself is no less interesting, both conceptually and practically (Chadabe, 1977). We have described the major differences in studio process in terms of the manipulation of the sound itself; one deals directly with the sound, and the role of notation is always subservient to that process. Besides having this almost tactile involvement with sound, the studio composer can also incorporate other aspects of machine-aided composition in the process. Let us examine some of them.

Analog and Digital Control

One useful distinction to describe the possible types of process is in terms of their analog and digital properties. In analog processes, the manipulation is continuous and the result is understood as a qualitative difference. A knob is turned and adjusted until the right pitch or loudness is achieved. In filtering and equalizing, the qualitative aspect of timbre is quite amenable to this kind of modification. A simple TOTE operation (test, operate, test, exit) suffices to describe the type of interaction involved. In a digital process, one actually specifies a precise numerical value for the parameter to be changed. One can also initiate a specific operation with values assigned to its variables where some intermediate algorithm is used by the machine to create the desired change. The result, whether foreseeable or not, is accurate and reproducible. For the composer who is used to precision only in the terms of musical notation, this type of detailed sound control may seem awkward at first when applied to unfamiliar variables. Ultimately it provides a greater degree of control. Although each type of process (analog and digital) has its advantages and drawbacks, together they function quite complementarily. Neither process is superior in any absolute sense, though they are often discussed as if one were. The point is that in an electroacoustic system, the composer can *choose* the type of process to use and adapt it to the task at hand.

However, it is also true that digital technology in the form of the computer has created a powerful tool for the design of compositional systems, or what are commonly called computer music systems. Fortunately, although digital processes are inherent to the machine, analog processes can also be simulated by it. Therefore, the choice of a computer system does not preclude a wide range of processes to be implemented. (There is also a trend in analog studio design to include more and more digital operations within its traditional processes.) From a quick look at the major professional journal in the field, namely the *Computer Music Journal*, one will see that research in computer music is currently more dominated by technical matters than philosophical ones, as is probably inevitable at this stage of a field which is being rapidly propelled by technological forces that are not confined to music alone. On the other hand, the popular journals and the home computer industry tend to promote music systems which replicate existing models of music and the compositional or performance process. Although an overview of the field is beyond the scope of this book, I will attempt to describe its contributions to electroacoustic design in as accessible and non-technical a manner as possible (see also Buxton, 1977; Bateman, 1980).

In chapter 9 we described one of the major components of digital sound systems, namely the numerical representation of sound, and some of the technical advantages for signal processing which result from this fact. Of equal significance is the concept of machine programmability—the software that controls the hardware. A useful way to conceptualize the composer-machine communication involved in a computer music system is to identify the two locations and types of knowledge involved, namely the composer's own knowledge about meaningful sound structures, and the knowledge that is embodied in the machine programs (Truax, 1980). Both types of knowledge are procedural, that is, knowledge about how to perform certain actions, and because programs are step-by-step representations of procedures, the knowledge they embody is objective and *explicit* (Laske, 1978). The procedures may incorporate knowledge about how to generate or modify sound or sound structures. They may require direction from the user via the input of specific parameters, or they may be completely automated. They may incorporate randomness (at least in a repeatable or pseudo-random form) or utilize deterministic equations. Whatever they do, the program itself is an explicit representation of a body of procedural knowledge, and its organization represents an implicit model of the compositional process (Truax, 1976).

Although the design of a fine violin may distill centuries of practical knowledge about how to produce musical sound, its design does not assist (it only constrains) the composition of music for it. The difference between a conventional musical instrument and a computer music system is that the latter possesses a virtual memory and a central processing unit (CPU) which can perform logical operations on data in its memory and that involved in input/output (I/O) operations. Therefore, as early as the mid-1950s, before digital sound synthesis was possible, Lejaren Hiller (1959) at the University of Illinois programmed a computer to compose musical scores in a manner that tested some of the traditional compositional rules of harmony and counterpoint. The fundamental difference between this work, and that involved in "programming" a mechanical musical device such as a musicbox, carillon, or player piano, is that for the first time a machine participated in the *compositional* process, and hence was an objective representation of part of it. Among other things, this meant that so-called musical rules could be tried out on something other than aspiring music students, something that would in fact *test* their validity on the basis of the quality of the output. An objective, machine rendering of the rules avoids the addition of subjective factors, and the inadequacies of the result are informative as to what's missing in the rules, i.e., the hidden assumptions that have been made. Just as sound-generating machines implement and test our knowledge of acoustic models, so too, machine-assisted composition tests our knowledge of musical structures.

Generality and Strength

A useful concept with which to understand the variables involved in the design of machine-aided composition is the dialectical relation between the characteristics of generality and strength embodied in such systems. Moreover, as shown in Fig. 19, there is a corresponding pattern of user interaction that relates to the degree of each variable present. That is, the concept describes the communicational process as much as it does the structure of the system. By "generality" we mean the range of output of the system, whereas "strength" means the degree of efficiency with which this output can be achieved. The dialectic rule dictates that the stronger and more efficient the algorithm, the more restricted is its range of output, i.e., it is less general. Conversely, to increase the generality of output, one must use weaker methods, or as one would commonly say, more general methods. At the extreme left of the continuum of Fig. 19, the cost of the generality is the large amount of user information that must be supplied (for instance, a program that can generate any specifiable structure on the basis of the user describing it element by element). At the extreme right, the process is automated (i.e., it requires little or no user input), but the range of results is restricted. At both extremes, there is little user interaction involved in the process. Towards the middle lies the range of what are called "interactive systems," where the user provides data to control the algorithmic processes of the machine and is constantly evaluating and optimizing the results as in the TOTE pattern.

Therefore, we can refer to the design *of* the system, as well as design *with* the system. In the case of complete automation of the process (where all human knowledge relevant to the process is externalized in a program), we could speak of design *by* the system—a case of artificial intelligence. However, although programs with a fair degree of automation have been written, we are far from any such "ultimate" composition system. The idea that it could exist needn't been viewed with alarm that machines are taking over, because its existence would only be proof of the explicitness of human knowledge about the musical process, and thus far, music has proved to be extremely

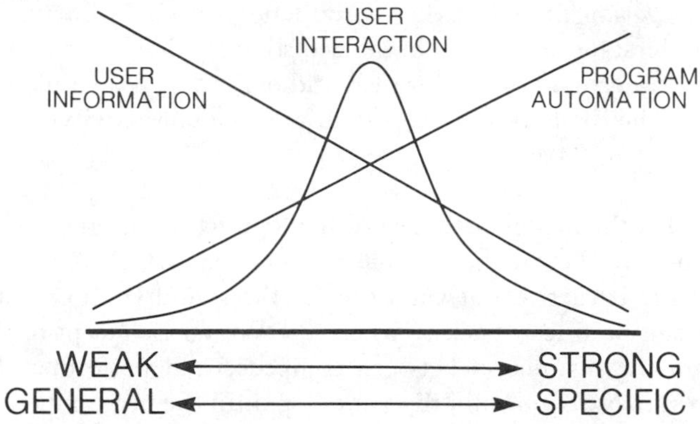

Fig. 19. Variation of user information, program automation, and user interaction as a function of the generality and strength of a computer music system.

subtle and complex. However, experience with software design also shows that the 19th-century view of music as completely subjective, intuitive and inexplicable is also false. The general haze that this concept creates around music serves only to isolate it as the privileged preserve of the talented few, with no relation to other forms of human activity. It is more valuable to discover that the introduction of a machine into the process is not an alienating act, but precisely because of the machine's objectivity it is the factor that *distinguishes* human knowledge into that which can be made explicit, tested and shared, and that which remains uniquely human, beyond the capability of the machine.

Moreover, the explicitness and memory of the computer system means that its pattern of use by the composer can leave a "trace," something that the traditional compositional process seldom does, or only in the form of musical notebooks or score fragments. The trace of an interactive compositional process is sometimes called a *protocol,* and its existence suggests that musical activity becomes an observable phenomenon, open to empirical study (Truax, 1976). By contrast with such measures of the elements of musical ability as the Seashore test (Seashore, 1938), protocol analysis offers the possibility of the analysis of those abilities in action, and hence can lead to a model of musical performance (Laske, 1977). Performance, in this sense, links all forms of musical activity, including listening, generating, and evaluating musical structures, and other activities found in a computer music system. Some educators, such as Jeanne Bamberger (1973), have seen the possibilities of such systems for music education because they can be used to foster musical *thinking*, not just the reproduction of musical artifacts of the past. If we understand music as "organized sound," then a flexible machine system that allows sound to be designed and organized is a valuable tool for understanding the dynamics of this essentially human activity.

Conclusion

To conclude this theme, let us return to the distinction in types of composition with which we began the section, namely that which is performed in real-time, and that carried out via scores or the sound studio. Historically, this division can be traced back to where the Western concept of the musician split into the distinction between composer and performer. In traditional cultures, they are one and the same. Up until the beginning of the 19th century in Europe they were usually the same person wearing two different hats. The court or church composer was expected to be a virtuoso performer, conductor, and the creator of original music as well. Beethoven is often cited as the first Western composer who attempted to gain independent recognition as a composer, although in his earlier years he also established his reputation as a pianist. Therefore, the split is relatively recent, and one can speculate whether the direction of electroacoustic technology as outlined here may yet lead in the future to a *re-integration* of those roles.

First, it should be noted that the difference between composition in real-time and non–real-time is not absolute; elements of each exist in the other. Anyone who has worked in a studio knows that there is a considerable physical performance component involved, and likewise, improvisational composition usually involves some amount of at least mental pre-planning. Some would contend that to be successful it even requires such prior organization. The barrier to the union of the two processes is the complexity of information flow and control that is required, and the current restrictions are technical on the one hand (in terms of the amount of data involved), and conceptual on the other (in terms of one's mental ability to control such complexity). However, as technology in this area becomes more powerful (as it does each year), the problem of generating large amounts of data quickly enough will gradually be solved. What is more critical, though, is our knowledge of how to represent and control such information once it is available.

Computer systems for interactive composition are gradually becoming more musically powerful as more tools are being developed to assist the process. Similarly, with advances in hardware, more signal processing can be performed in real time. The two developments assist each other in that as the complexity of sound production increases, what one needs are more powerful methods for its organization and control. Experience with interactive systems often leads to greater insight into how such organization should be handled, and eventually to programs that assist the process.

The significance of such developments is that they can lead to new ways of thinking about sound, as well as to new kinds of electroacoustic design. Moreover, the incorporation of more of the intelligence that is at the basis of electroacoustic design into the software component means that the tools of the future can change such artificial dichotomies as the split role of the performer and composer; they may yet become re-integrated into a single act, assisted by machines that reflect and embody our own knowledge. The technology itself may be directed by economic forces that need it for other purposes, but it is only those efforts which use that technology to establish new patterns of communication that realize the positive potential for net gain from such tools.

Discography

Selected electroacoustic works by composers referred to in chapter 13.

Amirkhanian, C. *Just, Heavy Aspirations.* 1750 Arch Records, S 1752; *Dzarim Bess Ga Khorim.* Fylkingen Records FYLP 1010; *Lexical Music.* 1750 Arch Records S 1779.

Appleton, J. *Georganna's Farewell.* Folkways FTS 33442; *Four Fantasies for Synclavier.* Folkways FTS 37461.

Barrière, F. *Cordes-çi, Cordes-ça.* EMI C053-12112.

Bayle, F. *L'oiseau-chanteur.* Candide 31025; *Solitude.* Philips 6740-001; *Tremblement de terre très doux.* INA-GRM 6101 BA.

Behrman, D. *On the Other Ocean, Figure in a Clearing.* Lovely Music LML 1041.

Berio, L. *Thema (Omaggio a Joyce).* Turnabout TV 34177; Philips 836 897 DSY.

Bodin, L. G. *For Jon (Fragments of a Time to Come).* Folkways FTS 33443; *Bilder.* Folkways FTS 33442; *Nastan & Plus.* Fylkingen Records FYLP 1010.

Body, J. *Musik Dari Jalan.* Kiwi SLD 54.

Boerman, J. *Composition 1972, Alchemie 1961, De Zee.* Composers' Voice CV 7701.

Cage, J. *Fontana Mix.* Turnabout TV 34046S; *Solos for Voice 2.* Odyssey 32 16 0156.

Chadabe, J. *Rhythms.* Lovely Music VR 1301; *Ideas of Movement at Bolton Landing.* Opus One No. 17.

Chopin, H. *Audiopoems.* Tangent TGS 106; *Definition des Lettres Suivantes.* Fylkingen Records FYLP 1010.

Celona, J. *Music in Circular Motions.* Folkways FTS 37475.

Clozier, C. *Lettre à une Demoiselle.* EMI C061-11632; *La Discordatura.* EMI C053-12112.

Dashow, J. *Second Voyage.* CRI SD 456.

Dodge, C. *Speech Songs, In Celebration, The Story of Our Lives.* CRI SD 348; *Any Resemblance is Purely Coincidental.* Folkways FTS 37475.

Eimert, H. *Selektion I.* Philips 835 485/86 AY.

Ferrari, L. *Presque Rien No. 1.* DGG 2543004.

Gould, G. *The Idea of North.* CBC Learning Systems PR-8; *The Latecomers.* CBC Learning Systems PR-9.

Hambraeus, B. *Tides, Intrada: "Calls", Tornado.* McGill Records 76001.

Hanson, S. *Au 197,0.* Fylkingen Records FYLP 1010.

Haynes, S. *Prisms.* Folkways FTS 37475.

Keane, D. *In Memoriam: Hugh Le Caine.* Music Gallery Editions MGE 29.

Koenig, G. M. *Funktion Blau.* Philips 6526 003; *Funktion Grün.* DGG 137 011; *Terminus X.* Philips 836 993 DSY.

Lansky, P. *Six Fantasies on a Poem by Thomas Campion.* CRI SD 456.

Le Caine, H. *Dripsody*. Folkways FMS 33436.
Luening, O. *Synthesis for Orchestra and Electronic Sounds*. CRI SD 219.
Luening, O., & Ussachevsky, V. *Concerted Piece for Tape Recorder and Orchestra*. CRI 227 USD.
Maderna, B. *Continuo*. Philips 836 897 DSY.
Orchard, I. *Skeena, River of the Clouds, Fortunate Islands, From the Mountains to the Sea, People in Landscape*. Available from Sound and Moving Image Division, Provincial Archives, Parliament Buildings, Victoria, B.C., Canada V8V 1X4.
Parmegiani, B. *Danse*. Candide 31025; *De Natura Sonorum*. INA-GRM AM 714 01.
Pennycook, B. *If Carillons Grew Wings*. Redwood Records ES-10; *Speeches for Dr. Frankenstein*. Folkways FTS 37475.
Piché, J. *Heliograms*. Melbourne SMLP 4045.
Pousseur, H. *Trois Visages de Liege*. Columbia MS 7051.
Reich, S. *Come Out*. Odyssey 32 16 0160; *It's Gonna Rain*. Columbia MS 7265.
Riley, T. *Shri Camel*. Columbia M 35164; *Persian Surgery Dervishes*. Shanti 83 501/502.
Risset, J. C. *Mutations I*. INA-GRM AM 564-09; *Inharmonic Soundscapes*. Tulsa TS78-208.
Schaeffer, P. *Etude aux Objets*. Philips 6521 021; *Objets liés*. Candide 31025.
Schaeffer, P., & Henry, P. *Symphonie pour un homme seul*. Philips 6510 012.
Schwartz, T. *New York 19*. Folkways FP 58; *Millions of Musicians*. Folkways FP 60; *Music in the Streets*. Folkways FD 5581; *1, 2, 3 and a Zing Zing Zing*. Folkways FC 7003.
Shinohara, M. *Mémoires*. Philips 836 993 DSY.
Smalley, D. *Pentes, The Pulses of Time, Chanson de Geste*. Univ. of East Anglia UEA 81063.
Stockhausen, K. *Gesang der Jünglinge*. DGG 138811; *Kontakte*. Candide 31022, Vox 678011, Wergo 60009, tape version: DGG 13811; *Hymnen*. DGG 2707 039.
Subotnick, M. *Silver Apples of the Moon*. Nonesuch H 71174; *The Wild Bull*. Nonesuch H 71208; *Touch*. Columbia MS 7316; *Until Spring*. Odyssey Y 34158; *Sidewinder*. Columbia M 30683.
Takemitsu, T. *Water Music*. RCA VICS-1334.
Truax, B. *She, a Solo, Trigon, Sonic Landscape No. 3, Nautilus*. Melbourne SMLP 4033; *Love Songs, Androgyny, The Blind Man, Aerial, Ascendance, Arras*. Melbourne SMLP 4042/43.
Ussachevsky, V. *A Piece for Tape Recorder*. CRI 112; *Of Wood and Brass*. CRI 227; *Linear Contrasts, Metamorphosis*. CRI SD 356.
Varèse, E. *Déserts*. Columbia MS 6362, Angel S 36786, CRI SD 268; *Poème Electronique*. Columbia MS 6146.
Xenakis, I. *Concret P-H II, Bohor I, Diamorphosis II, Orient-Occident III*. Nonesuch H 71246.

Bibliography

Alten, S. R. (1981). *Audio in media.* Belmont, CA: Wadsworth.

Anderson, L. M., Mulligan, B. E., Goodman, L. S., & Regen, H. Z. (1983). Effects of sounds on preferences for outdoor settings. *Environment and Behavior, 15* (5), 539–566.

Appleton, J. H., & Perera, R. C., eds. (1975). *The development and practice of electronic music.* Englewood Cliffs, NJ: Prentice-Hall.

Backus, J. (1969). *The acoustical foundations of music.* New York: Norton.

Bamberger, J. (1973). Learning to think musically (a computer approach to music study). *Music Educators Journal, 59* (7), 53–57.

Baron, R. A. (1970). *The tyranny of noise.* New York: St. Martin's.

Bateman, W. (1980). *Introduction to computer music.* New York: Wiley.

Bateson, G. (1972). *Steps to an ecology of mind.* New York: Ballantine.

Battcock, G., ed. (1981). *Breaking the sound barrier.* New York: E. P. Dutton.

Beeby, A. E. (1966). *Sound effects on tape.* London: Tape Recording Magazine.

Benade, A. H. (1976). *Fundamentals of musical acoustics.* London: Oxford University Press.

Beranek, L. L., Blazier, W. E., & Figwer, J. J. (1971). Preferred noise criterion (PNC) curves and their application to rooms. *Journal of the Acoustical Society of America, 50,* 1223–1228.

Berland, T. (1970). *The fight for quiet.* Englewood Cliffs, NJ: Prentice-Hall.

Bever, T. G., & Chiarello, R. J. (1974). Cerebral dominance in musicians and nonmusicians. *Science, 185,* 537–539.

Birdwhistell, R. L. (1970). *Kinesics and context.* Philadelphia, PA: University of Pennsylvania Press.

Bolinger, D. L., ed. (1972). *Intonation.* Harmondsworth, England: Penguin.

Bragdon, C. R. (1970). *Noise pollution: The unquiet crisis.* Philadelphia, PA: University of Pennsylvania Press.

Bragdon, C. R. (1979). *Noise pollution—A guide to information sources.* Detroit, MI: Gale Research.

Brüel, P. V. (1976). Do we measure damaging noise correctly? *B & K Technical Review,* No. 1, 3–25.

Bruneau, T. J. (1973). Communicative silences: Forms and functions. *Journal of Communication, 23,* 17–46.

Bryan, M. E., & Tempest, W. (1973). Are our noise laws adequate? *Applied Acoustics, 6,* 219–232.

Buchner, A. (1959). *Mechanical musical instruments.* London: Batchworth. (Reprinted, Greenwood Press).

Burns, W. (1968). *Noise and man.* London: Wm. Clowes.

Buxton, W. (1977). A composer's introduction to computer music. *Interface, 6,* 57–72.

Campbell, J. M. (1983). Ambient stressors. *Environment and Behavior, 15* (3), 355–380.

Cantril, H., & Allport, G. W. (1935). *The psychology of radio.* New York: Harper & Bros. (Reprinted, New York: Arno Press, 1971).

Cardinell, R. L. (1948). Music in industry. In D. Schullian, & M. Schoen, eds. *Music and Medicine*. New York: Schuman.

Chadabe, J. (1977). Some reflections on the nature of the landscape within which computer music systems are designed. *Computer Music Journal, 1* (3), 5–11.

Chevrie-Muller, C., Seguier, N., Spira, A., & Dordain, M. (1978). Recognition of psychiatric disorders from voice quality. *Language and Speech, 21,* (1) 87–111.

Chomsky, A. N. (1965). *Aspects of the theory of syntax*. Cambridge, MA: M.I.T. Press.

Chopin, H. (1981). *Poesie sonore internationale*. Paris: Editions Jean-Michel Place.

Chorafas, D. N. (1981). *Interactive videotex*. New York: Petrocelli.

Clynes, M. (1978). *Sentics*. New York: Doubleday.

Clynes, M., ed. (1982). *Music, mind, and brain: The neuropsychology of music*. New York: Plenum.

Cogan, R., & Escot, P. (1976). *Sonic design: The nature of sound and music*. Englewood Cliffs, NJ: Prentice-Hall.

Cole, R. A., ed. (1980). *Perception and production of fluent speech*. Hillsdale, NJ: Lawrence Erlbaum Associates.

Costanzo, F. S., Markel, N. N., & Costanzo, P. R. (1969). Voice quality profile and perceived emotion. *Journal of Counseling Psychology, 16* (3) 267–270.

Cross, L. (1968). Electronic music: 1948–1953. *Perspectives of New Music, 7* (1), 32–65.

Crystal, D. (1969). *Prosodic systems and intonation in English*. Cambridge, England: Cambridge University Press.

Crystal, D. (1975). *The English tone of voice: Essays in intonation, prosody and paralanguage*. London: Edward Arnold.

Culshaw, J. (1972). *The Ring resounding*. New York: Time-Life.

Dauenhauer, B. P. (1973). On silence. *Research in Phenomenology, 3,* 3–27.

Davis, B. (1975). FM radio as observational access to wilderness environments. *Alternatives, 4* (3), 21–27.

Denes, P. B., & Pinson, E. N. (1963). *The speech chain*. Garden City, NY: Anchor.

Deutsch, D., ed. (1982). *The psychology of music*. New York: Academic.

Deutsch, H. A. (1976). *Synthesis, an introduction to the history, theory & practice of electronic music*. New York: Alfred.

Dixon, N. F. (1971). *Subliminal perception*. London: McGraw-Hill.

Doelle, L. L. (1972). *Environmental acoustics*. New York: McGraw-Hill.

Dubos, R. (1965). *Man adapting*. New Haven, CT: Yale University Press.

Duerden, C. (1970). *Noise abatement*. London: Butterworths.

Dwyer, T. (1971). *Composing with tape recorders*. London: Oxford University Press.

Eiamas, P. D. (1975). Speech perception in early infancy. In L. B. Cohen & P. Salapatek, eds. *Infant perception: From sensation to cognition,* Vol. 2. New York: Academic.

Eisenberg, R. B. (1976). *Auditory competence in early life: The roots of communicative behavior*. Baltimore, MD: University Park Press.

Eisenstein, S. M. (1942). *The film sense*. New York: Harcourt, Brace & World.

Erickson, R. (1975). *Sound structure in music*. Berkeley, CA: University of California Press.

Feldstein, S. (1972). Temporal patterns of dialogue: Basic research and considerations. In A. W. Siegman & B. Pope, eds. *Studies in Dyadic Communication*. New York: Pergamon.

Felsenthal, N., Shamo, G. W., & Bittner, J. R. (1971). A comparison of award-winning radio commercials and their day-to-day counterparts. *Journal of Broadcasting, 15,* 309–315.

Finkelman, J. M. (1975). Effects of noise on human performance. *Sound and Vibration,* September, 26–28.

Gammond, P., & Horricks, R., eds. (1980). *The music goes round and round*. London: Quartet Books.

Gazzaniga, M. S. (1972). One brain—two minds? *American Scientist, 60* (3), 311–317.

Gerzon, M. (1975). Dummy head recording. *Studio Sound,* May, 42–44.

Giansante, L. (1979). The soundscape: What it is, how it works, and why it's important. *Media and Methods,* November, 44–47.

Goodey, B. (1974). *Images of place: Essays on environmental perception, communications and education.* Birmingham, England: University of Birmingham, Centre for Urban and Regional Studies.

Goodman, F. D. (1972). *Speaking in tongues: A cross-cultural study of glossolalia.* Chicago, IL: University of Chicago Press.

Gould, G. (1966). The prospects of recording. *High Fidelity Magazine, 16* (46), 46–63.

Grele, R. J., ed. (1975). *Envelopes of sound.* Chicago, IL: Precedent Publishing, Inc.

Griffin, D. R. (1959). *Echoes of bats and men.* Garden City, NY: Anchor.

Guignard, J. C., & Johnson, D. L. (1975). The relation of noise exposure to noise induced hearing damage. *Sound and Vibration,* January, 18–23.

Hale, J. (1975). *Radio power, propaganda and international broadcasting.* London: Paul Elek.

Hawkins, M. M. (1980). "An Exploratory Study of Response to Sound (Including Noise) Occurring in Rural Hampshire and Wiltshire" (Contract Report 80/11). Southampton, England: University of Southampton, Institute of Sound and Vibration Research, August.

Hiller, L. A., & Isaacson, L. M. (1959). *Experimental music.* New York: McGraw-Hill.

Hockett, C. F. (1960). The origin of speech. *Scientific American, 203* (3), 88–96.

Howe, H. S. (1975). *Electronic music synthesis.* New York: Norton.

Ihde, D., & Slaughter, T. F. (1970). Studies in the phenomenology of sound. *International Philosophical Journal, 10,* 232–251.

Ihde, D. (1976). *Listening and voice.* Athens, OH: Ohio University Press.

Innis, H. A. (1972). *Empire and communications.* Toronto, Ontario: University of Toronto Press.

Jakobson, R. (1978). *Six lectures on sound and meaning,* J. Mepham, trans. Cambridge, MA: M.I.T. Press.

Jaffe, J., & Feldstein, S. (1970). *Rhythms of dialogue.* New York: Academic.

Jessop, J. (1971). Radio as music: Glenn Gould in conversation with John Jessop. *The Canada Music Book/Les Cahiers Canadiens de musique,* No. 2, (Spring–Summer), 13–30.

Kaegi, W. (1971). Music and technology in the Europe of 1970. In *Music and Technology.* Paris: La Revue Musicale.

Karkoschka, E. (1972). *Notation in new music,* R. Koenig, trans. New York: Praeger.

Keane, D. (1980). *Tape music composition.* London: Oxford University Press.

Key, M. R. (1975). *Paralanguage and kinesics.* Metuchen, NJ: Scarecrow Press.

Kimura, D. (1964). Left-right differences in the perception of melodies. *Quarterly Journal of Experimental Psychology, 16,* 355–358.

Kimura, D. (1973). The asymmetry of the human brain. *Scientific American, 228* (3), 70–78.

Kryter, K. D. (1959). Scaling human reactions to the sound from aircraft. *Journal of the Acoustical Society of America, 31,* 1415–1429.

Kryter, K. D. (1970). *The effects of noise on man.* New York: Academic Press.

Langer, S. K. (1951). *Philosophy in a new key.* New York: Mentor.

Laske, O. E. (1974a). Musical acoustics (sonology), a questionable science reconsidered. *Numus West,* No. 6, 35–40.

Laske, O. E. (1974b). On the understanding and design of aesthetic artifacts. In P. Faltin & H. P. Reinecke, eds., *Musik und Verstehen.* Cologne, Germany: Arno Volk Verlag.

Laske, O. E. (1975a). Introduction to a generative theory of music. *Sonological Reports,* No. 1B. Utrecht, The Netherlands: Utrecht State University, Institute of Sonology.

Laske, O. E. (1975b). Toward a theory of musical cognition. *Interface, 4,* 147–208.

Laske, O. E. (1976). Toward a theory of musical instruction. *Interface, 5,* 125–148.

Laske, O. E. (1977). *Music, memory and thought.* Ann Arbor, MI: University Microfilms International.

Laske, O. E. (1978). Considering human memory in designing user interfaces for computer music. *Computer Music Journal, 2* (4), 39–45.

Laske, O. E. (1980). Toward an explicit cognitive theory of musical listening. *Computer Music Journal, 4* (2), 73–83.

Lazarsfeld, P. F. (1940). *Radio and the printed page.* New York: Duell, Sloan & Pearce. (Reprinted, New York: Arno Press, 1971).

Leathers, D. G. (1976). *Nonverbal communication systems.* Boston, MA: Allyn & Bacon.

Lomax, A. (1962). Song structure and social structure. *Ethnology, 1,* 425–451.

Lusseyran, J. (1963). *And there was light.* E. R. Cameron, trans. Boston, MA: Little, Brown & Co.

MacColl, E. (1968). Concerning the radio ballads. In E. MacColl & P. Seeger, *I'm a Freeborn Man, and Other Original Radio Ballads.* New York: Oak Publications.

McAdams, S., & Bregman, A. (1979). Hearing musical streams. *Computer Music Journal, 3* (4), 26–43.

McLuhan, M. (1964). *Understanding media: The extensions of man.* New York: Signet Books.

McNabb, M. (1981). Dreamsong: The composition. *Computer Music Journal, 5* (4), 36–53.

Markel, N. N. (1965). The reliability of coding paralanguage: Pitch, loudness, and tempo. *Journal of Verbal Learning and Verbal Behavior, 4,* 306–308.

Markel, N. N. (1969). *Psycholinguistics: An introduction to the study of speech and personality.* Homewood, IL: Dorsey.

Martin, J. (1978). *The wired society.* Englewood Cliffs, NJ: Prentice-Hall.

Mathews, M. V. (1969). *The technology of computer music.* Cambridge, MA: M.I.T. Press.

Mehrabian, A. (1972). *Nonverbal communication.* Chicago, IL: Aldine-Atherton.

Mendelsohn, H. (1964). Listening to radio. In L. A. Dexter & D. M. White, eds., *People, Society and Mass Communication.* London: Macmillan.

Merriam, A. P. (1964). *The anthropology of music.* Chicago, IL: Northwestern University Press.

Meyer, L. B. (1956). *Emotion and meaning in music.* Chicago, IL: University of Chicago Press.

Meyer, L. B. (1967). *Music, the arts and ideas.* Chicago, IL: University of Chicago Press.

Miller, G. A. (1967). *The psychology of communication.* Harmondsworth, England: Penguin.

Miller, J. D. (1974). Effects of noise on people. *Journal of the Acoustical Society of America, 56,* 729–763.

Minsky, M. (1981). Music, mind and meaning. *Computer Music Journal, 5* (3), 28–44.

Moles, A. (1966). *Information theory and esthetic perception.* Urbana, IL: University of Illinois Press.

Moore, B. C. J. (1982). *An introduction to the psychology of hearing,* 2nd ed. London: Academic.

Moorer, J. A. (1977). Signal processing aspects of computer music—A survey. *Computer Music Journal, 1* (1), 4–37.

Moorer, J. A. (1978). How does a computer make music? *Computer Music Journal, 2* (1), 32–37.

Moray, N. (1969). *Listening and attention.* Harmondsworth, England: Penguin.

Morris, C. W. (1938). *Foundations of the theory of signs, International encyclopedia of unified science,* Vol. 1, No. 2. Chicago, IL: University of Chicago Press.

Morris, C. W. (1955). *Signs, language, and behavior.* New York: Braziller.

Nettl, B. (1964). *Theory and method in ethnomusicology.* London: Collier-Macmillan.

Nisbett, A. (1972). *The technique of the sound studio,* 3rd ed. Norwich, England: Focal Press.

Noise Abatement Commission. (1930). *City noise.* City of New York: Department of Health.

Olson, H. F. (1967). *Music, physics, and engineering.* New York: Dover.

Ong, W. J. (1982). *Orality and literacy: The technologizing of the word.* London and New York: Methuen.

Ornstein, R. E. (1969). *On the experience of time.* Harmondsworth, England: Penguin.

Ostwald, P. F. (1963a). *Soundmaking.* Springfield, IL: C. C. Thomas.

Ostwald, P. F. (1963b). Sonic communication in medical practice and research. *Journal of Communication, 13,* 156–165.

Ostwald, P. F. (1973). *The semiotics of human sound.* The Hague, Netherlands: Mouton.

Ostwald, P. F., & Peltzman, P. (1974). The cry of the human infant. *Scientific American, 230* (3), 84–90.

Ostwald, P. F. (1977). Sounds in human communication. In P. F. Ostwald, ed. *Communication and Social Interaction.* New York: Grune & Stratton.

Partch, H. (1974). *Genesis of a music,* 2nd. ed. New York: Da Capo Press.

Payzant, G. (1978). *Glenn Gould, music and mind.* Toronto, Ontario: Van Nostrand Reinhold.

Pearce, W. B., & Conklin, F. (1971). Nonverbal vocalic communication and perceptions of a speaker. *Speech Monographs, 38,* 235–241.

Pellegrino, R. (1983). *The electronic arts of sound and light.* New York: Van Nostrand Reinhold.

Pierce, J. R., & David, E. E. (1958). *Man's world of sound.* New York: Doubleday.

Pittenger, R. E., Hockett, C. F., & Danehy, J. J. (1960). *The first five minutes: A sample of microscopic interview analysis.* Ithaca, New York: P. Martineau.

Plomp, R. (1976). *Aspects of tone sensation: A psychophysical study.* New York: Academic.

Price, A. J. (1972). Community noise survey of greater Vancouver. *Journal of the Acoustical Society of America, 52* (2), 488–492.

Reik, T. (1949). *Listening with the third ear.* New York: Farrar & Strauss.

Reynolds, R. (1975). *Mind models: New forms of musical experience.* New York: Praeger.

Rodda, M. (1967). *Noise and society.* London: Oliver & Boyd.

Roederer, J. G. (1975). *Introduction to the physics and psychophysics of music,* 2nd ed. New York: Springer.

Rosen, S. (1962). Presbycusis study of a relatively noise-free population in the Sudan. *Transactions, American Otological Society, 50,* 135–152.

Rosen S. (1973). *The autobiography of Dr. Samuel Rosen.* New York: Knopf.

Runstein, R. E. (1974). *Modern recording techniques.* Indianapolis, IN: Howard W. Sams.

Russcol, H. (1972). *The liberation of sound: An introduction to electronic music.* Englewood Cliffs, NJ: Prentice-Hall.

Salzinger, K., & Salzinger, S., eds. (1967). *Research in verbal behavior and some neurophysiological implications.* New York: Academic.

Sargant, W. (1959). *Battle for the mind.* London: Pan Books.

Saussure, F. de (1966). *Course in general linguistics,* C. Bally & A. Sechehaye, eds., W. Baskin, trans. New York: McGraw-Hill.

Schafer, R. M. (1969). *The new soundscape.* Vienna: Universal Edition.

Schafer, R. M. (1970). *The book of noise.* Wellington, New Zealand: Price, Milburn.

Schafer, R. M. (1973). *The music of the environment.* Vienna: Universal Edition.

Schafer, R. M. (1976). *Creative music education.* New York: Schirmer.

Schafer, R. M. (1977). *The tuning of the world.* New York: Knopf.

Schiller, H. I. (1969). *Mass communication and American empire.* New York: A. M. Kelley.

Schiller, H. I. (1973). *The mind managers.* Boston, MA: Beacon Press.

Schrader, B. (1982). *Introduction to electro-acoustic music.* Englewood Cliffs, NJ: Prentice-Hall.

Schwartz, T. (1973). *The responsive chord.* Garden City, NY: Anchor.

Seashore, C. E. (1938). *The psychology of music.* New York: McGraw-Hill.

Sebeok. T. A., ed. (1960). *Style in language.* Cambridge, MA: M.I.T. Press.

Shumway, G. (1970). *Oral history in the United States: A directory.* New York: Columbia University Press.

Shurcliff, W. A. (1970). *SST and sonic boom handbook.* New York: Ballantine.

Simon, H. A. (1969). *The sciences of the artificial.* Cambridge, MA: M.I.T. Press.

Simpkins, J. D., & Smith, J. A. (1974). Effects of music on source evaluations. *Journal of Broadcasting, 18,* 361–367.

Smythe, D. (1981). *Dependency road: Communications, capitalism, consciousness, and Canada.* Norwood, NJ: Ablex.

Soramaki, M., & Haarma, J. (1981). *The international music industry.* Helsinki: Finnish Broadcasting Company, No. 20.

Southworth, M. (1969). The sonic environment of cities. *Environment and Behavior, 1* (1), 49–70.

Sterling, C. H., & Kittross, J. M. (1978). *Stay tuned, a concise history of American broadcasting.* Belmont, CA: Wadsworth.

Stevens, S. S., & Warshofsky, F. (1965). *Sound and hearing.* New York: Time-Life.

Still, H. (1970). *In quest of quiet.* Harrisburg, PA: Stackpole.

Strange, A. (1972). *Electronic music, systems, technique and controls.* Dubuque, IA: Wm. C. Brown, (2nd ed., 1983).

Sundberg, J. (1980). To perceive one's own voicee and another person's voice. In Sundberg, J., ed. *Research Aspects on Singing.* Stockholm: Royal Swedish Academy of Music, Publication No. 33.

Supa, M., Cotzin, M., & Dallenbach, K. M. (1944). Facial vision: The perception of obstacles to the blind. *American Journal of Psychology, 57,* 133–183.

Tempest, W., ed. (1976). *Infrasound and low frequency vibration.* London: Academic.

Thom, R. (1982). *Audio craft.* Washington, DC: National Federation of Community Broadcasters.

Tobias, J. V., ed. (1972). *Foundations of modern auditory theory.* New York: Academic.

Torigoe, K. (1982). "A Study of the World Soundscape Project". Toronto, Ontario: York University, M.F.A. thesis.

Trager, G. L. (1958). Paralanguage: A first approximation. *Studies in Linguistics, 13* (1,2), 1–12.

Truax, B. D. (1974). Soundscape studies: An introduction to the World Soundscape Project. *Numus West,* No. 5, 36–39.

Truax, B. D. (1976). A communicational approach to computer sound programs. *Journal of Music Theory, 20* (2), 227–300.

Truax, B. D. (1977). The soundscape and technology. *Interface, 6* 1–8.

Truax, B. D., ed. (1978). *Handbook for acoustic ecology.* Vancouver, British Columbia: A.R.C. Publications.

Truax, B. D. (1979). A structural model for the analysis of radio program organization. Unpublished manuscript.

Truax, B. D. (1980). The inverse relation between generality and strength in computer music programs. *Interface, 9,* 49–57.

Truax, B. D. (1982). Timbral construction in 'Arras' as a stochastic process. *Computer Music Journal, 6* (3), 72–77.

Trythall, G. (1973). *Principles and practice of electronic music.* New York: Grosset Dunlap.

Varèse, E. (1966). The liberation of sound. *Perspectives of New Music, 5* (1), 11–19.

Vygotsky, L. S. (1962). *Thought and language.* Cambridge, MA: M.I.T. Press.

Waserman, M. (1975). *Bibliography on oral history.* New York: The Oral History Association.

Watzlawick, P., Beavin, J. H., & Jackson, D. D. (1967). *Pragmatics of human communication.* New York: Norton.

Waugh, L. R., & van Schooneveld, C. H., eds. (1980). *The melody of language (intonation and prosody).* Baltimore, MD: University Park Press.

Webster, J. C. (1969). SIL—past, present, and future. *Sound and Vibration, 3* (8), 22–26.

Webster, J. C. (1974). Speech interference by noise. *Proceedings, Inter-Noise 74,* Institute of Noise Control Engineering, 558.

Wetherill, E. A. (1975). Noise control in buildings. *Sound and Vibration,* July, 20–23.

White, F. A. (1975). *Our acoustic environment.* New York: Wiley.

Wolvin, A. D., & Coakley, C. G. (1982). *Listening.* Dubuque, IA: Wm. C. Brown.

Woolfe, R. (1980). *Videotex.* London: Heyden & Sons.

World Soundscape Project. *The Music of the Environment Series,* R. M. Schafer, ed. Vancouver, British Columbia: A.R.C. Publications.

(1973). No. 1, *The Music of the Environment.*

(1978a). No. 2, *The Vancouver Soundscape.*

(1977a). No. 3, *European Sound Diary.*

(1977b). No. 4, *Five Village Soundscapes.*
(1978b). No. 5, *Handbook for Acoustic Ecology.*
Xenakis, I. (1971). *Formalized music.* Bloomington, IN: Indiana University Press.
Yale, D. R. (1970–1971). The politics of Muzak: Big brother calls the tune. *Student Musicologists at Minnesota,* 80–106.
Yates, A. J. (1963). Delayed auditory feedback. *Psychological Bulletin, 60,* 213–232.
Young, L. (1972). Estimating radio reach. *Journal of Advertising Research, 12* (5), 37–41.
Zapf, D. (1981a). The World Soundscape Project revisited. *Musicworks,* Spring, No. 15, 4–5.
Zapf, D. (1981b). Inside the soundscape, the compositions of Hildegard Westerkamp. *Musicworks,* Spring, No. 15, 5–8.

Name Index

Italic page numbers indicate bibliographic citations.

Subject Index